For Jim Badley

With the best wishes of an Ancient Mariner

Fred Matthews

SAILOR STOKER ODDBALL

FREDERICK MATTHEWS

VIPER

Published in UK by

VIPER

The Studio,

Rabbits Farm, Rabbits Road

South Darenth, Kent DA4 9JZ

ISBN 1 900013 20 7

© VIPER 1995

Cover Design by
Carol Johnstone, Chris Johnstone
and Mike Bowra

THIS IS ALL I ASK
by
Gordon Jenkins

© 1958 Massey Music Co. Inc., USA
Assigned to TRO ESSEX MUSIC LTD., London SW10 OSZ

International Copyright Secured.
All rights reserved. Used by permission

CONTENTS

		Page
LIST OF ILLUSTRATIONS		3
FOREWORD		5
PREFACE		7
ACKNOWLEDGEMENTS		9
PART ONE	SAILOR	11
PART TWO	STOKER	47
PART THREE	ODDBALL	153
EPILOGUE		199

LIST OF ILLUSTRATIONS

1921	SCHOOL PHOTOGRAPH	91
1928	THE FLAT IN WHIMPLE STREET, PLYMOUTH	91
1928	PLAYING THE LEAD IN THE DOGS OF DEVON	92
1931	GRAVESEND SEA SCHOOL	92
1931	REFERENCE FOR THE SEA SELECTION OFFICER	93
1932	SS TAMAROA WAGE SLIP	94
1932	ROYAL NAVY CLASS MATES	95
1932	SHORTLY BEFORE LEAVING FOR THE USA	95
1934	THE AUTHOR IN MALTA	96
1939	THE AUTHOR IN STOKE'S BAY, GOSPORT	96
1942	THE DRAMATIC END OF HMS MEDWAY	97
1943	BEIRUT — THE AUTHOR WITH TWO LSF FRIENDS	98
1943	LS 1— THE FIRST OPERATIONAL CAIQUE	98
1944	GUNNERS PERRY AND MacCORMACK	99
1944	ZAHLE, BEIRUT— SBS REST CAMP	99
1944	THE TURKISH OFFICERS' CLUB	100
1944	THE AUTHOR ON LS 3	101
1944	MEMBERS OF THE LSF ON KHIOS	101
1944	THE OPERATIONAL AREA OF THE LSF	102

FOREWORD

The most fascinating qualities of this book are its openness, its completeness and the character of Fred himself, which comes out very strongly in the early pages describing an urgent, embattled childhood in Plymouth.

Fred Matthews is one of the most imaginative and yet essentially downright people I have ever known; full of ideas and an almost youthful enthusiasm for life in all its forms — at his action station in a submarine under furious attack by destroyers; in a fierce fight with German soldiers on a Greek island; or in bed with one of the women he loved — genuinely and desperately — all his life.

After one year at Sea School, Fred ships as seaman boy successively in two large merchant vessels, then a sailing barge. And in 1932 he joins the Navy as a stoker, serving in a survey sloop, a cruiser, three destroyers and finally submarines.

The outbreak of World War 2 finds him, now a leading stoker, in the submarine *Otway*. While in Malta he hears from his current girlfriend that she is expecting. He is deeply affected and conscience stricken, and on his return to England in February 1940 they are married.

After a period during which the *Otway* helps to cover the evacuation from Dunkirk, she is ordered to Wallsend-on-Tyne for a major refit. It is here that one of Fred's great romances is played out (and most movingly described). The calm and kindly Dorothy, who invites him to her home and bed, is in fact a virgin; and although he causes her excruciating pain at their first encounter, she never ceases to love him.

But fate turns against them when he is promoted to acting petty officer and drafted to H M Submarine *P36*, bound again for Malta. For Fred the real war now begins; with attacks on enemy convoys and savage counter attacks, one continuing for seven hours ... 'The destroyers came at us from all directions ... like express trains ... soul-shattering patterns of depth charges ... sending us tumbling against each other ... all you could do was hang on to overhead valves or pipes for dear life or grim death.'

Fred's first sortie with the Levant Schooner Flotilla takes him in a 27ft sailing boat with a Greek commanding officer on a reconnaissance voyage to the Italian held islands of Patmos and Mykonos. Then to the tiny island of Sirina, where they are shipwrecked and forced to spend nine days living rough on the island, before escaping to Turkey in a local caique which they have commandeered.

Fred now serves in a number of different LSF boats, and also takes part in a commando raid on the island of Piskopi, which ends in a pitched battle with the German garrison. During the fight, with bullets and grenades flying, Fred hurls an explosive charge into the enemy position; then up and over the mountains to his hidden folboat and away.

Throughout his life, Fred has been in love with love. From his very first experience, at fourteen, with a married woman more than twice his age, who finds him fondling her young daughter. She first reduces him to tears with ferocious threats of prison or worse, then orders him to strip and get into bed, whither she follows and proceeds to introduce him with great care and practised caresses to the art of making love.

Thereafter women of all kinds seem to dominate his leisure hours. And on the way home from the Mediterranean he spends three whole days in Haifa with the super passionate Sonia, who hardly pauses all night and every night in her athletic enjoyment of his eager body.

Altogether a book of many colours with frequent blazing highlights.

Adrian Seligman
June 1995

PREFACE

This book is a direct result of a letter I received in 1983 from Adrian Seligman DSC, the most outstanding of the many commanding officers I served under during the Second World War. It was Adrian, with his foresight and charisma who formed and commanded the Levant Schooner Flotilla with remarkable success, until the Admiralty decided they needed his extraordinary talents elsewhere.

The Levant Schooner Flotilla was quite unique, the like of which will never be seen again, of this I am quite sure.

I was one of the many 'oddballs' from the four services who were attracted, cajoled and curiously drawn to this illustrious group of men and boats and it was Adrian who moulded us into a force which most certainly had to be reckoned with by the German forces in the islands of the Aegean Sea.

In his letter, Adrian suggested that with my memories and experiences, I should make the effort and record my life in the form of a book. But it was some ten years later that I found the required motivation to respond to his suggestion. I travelled the world, renewed old acquaintances, attended numerous reunions and finally felt the time was right to tell my story up until my demob from the Royal Navy in 1945.

When I think of the officers I obeyed, respected and served with during my time in the Navy, I often recall the words of George Orwell, who said, 'All animals are born equal, only some are more equal than others.'

These men were privileged to have been born into circumstances which gave them the opportunity to receive a first class education, whilst at the same time enjoying the comforts of a well-appointed home. They were not required to go out into the world ill-equipped at the tender age of fourteen years, as in my case, to earn their keep.

With the greatest respect to them, I would say that no amount of study or research could ever enable them to comprehend what life was like for one such as I in that period. I have never been jealous of them, only envious. However, where in the hell would we have been without their leadership during those war years.

Although some of the dates, places and names have faded from my memory with the passing of time, the events of my life during that period are engraved forever. I am extremely proud to have been associated with some of those events, but there are others about which I find it difficult to believe that I could have acted in such a way. But I did, and I cannot turn back the clock, what has been done cannot be undone and you will no doubt judge me as you see fit.

This book is dedicated to the memory of the many thousands of gallant men who did not return home to grow old as we who are left grow old.

F. Matthews, May 1995

ACKNOWLEDGEMENTS

I am indebted to John Wingate DSC, whose good advice brought me down to earth with regard to getting a book published. He also gave me permission to quote from his excellent book — *The Fighting Tenth* — of which both he and myself were part; to recall with pride.

I must also mention two war time contemporaries of mine, Tommy Gould VC and Jim Steel DSM. These two intrepid sailors together with other ex-submariners, namely Jan Ham, Graham Hamley, Albert Worrillow and Roy Wilson continually nagged me to get my story down into print. They were, I suspect, fed up to the teeth with hearing all about my adventures, when in fact it was probably my turn to buy the beer.

Finally, I must thank Philly Chadwick for converting my scribbled longhand into a more acceptable form of reading via a word processor.

PART ONE - SAILOR

CHAPTER 1

During early 1944 I found myself in a situation that is embedded in my mind and will probably remain so for the rest of my life. What had seemed a real adventure in the beginning had turned into something of a disaster.

There I was on an enemy held island in the Aegean Sea, in company with a detachment of Special Boat Squadron raiders, attempting to steal a landing craft from under the noses of the German garrison. I was only a petty officer stoker, to be honest more interested in women and rum than fighting, God only knows what I was doing there with them. And things had not gone as planned, on our approach to the harbour, a dog, of all things, alerted the Germans to our presence and a fierce fire-fight ensued, wounding several of our party.

Eventually, we made our escape back into the hills to lick our wounds and fifty years later I can remember quite vividly the moment when I collapsed on the ground at our hideout, exhausted, drenched in sweat and shaking like a leaf. I remember finding a corner amongst the rocks in which to curl up and the feeling of the blood coursing through my veins will live with me forever.

I was in turmoil and a multitude of thoughts continually entered my head. Thoughts of my wife and family at home. The other women in my life who I loved. The decisions that had to be made if ever I got off the island in one piece and made it back home.

From the moment I left home to go to sea at the age of sixteen my life had been one long adventure, full of wine, women and song and I did not want it to end on some unknown island far from home. As I drifted off to sleep my whole life seemed to unfold before my very eyes and as I sit writing now once again my life up to and during that period seems to fill my every thought.

I was born in 1914, ten days before the outbreak of World War 1, either the twelfth or thirteenth child of an apparently ill-matched couple, but a pair who obviously had one thing in common if the number of kids they produced is anything to go by.

My mother had been a hard working Cornish girl from St Ives, previously married for a brief period to a tin miner who set off for fame and fortune in California only to be killed in an accident there. She was semi-religious, but brainwashed I suspect by the conditions which prevailed during her formative years. Conditions which also existed to a great extent during the early years of my life.

When one considers the standards by which we live today, it is difficult to believe that in the period to which I refer it was almost a crime to be out and about during Sunday and evening church services.

My father, an agnostic, was a very intelligent man with a wonderful memory. A journeyman brass moulder from Wolverhampton, he was a practical joker, solid drinker, smoker and a gambler who would bet on anything.

The first meeting between my parents, so I understand, occurred when she came up to Plymouth from St Ives for a shopping trip and he was in Plymouth doing a wheel-casting job for Plymouth tramways. Any sailor who has ridden on the top deck of a tram to the dockyard or barracks and who swears that the trams had four square wheels is quite wrong. My father was adamant that they all had three square and one triangular.

The story goes that a few months after the outbreak of war, father and a couple of his pals were having a few pints on a Saturday afternoon after leaving work prior to going home for their dinner. Emerging from the pub and 'Franz List' I suspect, they walked straight into the arms of a big recruiting sergeant who promptly signed them up and sent them off to war. The silly old sods should have stayed in the boozer — they were all over forty anyway!

My mother did not discover his whereabouts until the following week when she received a postcard sent by him from an army camp at Tidworth, so she promptly packed her bags and marched us kids off to her mother in St Ives for the duration. There were only five of us children surviving by this time as various epidemics had taken their toll of some of my brothers and sisters.

My grandmother was a very formidable woman of Irish stock. Her name was Elizabeth Adams, née McGuiness, a widow who ran two fish businesses, the main one from large premises on Tregenna Hill where we all lived. She ran her businesses like a regimental sergeant major, everyone had a job to do, no matter how young they were. She was a very enterprising woman and took in boarders, one of whom was Leslie Henson, the actor — older readers may remember him for his saucer-like eyes.

My brother and I, he was six years my senior, shared an attic bedroom into which the beam from the Godreavy Lighthouse flashed continuously.

Because of my age, memories of these war years are very few, but as I look back, I realise that this was indeed a good period of my life, there was discipline, affection, good grub and cleanliness. I have only two or three outstanding memories of these years, the most vivid being taken to Porthminster beach on one occasion by my elder sisters and brother.

As we approached the sea front from the top of Tregenna Hill, the air was full with the odour of sulphur, growing stronger the nearer we came to the shore. The reason for this became abundantly clear as we set foot upon the sand. There, so far as our young eyes could see, along its entire length, were hundreds of shattered wooden cases containing matches. Apparently they had come from a ship which had been torpedoed off the coast.

Porthminster beach at this time was also the graveyard for old worn out fishing boats, their black hulks were drawn up in neat rows just above the high-water line where they were left to die in peace after a lifetime of service and they also provided nesting places in the sand for young courting couples.

When I started school, at a little place down by the harbour in St Ives, it was a period of high tides and one morning the sea came into the classroom carrying the desks and seats with it and us kids had to cling to them and wait to be rescued. Being rescued from the sea seems to have cropped up many times in my life.

Near the end of the war in 1918 my mother and I set off for Plymouth to search for somewhere to live. Apparently she had received word from my father that he was on his way home from the Army and wanted to live in Plymouth. I remember quite clearly our first night in the town, walking from the railway station with me clutching her hand like an anchor. We walked down through gas-lit streets with our own handmade lantern into Southside Street, on to the fish market and so to Castle Street for our first night's lodging.

A day or so later, mother found rooms for us all in Whimple Street which was about five minutes walk from both the town centre and the fish market on the Barbican. The rooms were at the top of a house which was shared by about fourteen people, including ourselves. We had an all-purpose room, where we ate and spent our leisure time and leading off this room to the back was a small bedroom. There was a tiny kitchen, which had a gas cooker and larder food cupboard, and room for just one person. To the front we had a large room that was only used on special occasions. This contained a polished table, a set of chairs with plush seats and a long kind of settee to match, the usual potted plants, a couple of china cabinets and also a double bed, which could be hidden or screened. To complete our rooms, there were two bedrooms above.

Every drop of fresh water that we used had to be carried up to the flat in clay pitchers or other containers from a tap situated in the back courtyard. Likewise, every drop of dirty water had to be carried down as there was no internal plumbing of any kind. This meant that four flights of stairs had to be negotiated in each direction. It seems incredible today.

The all-purpose room contained a large wooden table which was almost snow white due to it being continually scrubbed, a number of wooden chairs, a couple of high-backed wooden chairs with arm rests and a loose cushion seat. Beneath the large wooden table there were a number of flat cross pieces fitted to give it strength and stability.

It was upon these cross pieces that I used to deposit small crusts of bread which I could not eat. The inevitable result being that whenever the table was scrubbed, a fall of hard crusts occurred and a cat and mouse game arose with my mother as she would chase me with a sweeping brush. However, I was nobody's fool and would drag my father's chair into a corner and hide behind it in a flash, defying her and the world at large. This was my stronghold, but unfortunately for me it had bars running down its back which would allow for the passage of a broom handle. I suffered quite a few thrusts from this weapon until she gave up under pressure of other work to be done.

My greatest memory of her was her industry. She was continually on the go, scrubbing, mending, cooking and washing, dancing from room to room, singing the latest songs. What the hell she had to sing about God only knows.

There wasn't any radio in those days. Therefore, if ever the clock had stopped and she needed a time check, I would gallop down four flights of stairs, run up the length of the street, glance at the clock tower of St Andrew's Church, remember the time, then race back over the same course to tell her.

To the local tradesmen, she was public enemy number one as she gave them hell if they tried to sell her anything she considered substandard. We children continually had to take things back to the shop to be changed.

She was a very tenacious woman and would never give in to what some of us regard as fate. On one occasion she sent me on an errand, wishing to get the chore over quickly, I ran down the stairs, raced along the passage only to trip over the front door step. The half-crown which I held in my hand rolled into the storm drain in the road. Well, within the hour she must have had about a dozen council workmen at the scene. The half-crown as I recall, was recovered or we would still be there today. Oh how I wish that could be!

Below us lived a family of five. Opposite them on the same floor in a large room at the front of the house there lived a semi-recluse woman. Her room was crammed with furniture and possessions and always smelt of incense.

The ground floor had a shop at the front which was occupied by a wonderful old watchmaker and his housekeeper. His shop was an Aladin's cave, the contents of which would I am sure fetch a King's ransom today. His shop was packed with every type of clock you could imagine. There were grandfather clocks with all sorts of working movements incorporated within the clock face — moving ships, moons and stars. There were cuckoo clocks, chiming clocks and dozens of beautiful watches in glass cases.

The house had a long narrow back courtyard separated from the house next door by an eight or nine foot wall. At the far end of the yard there stood a wash-house with a coal-fired copper for boiling the dirty linen etc. Adjoining the wash-house was the one and only toilet, shared of course by everyone living in the house. This toilet unfortunately backed onto a bakery and although warm in winter was continually overrun with cockroaches burrowing through the plaster walls. My father was forever replastering the holes they made in the wall. Heaven only knows why they preferred our toilet to their own lovely bakery, but perhaps cockroaches have no sense of smell?

After dark, the only lighting in this condemned cell was the candle and matches you brought with you. This was also a deterrent to the cockroaches, but even so a teenage girl living in the flat below ours was wont to spend hours in this place reading, so if you were breaking your neck, well, you had to turf her out first. There is always one isn't there!

When twilight fell and play outside was suspended for the day, the rest of the evening before bedtime was usually spent around our large table in the all-purpose room either reading or playing games — mainly card games which explains why we were all very good at playing cards.

My eldest sister, who died aged ninety, played cards until she was eighty-seven years old, every week at the local church hall. She could still remember every card played by her partner and her opponents and also make a shrewd guess as to which cards they still held in their respective hands.

Occasionally, whilst reading or playing games, we would look towards the flypaper hanging from the ceiling, perhaps looking to see whether there was room for just one more victim to find its resting place. Often there was not, which meant that one of us would be sent to the shops with a penny to buy a new one. How I loved pulling it up from its circular container into a two-foot long sticky curl.

Whoever broke the solitary gas mantle in this room — accidentally stabbing it with a match when trying to light it — received a tongue lashing from dad because I believe it cost about four pence to replace, which was a lot of money in those days.

We did not have many luxuries in our house, although my father never kept my mother short on money, he also made sure the local publicans and bookies never went short. But he was basically a good man.

School was just down the hill, about three minutes walk in the direction of the Barbican from where many pupils came, sons and daughters of fishermen and the like, people who often had to send their children to school without shoes. By this time attendance was compulsory, with a person known as the 'Boardman', whom we kids looked upon as an ogre — chasing you up if you were absent from school.

One of my school pals was Billy Glanville, who in 1986 was the Lord Mayor of the City of Plymouth. Bill and I went from the Infant's classes at Palace Court School to the boys section in 1921 and we thought nothing of giving the caretaker a hand at carrying the buckets of coal up from the yard to the various classrooms. During our holidays, at weekends and most summer evenings, we swam from the Hoe foreshore, made tents from old sacks tied to the iron railings or played football.

A few years ago, I met Bill in his official capacity at a dedication service in St Nicholas's Church, HMS *Drake*, Devonport. This was the first time I had knowingly seen him for about sixty years, but we recognised each other almost immediately. It was then that I discovered he was one of my rescuers in 1942, when I was a survivor of the sinking of HMS *Medway*. He was a survivor during the war of the battleship HMS *Barham,* which exploded after being torpedoed with the loss of about nine hundred lives. We later had a private meeting in the Lord Mayor's parlour to talk over old times and to see each others treasured photographs.

Opposite our school there lived a dear old Italian ice-cream vendor with a peg-leg. His pitch was at the far end of the street in which I lived. This meant that his cart had to be manhandled along the cobble stoned street, then up the hill also of rough cobbled stones and finally along our tarmac street to his pitch. Invariably a number of kids were harnessed to the cart to do the donkey work and naturally the reward was an ice cream.

In winter his vehicle was adapted for roasting chestnuts. He would be there in all weathers, hour after hour, all day and evening long winter and summer, for what? I don't believe he ever became rich or left behind any money when he died. He was just one of the many unfortunates who were without a limb at this time because of a tragic war not long ended and not of their making, but who were determined to make a fair living. There were no supplementary benefits to be had in those days, perhaps only a small pension for the loss of a limb.

General election time really brought the politicians out of the woodwork, with bags of coal and other goodies being given to needy families, although why these families were only in need at election times, only the politicians knew. We kids received bags of sweets, seemingly from heaven itself, to march up and down outside the polling centre chanting 'Vote, Vote, Vote for Lady Astor.' What a lot of old 'cobblers', but it certainly worked in our neck of the woods, solid Tory.

They were difficult times and money was short with most working class families. It was common practice for a fathers best or Sunday suit, together with other items, to be taken to the pawnshop on Monday and then redeemed the following payday.

Cake shops would sell off stale bread, cakes and buns cheaply to eager children who waited outside for the shop to open. The same system was also operated by grocers with the residue from their tins of various biscuits, all broken up and mixed together and sold cheaply, there was no individual packaging in those days.

The coming of the herring season was a festival in itself, the highlight of the year. Dozens of fishing trawlers and drifters would be packed together just like sardines, side by side across Sutton Pool on the Barbican, with just fenders between them. The aroma of the place at this time had to be experienced in order to be fully appreciated. Nothing unpleasant, just an odour of fresh fish, brine, rope, paint, canvas, tar and oil. This, plus the noise of what seemed to be a thousand foreign tongues was truly fascinating. The noises in fact came from the women of Yarmouth or Lowestoft who followed the fishing fleet and who, whilst they were talking and singing, would be busy gutting and packing the fish into boxes for despatch to all parts of the country.

Picture in your mind if you can, small down to earth cafés packed with fishermen and their kindred folk, all with great big steaming mugs of tea and bacon sandwiches and not a kipper in sight — this was vibrant life indeed!

I would return home triumphantly from the harbour with the fingers on each hand thrust through the gills of a herring, two on the longer fingers, sometimes with as many as twelve fish in total. The smell of them being cooked, soused in vinegar with bay leaves, was unforgettable.

A short distance down the hill from where we lived there was a narrow thoroughfare named Lower Lane. It would allow the passage of a lorry or horse-drawn cart, but in one direction only. At one end there was an ice-making plant where in summer we would gather with our bowls, jugs or basins collecting the scraps of ice which were continually breaking off from the large blocks that were being manhandled into the lorries and carts. The ice blocks were delivered to butchers, fish shops, hotels or large private houses with ice boxes. There were not many refrigerators about in those far off days.

In the evenings the lane would be silent, except for the occasional hiss from the roof of the ice-making plant, but not for very long as this lane was normally transformed into our football pitch. We were not permitted to play football on Plymouth Hoe, which was ten minutes walk away, or in any of the parks, the park-keepers were men with a mission then.

Our ball was constructed out of pressed wet paper, wrapped in an old rag firmly tied with string. Eleven boys on each side? Well, you have just got to be kidding — our minimum must have been about sixteen aside.

Our goalkeepers, the unlucky ones who drew the short straw or the ones who could not fight, also doubled as a lookout for the 'coppers'. Some of these gentlemen of the law were not above slipping a couple of farthings into the fingers of their uniform gloves they carried, which we discovered much to our discomfort when we were on the receiving end of a swish from these unorthodox weapons. This did us no lasting harm, but taught us to fear, or rather respect the law. It must have been respect because we always ran to them for help in an emergency.

Our neighbours on the other side of the courtyard wall were a naval man and his wife, with a son of about my own age. The man must have been something of a wireless buff, because one day he appeared in the courtyard and proceeded to rig up yards of aerial wire together with porcelain insulators from end to end. All this wiring was then led into the window of his kitchen-cum-living room which also had wires stretched across it.

The son called to me one day to tell me that his father had a crystal set, together with a couple of sets of earphones and was intending to tune into a broadcast coming direct from Hyde Park in London. The broadcast was of the most famous cowboy of our time, Tom Mix, who had come over from Hollywood bringing with him his equally famous horse, Tony. Well, it was just incredible, sheer magic, because none of us had actually heard Tom Mix speak, there were only silent films in those days.

At this time there was just one thing I thought about becoming and that was a bell boy on a great big ocean liner. They were continually seen on cinema screens at that time with little pill box hats and rows of brass buttons down their tunics. I could picture myself as such, more especially as I could actually see all these great transatlantic ships almost every day of the week from Plymouth Hoe.

Plymouth Sound, which is the harbour inside the breakwater, was truly the crossroads of life. At any one time one could see great passenger ships at anchor, maybe the *Mauritania* or some big French or German liner, a number of battleships, a squadron of cruisers, flotillas of destroyers, and various small merchant ships.

At regatta time, over near Drake's Island, there would be a number of the largest yachts one could ever see, King George V's *Britannia*, Tommy Lipton's *Shamrock* or was it *Westward*, and many others.

In amongst all these ships would be mail and passenger tenders constantly on the move between the liners which would arrive and depart, sometimes within the hour. These tenders would discharge the mail and passengers at the rail head in Millbay docks from where they could be transported to London in about four hours. There would also be literally dozens of naval barges and other craft moving between the ships and the dockyard just up the river in Devonport.

RAF flying boats would take off and land in the Sound and taxi to their moorings in the inner harbour at Mount Batten. This was where Lawrence of Arabia was stationed at the time. The flying boats were the 'Blackburn Irises' one of which I actually saw turn over, nose first and sink after landing near to the Mallard Buoy. With such surroundings it is no wonder I was drawn to a life at sea in later life.

CHAPTER 2

I can only remember about half a dozen or so of my mothers's brothers and sisters. The most prominent being Johnny Adams, a tough fisherman and a great rugby football player for Camborne and other clubs in the area. There was also Aunt Nannie, married to a sailor who deserted the Royal Navy when he was in his thirties. I was too young to remember much about him except for one period when he stayed with us in Plymouth for a few days.

He was painting the front of a cupboard for mother — the painting was a vase of daffodils and narcissus which to me at that tender age was one of the loveliest pictures I had ever seen close up. There is a punch line to this little story, he seemed to be determined to finish this lovely picture on a particular evening and in order for him to be able to complete this 'masterpiece' it became necessary for me to hold a lighted candle close to him. Only he knew then that come the morning, he would disappear from our lives forever. What an artist! I wonder whatever happened to him? He just sailed off to his island of dreams and I do hope he reached it.

My father had eleven brothers and sisters who all lived to be over ninety years of age. Three of these brothers, who were boilermakers and coppersmiths, emigrated to Australia in the 1880s, settling in Melbourne, where during the course of making money they proceeded to populate the place. A glance at the Melbourne telephone directory today will confirm this. In 1968, one of these brothers, Edward, who had eleven children, was the State of Victoria's oldest man at the grand age of 104.

His brother Bill, whom I met when he returned to England for a holiday, told me that the three of them travelled to Australia in a sailing ship, which took three months to get there and they only paid for their passage. All their food had to be purchased daily from the purser and was cooked on a steel plate on the upper deck in a makeshift oven which they had made themselves.

One of my dad's sisters, Elizabeth, married a singer, a certain George Morgan, who was part of a double act named *Morgan and Stuart*. I can remember them appearing on the bill at the Palace Theatre in Plymouth in the early twenties. They made quite a bit of money from tours to South Africa, Australia, Canada and the USA. He died shortly after this leaving my aunt quite wealthy. At one time she was the sole owner of the Redcliffe Hotel in Paignton. One of her grandsons, Peter Morgan CBE, settled in the West Indies where he became the only white member of the Senate and then the High Commissioner for Barbados in Canada.

My brother, Bert, was not considered to be very bright at school, but he certainly made up for this later in life. He left school at fourteen to become a barber's boy preparing the customers with lather ready for the man with the razor. He then moved on to work in the Grand Hotel in Torquay and later became a steward with Imperial Airways and assistant purser with P&O on the

'Strath' liners. After the war, he was in the employ of the film star James Mason and accompanied him to New York and Hollywood, there to become an American citizen as he loved the USA so much. When James Mason returned to Europe to resume his film career here, my brother decided to remain in America and continued working with other film stars. This was unfortunate for me in a selfish way, as occasionally I was lucky enough to receive one or two suits which James Mason discarded.

I do not ever remember my brother once being ill, but sadly he collapsed in a New York street and died the following day in hospital. This was in 1968 when he was in the employ of Jason Robards who attended his funeral service together with several other stars.

On his journey through life he became quite an entertainer himself, although not professionally. He could dance, sing, play various instruments including the piano — all quite well. He was also a great conversationalist — not just on theatrical matters, but wide ranging subjects, both past and present. I have heard it said that when he left a room it was as if a light had been switched off.

He once confided in me that when he retired, he planned to secure a small house on Malibu Beach, California. That is what dreams are made of and sometimes they come true, but unfortunately not for him.

My eldest sister Violet, sixteen years my senior, was really the 'dogsbody' of the family, she was detailed to keep her eye on all the younger children in the family, in addition to her domestic work in private houses. She also was not considered by her teachers to be very bright, but that was probably because she was hardly ever there always being kept at home to look after children.

However, she went on to serve for three years in the WRACs during the first war and was a Wren in the second. At eighty-seven years of age, although a little frail, was as bright as a button, read about six library books a week, was a keen card player and a great intelligent talker.

Incidentally, she married a brilliant chap named Philip who was unfortunately caught in a German gas attack during the first war which badly affected his lungs. Also, as a result of hand grenades that burst near him, small splinters of metal would occasionally work their way to the surface of his skin on his backside and lower back.

There is not a great deal that I can write about my elder sister Gladys, twelve years my senior. She was a good looking girl like mother and worked in the railway buffets, eventually marrying a fitter working in the naval dockyard.

My youngest sister, Irene, ten years my senior, was a great pal to my brother and they were always off skating together at the local roller rink. My mother used to examine their shoes for evidence of the clips biting into them, which she claimed weakened the shoes.

She also used to examine my shoes, with her tongue for traces of salt water, to check if I had been to the beach. What a detective she would have made!

However, I return to the story of my life with a tragedy which I was unable to comprehend at the time. I was ten and a half years old when my mother was admitted, at the age of fifty, to hospital for an operation. I later found out that she had previously been in hospital for a suspected growth, but had apparently bribed a nurse to obtain her clothes and absconded.

This time, however, there was to be no escape from the surgeon's knife. The doctors said that the operation was successful, but a couple of days later, complications set in. Friday 20th February 1925, will remain rooted in my memory until it is my turn to follow her. My father, who had obviously been told to expect the worst, kept me home from school that day and we both went to see her in the morning. She kissed me and asked me to return home to fetch my sisters. We were met halfway by dad who told us that mother had passed away. I have often wondered how different life would have been for me had she lived.

The magnitude of her dying did not register with me at that time. It was not until my late teens that I realised what a loss I had suffered at such a vital period in my life.

To me, there was great confusion at her death, which is probably why her absence did not sink in as it should have done. There were relatives from everywhere, heaps of them, with Grandmother Adams from St Ives — then in her late seventies — taking charge as she always did.

I can remember her funeral as if it was yesterday. There were black horses and carriages and all the women wore black with veils over their faces. The men and boys were in black or dark grey with black diamonds of cloth or arm bands stitched to their sleeves. We even had white handkerchiefs with black borders.

After the funeral, grandmother decided that I must return home with her until the readjustment of our household. This, as it happened, was for only a month or so. I then returned to Plymouth and a family which consisted of dad, my sister Irene and my brother. Irene eventually married her sailor and they moved in with us and my brother soon left to start his hotel job. Make no mistake about it a mother is the hub around which a family revolves and she was sorely missed by us all.

Life had to go on and I joined the Boys' Brigade, the headquarters of which were on the Barbican. An ex-army captain, Percy Harvey, was our leader and he was a wonderful man whose influence on my life was invaluable.

In the late fifties and early sixties, I was working in circumstances which allowed me to take an early morning swim from Plymouth Hoe before starting at the office around 10.00 am. Invariably, I would pass Captain Harvey on his way to the Hoe where he would sit for hours to read his newspaper and gaze seaward, perhaps to the Point where we all used to camp. He would always have his army officer's haversack over his shoulder containing his newspaper, flask and sandwiches and it would always be the same routine greeting between us.

'Good morning Sir', from me.

'Good morning Fred', from him, as he pointed towards the Hoe with his favourite pipe.

One evening I sat down to read the local evening paper and discovered that he had been found dead, sitting in a seat facing the sea. He had long been retired, but deserved many more years. I was about forty-six years old at the time and he must have been in his late seventies.

The Boys' Brigade, which I loved, assembled two or three times a week, the main attendance was on Sunday evenings for a service followed by a talk from a speaker who was nearly always a local celebrity. Another evening would be devoted to drills and band practice in the drill hall at Millbay, near the Hoe.

The summers were really special. On Friday afternoons, after school, we would pack our haversacks with enough food to last until Sunday evening, then off we would go to our weekend camp at Renny Battery — an army camp. We would always be accompanied by one of our officers, nearly always it was Lieutenant George Parr, who died a few years ago at the age of eighty, a great chap from a great family.

The journey to our camp was quite an adventure in itself. We walked with our kit from the headquarters along the Barbican fish market to Phoenix Wharf, where we caught a ferry across a short stretch of water to the village of Turnchapel, situated quite near to the RAF base at Mount Batten. On this short trip we would invariably pass quite close to a number of flying boats gently rising up and down at their moorings. Sometimes we would see one arriving or departing with its great propellers rotating and blowing up spray towards us.

Stepping off the ferry, we were faced with one hell of a march to Fort Bovisand, which is situated facing one end of the Breakwater at the entrance to Plymouth Sound. For the first mile or so it was an uphill climb to Jennycliffe Bay, then about a half mile along the main road we turned off onto an unmade, well trodden, winding cliff path, along which we walked in single file carrying our gear. When we reached Fort Bovisand we still had another couple of miles to go across another rough cliff path to Renny Battery, the army gun emplacement commanding the entrance to Plymouth Sound.

There was an arrangement with the commanding officer of the Renny Battery whereby he allowed us the use of one of their store rooms in which we could keep our 'Bell' tents and cooking utensils etc. All our equipment had to be manhandled down a steep slope to two or three old flat abandoned gun emplacements where we set up camp about 40ft above the high water line.

Friday evenings we normally had just two tents erected holding about ten boys in each, we would have a cook-up, roast spuds in the fire, a singsong, then turn in exhausted. After breakfast on Saturday morning we would bring down another tent for Captain Harvey and the lads who arrived later in the day after work and then we dispersed to our various pursuits, swimming, fishing etc.

Sometimes on Sundays we would have a visit from George Parr's two younger sisters, Marian and Lottie, who would spend the day at Bovisand beach with their family. Marian and Lottie were lovely girls. I was very fond of both of them and after joining the Navy became engaged to Marian. Their father was a firm, but fair man and their mother was a wonderful woman who kept a lovely table — a good cook. Their father and elder brother Frank were the owners of pleasure boats which used to ply between the Barbican and Bovisand.

During one particular summer, we spent a whole week camping on Lord Astor's estate at Cliveden, Berkshire, and this is where my chanting 'Vote Vote, Vote for Lady Astor' really paid off.

How can I describe how I felt? Someone from my background being allowed in the grounds within sight of this great mansion. We dug our latrines, set up the tents and the Astors gave us full range of their stretch of the River Thames. We were allowed to use their punts and skiffs, which us young sea dogs from Plymouth could easily handle.

One day we were taken into the mansion to meet the Astors and have a meal, and afterwards we were allowed to get lost in the maze in the garden. We were also given a picture postcard of Cliveden autographed by members of the family. I remember Michael Astor signing my card, what an experience for such as I.

Another vivid memory of mine is of the General Strike of 1926 which even penetrated a placid Tory stronghold like Plymouth. My father and I stood and watched tram cars being stoned and overturned at St Andrew's Cross at the far end of our street. I remember it now, but could not understand it then.

I was by this time a member of both St Catherine's Church choir, for which I was paid, and St Andrew's School choir, for which I was unpaid. The school choir gave a concert at least once a week at various venues throughout the area. Also at this time, it was discovered that I was a fairly good solo singer, but rather nervous as I recall. However, I actually came third in the musical festival in Plymouth Guildhall with my rendering of *Off to Market Johnny* and also played the lead, Queen Elizabeth, in my school production of *Dogs of Devon*.

I was more or less a free agent in those days and allowed to do as I wished, within reason. Dad would be out most evenings boozing and playing cards with his pals. I cannot ever remember seeing him worse the wear for drink and never once did he lay a hand on me. Unfortunately, neither did he take any positive interest in me, except to advise me not to work in a foundry as he said the fumes would kill me. It didn't kill him though — he worked there until his late seventies.

One of my school teachers found me a part time job with a local photographer, apparently one of the top men of his profession. The pay was five shillings per week, which was very good in those days. The premises backed on to our school which enabled me to go there straight from school. Part of my job was to deliver framed photographs to various places, including the barracks and naval ships in the dockyard at Devonport.

On reflection I wish I had been given some definite advice at this time because the job had prospects. Alas, no advice was forthcoming and a life at sea was my destiny.

CHAPTER 3

A s I began to grow up I gradually became aware of a change in my attitude towards girls. This change came about when we acquired new neighbours, a naval couple in their mid-thirties with a good looking precocious daughter about twelve or thirteen years old.

The daughter was a little beauty who was given to inviting other girls of her own age group into her back yard. There they would dress up and parade around preening themselves and act out their fantasies.

I was really taken with the daughter who on occasions would look towards me rather coyly, knowing that I was watching her every movement. Her father was eventually posted abroad and her mother began to leave the daughter alone on three or four nights during the week to visit friends.

On these evenings, I would watch her leaning on the window ledge of their living room window just gazing out into her back yard, wearing only a nightdress. She would occasionally look towards me, quite provocatively, knowing I am sure that I was attracted to her.

One evening a plan came to me which I thought was foolproof and I decided to give it a try. We always kept our scrubbing brush upon the window ledge of our tiny kitchen in order that it would dry. This window was situated directly above the sloping roof of our neighbours small coal shed in the back yard, which was directly outside their back door. I figured that if I gave the brush a little push, it would drop onto the sloping roof and roll into the yard next door giving me a legitimate excuse to go around and recover it.

One evening I succeeded with my little plan and asked the girl if I could come around to get the brush. She agreed and came to the front door to let me in, still wearing just her nightdress. I then went to the yard, recovered the brush and bolted the back door. The passage from front to back was rather narrow and dark, so throwing caution to the wind I took the girl into my arms to kiss her. She responded immediately, which was a real milestone in life for me.

We acted out this little pantomime two or three times a week, just kissing and cuddling. We were very immature with regard to the birds and bees I'm afraid, but extremely happy in our own little way. Unfortunately, one evening our little private heaven was shattered by the unexpected return of her mother.

Directly outside the front door of the house was a gas-lit street lamp which shone into the passage whenever the front door was opened. On this occasion the light from this lamp fell upon us clasped together in a loving embrace. The first words spoken were from the mother who ordered her daughter to bed immediately, her bedroom was situated right at the top of the house, two floors above. I in turn was ordered up to the living room on the first floor.

I was then given the biggest tongue lashing I have ever received in my life including my years in both the Merchant and Royal Navy. I was threatened with borstal, prison, being struck by lightning and deportation to Canada or

Australia. She threatened to tell my father and sister and I was ordered to remain exactly where I was. I stayed rooted to the spot, until she returned from upstairs after castigating her daughter who was no doubt crying on her bed. I was by this time sobbing uncontrollably and between sobs tried to plead with her for forgiveness. After all I was only 14 years old!

She left the room and after what seemed an eternity returned — as I thought to continue the onslaught, but instead, without a word, she put an arm around me and led me into the front bedroom. I was now in a bad way, shaking and sobbing, but she told me to undress and get into bed. This I did and lay facing the wall. I had no sense of time, my head was in a turmoil, but after a while I felt her getting into bed with me. She then turned me around to face her and cradled me in her arms. It was then I realised that she was completely naked. Quietly, in a voice just above a whisper, she began to talk to me, telling me about the facts of life, what to do, what not to do and how to do it, all the time caressing me with her hands.

I began to feel easier under the influence of her caresses and just lay there cosily cradled in her embrace, but gradually I felt a change taking place, I became warm and elated — this was indeed a new phenomenon for me. I then became aroused and my partner, well aware of this, gently manoeuvred me into a position on top of her and made the insertion for me.

If I had wanted to escape, which by this time I do not believe I had any desire to do so, it would have been practically impossible because she had brought her legs up around me and held me tight with her arms. We were simply locked together.

I was carried away with a sense of well being, floating on air as it were, my head spinning — I was shaken with spasms, then just as suddenly, all was still and I was drained and exhausted. Life was never the same again for me.

When I look back after all these years, I must have thought that there was no such thing as life after sex, because this first experience was so painfully wonderful that I thought I was in the process of dying. Probably the fact that I had not been circumcised, plus my ignorance, were contributory factors to the severe pain I had to endure. I had torn a vital piece of skin and when I was eventually allowed to leave the bed, I was too frightened to look down or even touch myself for fear of what I might see or feel. I really thought that my 'pecker' had dropped off. Without a word passing between us, I hurriedly dressed and crept silently away to my house and the safe haven of my bed.

After that encounter nine days in a week would not have been sufficient. I had my work load, choir practice and concerts, Boys' Brigade, my part-time job and of course her. I was subjected to a mild form of blackmail as she threatened to tell my family what had happened with her daughter. As a result, I was bedded two or three times a week and to be honest blackmail was unnecessary. Growing in confidence, realising that I had suffered no permanent damage and that I would not go blind, I took to it like a duck takes to water and began to feel that I could take on all-comers, which I very soon did.

With my confidence growing, I was determined to have a similar relationship with the daughter. The real driving force behind my determination to possess her bodily was her precociousness and outstandingly youthful beauty. It was driving me crazy, especially as I had been taught what it was all about. I could have eaten her.

After much planning she finally succumbed to my advances, but initially we were always on edge, apprehensive, frightened, unable to relax and scared that her mother would find out. All this, coupled with her naivete, created tremendous problems and I invariably had a premature ejaculation. However, there were a number of occasions when we made it without any disastrous results, although the first time we did it, she cried bitterly and was quite upset. I knew exactly how she felt.

For myself, there was the satisfaction of having reached the target, but nothing could match the experience with her mother — she won hands down. She was definitely the top of the class — my first — and because of this very fact, must surely be considered my greatest encounter.

All good things must come to an end and one day, quite unexpectedly, she announced that her husband was coming home and would be leaving the Navy. That meant they would all be moving back to their home town in the North. I was shattered, just could not take it in. What would I do? She just couldn't go, but alas she did. In a way I suppose it was very fortunate for me, but the dramatic manner in which our affair ended left me feeling very low for quite some time.

When they left, my family moved into the house they vacated. This was indeed a luxury, electric lighting, fresh water from the tap upstairs, a kitchen sink and no other families in the house. The ground floor, however, was occupied during the day by a parcel delivery company.

On occasions when entering the front bedroom I could sense a presence, not ghostly, just warm and friendly. Happy days, but those evenings were gone forever. I was forced to start spreading my wings, to fly from the nest and go out hunting. After all, wasn't I now a fully trained hawk?

When I passed school leaving age, which was fourteen, a full-time job was arranged for me. Whispers of this had been rife for many months, but I had been far too busy to take note of them.

I suppose I should not blame my father and brother-in-law Philip too much for steering me into the direction they did, because at this period there were not many employment openings for youngsters without qualifications. They understandably thought that the job they had secured for me would be the envy of most boys, it was, at least to the lads of my immediate acquaintance.

Father and Philip were really in no position to foresee the advances which would be made in the field of my part-time job with the photographer, but surely they should have given some thought to my wages. I was receiving five shillings per week for a few hours part-time evenings and was expected to work full-time from eight to five daily and eight to twelve on Saturdays for seven and sixpence per week.

The school I was attending at this time allowed me to leave at a moment's notice. I had been in the same top class for two years and was now just over fourteen years old. I wanted to go to the Technical School, the entrance exam to which I had easily passed, but this school required me to stay until I was sixteen years old and there were uniforms and text books to buy in addition to other expenses. In essence the family could not afford the money.

So I had to take my first long trouser job. Philip was the manager and his assistant, a lady, left to get married about the time I reached school leaving age and so I was taken on to be groomed for stardom.

I didn't have a bike and public transport, which I could not afford, took a long roundabout route from my home to my place of work, so I walked. The walk was downhill to the north quay of Sutton Harbour and took about twenty-five minutes. Along this quay was the scene of great activity — there were goods trains continually coming and going and fishing boats were moored, together with small trading vessels. I would duck under a bar protecting a level crossing and walk down Commercial Road. This entire road, except for a public house, was taken up by timber yards, builder's merchants, corn and seed firms and one factory situated at the junction of a narrow lane, which we knew as Candleworks Lane. The stink from this place was appalling, as they produced glue and candles. A little further along was a railway good's depot, then another level crossing and about a hundred yards further on, our office.

The company for which I worked was one of the largest private contractors in the area specializing in the removal and transport of practically anything and everything. We had government contracts for transporting heavy guns for the Army and a couple of our heavy lorries were engaged in delivering daily coal supplies to Princetown Prison on Dartmoor. We moved most of the timber which was unloaded from ships in the nearby docks. Household removals were done by us and we were also agents for cattle cake and fertiliser, which were delivered to farms in the local area.

Our vehicles consisted of a few ex-army lorries, plus a couple of coal-burning traction engine lorries and a small number of Fords and other assorted trucks. We also had about thirty horses with their attendant vehicles, the bodies of which were made by our own coach builders, wheelwrights and blacksmiths.

The managing director was in my opinion a skinflint with no real forward looking interest in the company. He relied too much on Philip to run the business and keep the firm ticking over.

The conditions in our office were appalling even for the hard up days of 1929. The office was 'Dickensian', with one high sloping desk running practically the whole length of the room and we sat upon high wooden seated stools. Our tools of the trade were an antique Imperial typewriter and a letter press, which I suppose would fetch a fortune today. The lino covering the floor was worn and patched in places.

The boss had his own small private office just off the main one. He came in for about three or four hours on most days and that was his contribution.

My job, under Philip's direction, was checking workers time sheets and calculating their wages. They were paid by the hour, not by the week — one shilling per hour and sometimes they could only manage to get in about four or five hours per day. Although Philip was a sick man, which I did not appreciate at the time, he would move heaven and earth to obtain work for his men. I was the general 'dogsbody' and five o'clock could not come fast enough for me. All this for seven and sixpence a week, I must have been raving mad!

My private life at that time was going along quite well. I had finished with choirs, but I still loved the Boys' Brigade — although of course in the summer I could only join the camp on Saturday afternoons.

My best friend, who I will call George, was a right 'Jack the Lad', or thought he was. He was up to all the tricks imaginable and also had an eye for the girls, but he did not know what it was all about, did he? I was streets ahead of him and all the other lads of our age — look at the training I had received.

George and I used to help his grandmother with her washing most evenings. We would do the wringing for her with an old-fashioned upright mangle, one of us would turn the handle whilst the other would feed the sheets and towels etc. through the wooden rollers.

When the washing was finished his grandmother would reward us with sweets and then she would go to the *Valiant Soldier*, the local pub, accompanied by a younger woman who, would you believe, had a daughter of our age or a little younger. Well, George used to entice her into his grandmother's bed room for a romp on the bed, but he didn't really have a clue as to how to go about things, so of course I had to take over and sort her out.

George didn't know it at the time, but I was also 'fixing up' his younger sister, and her friend, the word must have gone around because before very long I was beating them off with a club.

A couple of years passed with the same old routine, I was absolutely bored stiff at work, but the evening leisure periods had some great compensations.

In Plymouth at this time there was a great character, a very wealthy gentleman named 'Casanova' Ballard, who built, at very great expense, a three or four story building named the Ballard Institute. It was in effect a boys' club and I spent quite a lot of my time there with many of my friends. Mr Ballard's generosity was boundless, no boy in need ever went without shoes or clothes, and even bicycles were given to some. Incidentally, this gentleman was frowned upon by the establishment. It was alleged that Mr. Ballard had tried to influence the outcome of a parliamentary election for the Drake division of Plymouth in favour of the Labour candidate who won the seat. A full judicial enquiry was held before such awesome justices as Talbot and Swift, with the object of unseating the candidate, Jimmy Moses.

I had to appear before the enquiry as a witness against Mr Ballard. It was alleged that he had told all the young impressionable boys at his club, if the Conservatives won the election he might have to close down his Institute and move to some other part of the country. Supposedly, this resulted in hundreds of boys going home to tell their parents, who would then certainly vote Labour.

As I recall, it was not Mr Ballard personally who suggested that this might happen, but some of his instructors. However, I was one of the fourteen and fifteen year old kids who had to stand petrified alone in the witness box to be questioned by such advocates as Sir Stafford Cripps and Mr Roland Oliver KC. At the time I was employed by a very prominent well known Tory. I had spoken to other people in our firm about what I had been told at Ballards and word of this had got to the boss who passed it on without telling me. Hence the frightening experience in court.

'Casanova' Ballard was a true philanthropist, seven days a week, fifty two weeks of the year — not just at election times. Some of the boys who were educated at Hoe Grammar School and had successful careers owe it all to him. His good work still goes on in the form of legacies, grants, and scholarships.

Carnival time was another wonderful time . There were processions, streets and buildings were decorated and sporting events and regattas organized. Dancing took place on the promenade of Plymouth Hoe, where it seemed every boy and girl in Plymouth met to flirt and pair off. The promenade would be packed from end to end with young people just walking up and down hoping to meet their dreamboat.

I have forgotten to mention a shattering blow I received when I was about fifteen and a half years old. Bored to tears with my job, but not daring to tell anyone directly, I visited the naval recruiting office in Devonport where I tried to join as a boy seaman, but imagine the shock to me of being told, after a preliminary medical examination, that I could never join the Navy because I had flat feet!

At work I was too concerned with my own trials and tribulations to really appreciate Philip's deteriorating health. He had become rather stout and breathless and was brought from his home to the office every morning in a little two wheeled trap drawn by a lovely little pony.

One morning, the trap arrived back at the office without Philip. The driver, who was a stable lad, informed us that Philip had collapsed and died whilst dressing for work.

My sister told me later that he had eaten his breakfast and suddenly paused whilst in the act of tying his shoe laces. He then asked her to bring to him their two daughters who were upstairs in their bedroom, he kissed them and sent them back upstairs. My sister told him that she would go to the shop across the road and telephone for the doctor, but Philip said that he did not think he would last until he arrived. Within minutes, he had passed away — a sad end to a very fine gentleman.

Within days of Philip's death, the dear little pony was found dead in her stall. I often wondered whether she missed her daily apple which Philip always gave her on arriving at the office.

Philip's death was the last straw as far as I was concerned with the company I worked for and I informed the managing director that I wanted to leave. He asked me to stay for a few weeks in order that a replacement be found, to which I agreed. I didn't have a clue then what I was going to do. I had been rejected for the Navy and did not at the time even consider trying to join one of the other forces.

One day I read in a magazine an article which featured the training of boys for entry into the Merchant Navy at a sea school, sponsored by the larger shipping companies and located in Gravesend, Kent. I immediately wrote to the school seeking entry. They in turn, sent me an application form and informed me of the necessary qualifications required before I could be accepted for entry. These were a medical certificate from my doctor, a character reference and a Board of Trade certificate for an examination in form and colour vision. Having obtained these, I duly sent them off to the school and waited for the outcome with my fingers crossed.

This was another period of my life when no advice was sought or given. Boy seamen were required to pay two pounds, which covered the charge for their working clothes of dungarees, jerseys, weather hat and a couple of blankets. The stewards paid six pounds for their uniforms. Nobody told me that stewards could earn a lot more money than a seaman ever would.

I can remember waiting for the result and wondering what life would be like, away from home and my friends. Well, one friend in particular, Marian, who with her sister Lottie used to visit our Boys' Brigade camp and we had been pals for years.

I had my moments of romance with both of them on separate occasions, but strangely enough, would you believe, we never engaged in any sexual activities. I have thought about this many times but have never arrived at a satisfactory explanation. Also, I am quite sure that neither of these girls were aware of my sexual activities with the other girls in my neighbourhood.

Marian was the love of my life. She was mine, but never was. There have been many times since that I have regretted not having taken advantage of her, at least it would have forced the issue. I am sure that after all the fuss had died down, we could have made it together, but all we ever did was to kiss and cuddle and make teenage plans for our forthcoming future. I remember the old song *At seventeen he falls in love quite madly with the eyes of tender blue.* I was just coming up to that age.

CHAPTER 4

Sometime during January 1931, I received an answer from the sea school, I had been accepted as a boy seaman and I packed my bags, said goodbye to my family and friends and set off for Gravesend, and a new life.

After arriving at Paddington, I found my way to Leadenhall Street where after an interview, which thankfully included three or four other boys, I was instructed to take a train to Gravesend, then find my way to the school, which was situated at the rivers edge on the lower reaches of the Thames. When I arrived there I was somewhat taken aback as the buildings resembled the prisons I had seen in films at the cinema. It looked a very bleak place indeed.

The main block in which we were housed, two to a cabin, had three decks, each divided into port and starboard. 'A' deck on the ground floor, 'B' deck on the first floor and 'C' deck on the second floor. The whole centre of this block was open plan. Each deck or landing was reached by ascending a steel ladder or stairway and the port and starboard sides were connected by bridges. There were occasions when we were required to step out of our cabins and look over the rail down to the ground floor where we could all be seen by the duty instructor.

Everything about our conditions were austere, plain and simple, with just the bare necessities in the cabins, dining hall, bathroom and classrooms. Some of the lads came from orphanages and poor homes and they took the surroundings and conditions in their stride, but others had to make quite a lot of adjustments.

Our daily routine was very rigorous from Monday to Saturday inclusive. In the mornings we had to queue in single file completely naked and you had to keep your hand over your private parts. We would move forward, one by one, until we came face to face with an instructor, clad in an oilskin apron, who would have before him a large round wooden tub filled with liquid soap. The instructor would then scoop up a load of this soap and plonk it on the top of your head ensuring that you had to shower — like it or not!

After a brisk rub down, we dressed and queued again, single file, in the dining hall, which had plain well scrubbed wooden tables and long wooden benches. On reaching the instructor we were given a large plate of porridge topped with a big soup ladle of molasses. At the same time we collected a plate with two thick slices of bread and margarine with a dollop of marmalade on the side. These were known to everyone as two dogs and were bought, sold and traded amongst us boys for almost anything.

On Sundays we were excused the compulsory shower and sometimes had a change of breakfast, normally egg and fried bread with two sausages, that was living for you.

We queued for practically everything. Our food was substantial and very plain. We would have a simple snack at lunch time and for dinner, meat and two veg, fish and chips or stew. In the evening, about an hour or so before lights out, we would have a mug of cocoa and a thick slice of bread and jam.

Pocket money had to be sent from home and we were only allowed out of the school on Saturdays, when we could do as we wished.

As a seaman, I was taught about the various parts of a ship, how to splice ropes and tie knots, boat pulling, which I knew all about, how to box the compass and what was very important, how to sail a ships lifeboat with a dipping lug sail, which would enable it to sail six points to the wind. We were also required to take part in lifeboat drill two or three times a week.

When we were considered to be fairly proficient at these tasks we were sent to our training ship moored in the Thames, within sight of the school. She was the *Triton*, commanded by Captain Chisholm who was a strict disciplinarian, and a right 'stinker' to us boys.

This ship was actually an old paddle steamer, the paddles of which had been dismantled. The housing on the port side contained our washing facilities and the starboard side our toilets and cleaning stores.

The main reason for being sent out to this vessel was to teach us the rudiments of shipboard life — the rules of the road. Movements of other ships up and down the Thames provided plenty of scope for such instruction. We were taught about navigation lights, the meaning of various flag signals, bridge work with the wheel, compass and telegraphs and lookout duties in the crows nest on the foremast and other vantage points. We were taught about swinging the lead, not in this case dodging work, but determining the depth of water beneath the ship.

The boys' quarters on board were in a hold, amidships. There were rows of bunks three high on each side and in the centre was a long wooden table with benches each side and this was where we took our meals.

I have already said that the captain was a hard man and I have a very good reason for this assertion. My period on this vessel was during the early winter when early morning frosts would shimmer on the wooden decks and fittings, but the captain would still have us out scrubbing the deck on our hands and knees. We would also have to clean the numerous brass fittings throughout the vessel including the binnacle, telegraphs and voice pipes. This would be done with linseed oil and bathbrick, which would leave your hands sore and cut, the only remedy being to rub vaseline into the wounds.

It turned out that I was more fortunate than the other boys on the vessel because I was selected by the captain's wife, who lived on board, to become her 'shore boy' or 'toyboy'. This meant that on about four mornings during the week I would be rowed ashore with a basket and a list to do her shopping. At the time I was convinced she fancied me.

My spell on the *Triton* eventually came to an end and I returned to the shore establishment where I was selected for a wireless watcher's course. In those days some of the smaller merchant vessels just carried one, or at most two, wireless operators. To supplement these men, a wireless watcher, who held a certificate of proficiency issued by the Postmaster General, was trained to recognize various signals, such as call signs and distress signals. On hearing any of these calls, he would then alert the qualified operator who would take over.

At the end of my training at the school, I was placed on the 'stand by' list, which was a list of the top twelve boys who were kitted out, ready to go to a ship anywhere at a moments notice. We all hoped that at least two of us would go together which occasionally happened, but no such luck in my case — I was fated to travel to my first ship alone.

In January 1932 my turn came and I was instructed to pack my kit bag and proceed to Victoria Docks in the east end of London, there to join the SS *Tamaroa* of the Shaw Saville and Albion Line, a subsidiary of the White Star Line and reputedly a skinflint company. As far as I was concerned they were all I received was two pounds per month — with overtime, if any, at sixpence per hour. I set off for London with dreams of sailing the seven seas to far away places with strange sounding names.

I arrived at Fenchurch Street Station and with my kit bag on my shoulder set off on the bus to Custom House, from there to Victoria Docks where I walked down a line of ships looking for my own ship. Eventually, I found the *Tamaroa*, a sister ship of the *Mataroa*. Their names originated from New Zealand, the country to which they plied their trade and to which they were both bound. These ships were passenger cargo vessels of about 8,000 tons, according to my discharge book which I have before me as I write. They had one funnel and six cargo holds. I looked up at this great tall ship and with my kit bag on my shoulder, took a deep breath and climbed the gangway where at the head was a seaman who had been posted there to check anyone coming on board. He directed me to the chief officer.

This austere gentleman, after a brief interview, ordered me to report to the bosun. The bosun, just my luck, was a native of Stornoway and they were reputed to be the toughest in the business. This one had to be the number one of his class because from day one my backside hardly ever touched the ground. I was his personal 'dogsbody' and he chased me from pillar to post, shouting at me a whole variety of commands, such as, 'Pick up this!' Fetch that!' Stow that away!' Where the hell have you been hiding!' And others that I can't repeat.

My primary duty was to fetch and serve the bosun's and carpenter's meals in a cabin they shared in the fo'c's'le. On occasions this was a very difficult operation, especially when a heavy sea was running, because the meals had to be brought from a galley across the open forward well deck, which could be awash with sea water.

When we left, a tug eased us out of the dock and into the River Thames where we turned and proceeded slowly downstream towards the open sea. I could hardly wait to catch a glimpse of Gravesend Sea School and the Triton. Eventually, on our starboard side, I saw the school coming up. All the lads on the *Triton* seemed to be waving to us, as I had done in my time to ships that were passing.

At the mouth of the river we turned to starboard into the English Channel and on to our first port of call, which was to take on fuel at Curaçoa in the Dutch West Indies.

I shared a cabin in the fo'c's'le with five others. They were four ordinary or able seamen, plus another deck boy such as myself and we two were known as the 'Peggys'. We shared the duty of clearing and washing up the dishes in the mess room after everyone had eaten.

On the second day at sea we headed towards the Azores and I gradually became aware I was not feeling too good, I had a bit of a headache and my tummy rose and fell with the movement of the ship. Well, this wasn't very good at all and I decided if I could avoid the bosun I would get to my bunk for a lay down, which I did. Suddenly, I was grabbed by the shoulder, 'Out you bloody get' he roared at the top of his voice.

One minute I was afraid I was going to die and the next minute I thought that it might be the only way to escape the bosun's wrath. I thought I would never get to New Zealand, not in a million years.

On day three, I was still sea sick and thought I would probably starve to death as I hadn't eaten for a couple of days and I didn't think I ever would again. Just seeing the bosun's and carpenter's meals was quite enough for me. All I wanted to do was to get to my bunk and die in peace.

On day four, I thought that perhaps the sea had gone down a bit because I was not feeling too bad. The other 'Peggy' assured me that there had been nothing wrong with the sea and that I was just getting my 'sea legs'. A week at sea and I could do the job standing on my head, it was a doddle.

We had two kinds of passengers, the first and the second class who used the main dining rooms and also 'A' and 'B' promenade decks. Then we had a number of teenage girls who were from orphanages. These girls lived aft, but they were not allowed to eat or mix with the first and second class passengers.

They were, however, allowed to move forward via the lower deck to relax on the fo'c's'le and forward well deck. I later found out that these poor kids had been conned into making this trip by female dragons in the employment exchanges and orphanages. These poor, underprivileged, kids had been told by their superiors that a wonderful new life was waiting for them on the other side of the world in a country flowing with milk and honey.

These children, sixteen years old plus, were being transported to New Zealand for onward passage to Australia where they were told they would be taken on at farms, ranches, and sheep stations as domestic servants, probably to marry some wealthy farmer. They were not told that they would have to work sixty or eighty hours a week and that it was probably a one-way ticket; it's difficult to run away in the outback. Anyway, this did not befall them all as quite a few of them must certainly have been in the family way by the time we reached New Zealand. Some of the seamen and firemen were having their wicked way with them before we were halfway across the Atlantic Ocean.

Apart from my other duties, I was also required to report early morning for scrubbing down the main promenade decks and to set out deck chairs for the first and second class passengers. At Curaçoa, which was my first foreign port, I was extremely disappointed, there was nothing there, just an overwhelming smell of fuel oil. We moved on and entered the Panama Canal, finally berthing at Panama City.

I remember very little about the Canal after a lapse of over sixty years, only the little tractors on each side of the ship pulling us through the locks, the alligators that basked in the sun and the awful smell of the place.

The crew and passengers were allowed to go ashore at Panama City, so with the other 'Peggy' I took advantage of this. We left the ship and within minutes of being ashore I was approached by a lady of the town, a half-caste or creole or something like that. She slipped a hand inside my shirt and fondled my chest saying 'Come with me sailor boy', or words to that effect. I don't to this day know how she knew I was a sailor, was it because of the smell, my blue dungarees or the way I walked? Anyway, I went along with her to what on reflection, was a right pantomime, with me top of the bill.

The outstanding feature of the matinee performance, which indeed it was, happened to be the setting for this great epic. It was a big room containing a large double bed, a bedside table and a bucket. The whole room was surrounded by see-through fly screens, these screens were taken up by small, black faced children who watched the whole show in total silence. I did not enjoy it one little bit and made my way back to the ship as fast as I could.

My other recollections of Panama City are of the land crabs coming out of their holes in the ground, the sudden darkness when night fell, and the bats and fire flies. Also, when I climbed the gangway for the last time before the ship sailed I had a stalk of bananas on my shoulder and within minutes the passengers had taken the lot, plucking them off in ones and twos.

Wellington, New Zealand, was our final destination, some eighteen days sailing time from Panama. However, the next port of call after Panama was the south sea island of Pitcairn. An obligatory stop to give passengers something for their memory books and the natives of the island a few welcome supplies and the opportunity to barter with passengers and crew.

The islanders would exchange curios they had made in exchange for articles of apparel, trousers, shirts, jackets, skirts etc. Money was useless to them really. The natives were fair skinned, lovely simple folk, descended from Fletcher Christian of the *Bounty* fame. It was indeed an experience to visit this place, because I had been a great reader of history.

On our arrival, many longboats were waiting for us in the bay, they apparently had seen us miles out to sea. When we stopped engines and dropped our ladders over the side the captain allowed the women and children to come aboard first, followed by the men with their wares, at which point all hell broke loose.

Barter was the name of the game in Pitcairn, with everybody talking or shouting at the top of their voice. But all too quickly, twilight fell and our floodlights were switched on over the sides of the ship and our friends departed, never to be seen again by most of us.

They sat in their boats singing lovely hymns, the cheerful sort, nothing heavy, as we looked down upon them and the hammerhead sharks which circled their small boats, no doubt attracted by the lights and activity. With a few blasts on the ship's siren we departed from these lonely, but lovely people, a lasting memory that I have never forgotten.

On and on we proceeded across the wide Pacific, day after day as the sun continued to pour down upon us from cloudless skies. The sea was like a mill pond, porpoises leaped across the bow of the ship and flying fish frequently surfaced before plunging back into the ocean before the hot sun dried them out.

All these simple, peaceful happenings were witnessed by me in off-duty moments when I was lying on my stomach, with my nose on the stem of the ship as it ploughed it's way towards New Zealand. I was just a young insignificant 'Peggy' who had been ordered out of the room by the other four ordinary or able seamen, who in turn, had invited four of the would be servant girls into our room, there to partake in 'tea and games'.

I was still a greenhorn, would you believe, even after all my experiences back home. Lying there, hour after hour, was a favourite pastime of mine, in a world where I was indeed like a fish out of water, but I learnt very quickly. I was happy even though I was the lowest form of animal life on the ship.

Even at this late stage of my life I am fascinated by sea travel and it is only a lack of resources which prevents me from never unpacking my suitcase until I am gently lowered over the side of a ship with a fond farewell. I guess I am just a romantic at heart!

CHAPTER 5

We arrived in Wellington sometime during February 1932 and it was fairly obvious why it was nicknamed 'Windy Wellington'. It blows a gale there and the first thing that I noticed, apart from the wind, was the wireless station way up on top of a hill. I believe it was called 2YA or something similar. We off loaded passengers and a certain amount of cargo, then proceeded to Lyttleton and then Auckland, a lovely place which incidentally sealed my fate as far as this ship was concerned and of which I will tell you later.

I really enjoyed my visit to New Zealand, but there was one thing which spoilt it for me and it left a lasting impression. The sight of grown men begging for food.

You will recall that the other 'Peggy' and myself were responsible for clearing up in the mess room and washing the dishes after we had all eaten. The other 'Peggy', who was due to be upgraded to ordinary seaman, had already served on the previous voyage and knew all the ropes. It was he who told me that in the larger ports of New Zealand we would not be required to clear away and wash up, the reason being that there would be plenty of volunteers for this task. These men were the unemployed — many of whom had been emigrants from England and had been lured to a new world of promise, but now they and their families were broke and hungry.

It was quite unbelievable to a young well-fed lad such as myself to witness the sight of these men with their 'doggy bags' queuing for hours to wait for scraps of food discarded by the crew. There would always be plenty left for them, us 'Peggys' saw to that. These poor souls did not know where their next meal was coming from and therefore endeavoured each day to be first in our food queue.

I understand that there was a kind of relief payment to the unemployed, but it was, so I was told, a very small sum for which they were called upon to contribute a few hours land reclamation work. Yet, a few brief years later some of these young men would be required to fight a bloody war. As I look back, I sometimes wonder whether God occasionally took a holiday from watching over us all.

However, I could not solve the problems of these unfortunate people. I was a healthy teenager looking for adventure in another land which takes me to an incident in Auckland where I met a smashing little sun bronzed 'filly'. She had me hooked and I could hardly wait for the end of our working day in order that I might get ashore to meet her. Across the harbour from our commercial docks was the naval base of Devonport — our ship had quite a bit of cargo for this base including clothing, bedding and other linen. One evening I was responsible for locking the doors of the entrances to the ship's holds, after the stevedores had gone ashore for the day. Eager to get ashore myself the suggestion was put to me by one of the other seamen from my room that he could lock up for me, I readily agreed and went off to my date ashore. As you have probably guessed certain items of cargo disappeared, although I was not to hear of this until a few weeks later when homeward bound.

Another interesting incident occurred in Auckland. The other 'Peggy' suggested that we take the dustbin ashore to the rubbish dump further along the dock, this was one of our duties in harbour instead of dumping it overboard as was the custom at sea. When I queried the reason why — because I could see that it was only half full — I was told to shut up and pretend it was quite heavy. I told you he knew all the ropes. Off we went with the bin across the forward well deck, along a passage way then down the forward gangway, along the dock to the rubbish dump, where we emptied the bin. Back we went along the dock only to pause momentarily amongst the thousands of cases of apples which were being loaded into our cold storage hold. Suddenly the other 'Peggy', quick as a flash, had the lid off the bin and a case of apples went inside. We then carried it aboard as if it was very light, alternating the weight on our arms.

Before returning to England we made a short trip up the coast to take on a cargo of lamb. We still had passengers on board, I don't know why, perhaps they were just going along for the ride.

The wrapped lamb was carried on the shoulders of Maori porters from the trucks at the rail head at Opua to the dock side for hoisting on board. In the main, these porters were itinerants who took their wives and children with them, living wherever they could. They were usually organized by a white ganger. Opua, then a small settlement, was probably deserted between ships, except for any wildlife that is, and the rail head was just a hut at the end of the line situated about three or four hundred yards from the dock side. All this, no doubt, has changed a great deal by now.

One of the dear old Maoris asked me in pidgin English if I had any jam, which actually I had in plenty. Seven pounds of it in fact, but telling him that I had just one tin to trade, we agreed on a deal. He could not afford to be caught with it so asked me to take it to the rail head where his daughter would be waiting to receive it, this I did. His daughter had been waiting very patiently for most of the day when I arrived but she quite understood what to trade and had no complaints. Jamless, but happy, I returned to the ship — as I have always said, win a few, lose a few.

We returned to Wellington and loaded the remainder of the cargo and took on board the passengers for England. We retraced our steps to Pitcairn and then on again to Panama. The trip across the ocean was uneventful and I wished at the time we could have called on Tahiti or Hawaii, but there would always be another trip, I told myself, or so I thought.

At Panama and Curaçoa I stayed on board, in fact I did not step ashore again until we berthed in Victoria Docks, London, on May 11th.

It was customary for the crew to collect their channel money on arriving in the English Channel, a couple of pounds or so to tide them over until they were formally paid off. It was also when crew members asked for permission to work on the ship during the spell in harbour between voyages. I was about to make my way to the bridge to speak to the chief officer about being accepted for the next trip when one of the junior officers — with whom I had become friendly — advised me that I should take my money and get as far away from the ship as possible. He had heard that there could be an enquiry into the circumstances surrounding the items of missing cargo which had disappeared in Auckland when I was responsible for locking up. So taking his advice, and as the other 'Peggy' had the wind up also, I left the ship as soon as it docked and walked out of the dock gates into the unknown, homeless and without a ship.

was a really frightened young man with no one to turn to for advice, two hundred and forty miles from my home in Plymouth and afraid to write to tell them of my plight. I did not know until later, much later in fact, that I could have returned to Gravesend Sea School and explained everything to them. They would have taken me in at no charge until they found me another ship, but I was so confused and needed time to think. So, with only a couple of pounds in my pocket, I booked into a seamen's doss house opposite Custom House station in Canning Town.

My accommodation was a square box-like affair containing a tiny bed, a chair and a locker. On the bed was a horse hair mattress supported by mesh-like chicken wire.

Some of the gentlemen with whom I shared this desirable residence were known to grill kippers on the wire which supported their mattresses and they accomplished this by passing a lighted candle to and fro beneath the wire holding the kipper. You could hardly breathe at times as there were only windows on the outer walls. I personally heard the caretaker on many occasions, walking through the passages between our cubicles, shouting, 'Put that bloody kipper and candle out!'

My meals, every single one of them, breakfast, dinner and tea, were exactly the same. I would buy a wrapped sliced loaf, half a pound of margarine and a tin of pork and beans, which I don't see in the shops today. When these items ran out, I replenished them with the same. I would sit on my little bed for every meal, spread the margarine on the bread and eat the beans with a spoon. For a change, I would make a sandwich with the little pieces of pork, if I could find them.

One of the men staying in the hostel informed me that I should be able to obtain unemployment benefit. Quite frankly, I hadn't given it any thought, but I took myself off to the nearest labour exchange with my insurance cards where I was informed that I could indeed obtain the dole, a sum of around five shillings per week, but I would have to attend a day school until they found a job for me. I told them that I was required at the shipping office daily down at the docks to register for work so they let me off the hook and I received the dole money the following Friday.

I toured the docks every day looking for work and on one occasion plucked up courage to go aboard one of the Blue Funnel Line ships. However, when making an enquiry from one of the officers on board about employment, I was asked whether or not I had seen a coffin coming on board. When I asked why, I was politely informed that there were never any jobs to be had unless someone had died. I was still learning!

After several weeks a little slice of luck occurred. On one of my daily trips to the docks I paused to watch a crane lowering a mast onto a large sailing barge.

I had seen hundreds of these barges moving up and down the river passing our school and I always marvelled as to how they kept afloat. To me they always appeared to be on the point of sinking as their gunwales were just a foot or so above the water line.

However, on this particular day as I stood watching the mast lowering operation, a well-built man in his fifties shouted up to me asking if I was looking for a job. Was I looking for a job? Well, you could have knocked me down with a three ton lorry. I was so desperate that I would have taken anything he had to offer, so I shouted back an answer to that effect.

'Come on down' replied the man who was the skipper, a smashing chap, as it turned out. He told me that one of the crew, his nephew, had fallen from the dock onto the barge and had been taken to hospital with suspected fractures. The results of the doctor's examination would not be known until later in the day when the barge would be loading down river ready to sail early the following morning. In any event, the skipper said that his nephew would have to miss the trip.

After asking me who I was, what work I had done etc. and hearing that I was from a sea school, he offered me the job at thirty shillings per week, plus my food. I jumped at it, the money was three times the amount I had been paid on the *Tamaroa* and I figured that the food had to be better.

I rushed back to the doss house to get my kit fearing that perhaps the barge would be gone when I returned, but she was still there when I arrived breathless after struggling with all my gear.

Off we went down river to load up with building materials, bags of cement, stone chippings and other things, leaving a layer of fine white dust over everything which had to be cleaned off further downstream. The barge itself was quite big with a large lee-board which had to be manhandled. The crew consisted of the skipper, his son, his younger brother and myself. They were really great people to be with, my memory falters a little over this period of my life, but I think their surname was Johnston — George, Edward and Tom.

On our way downstream we passed quite close to the *Triton* and who should be sat in an easy chair on the bridge, but the captain's wife. We could see each other quite clearly. She stared at me with a puzzled look on her face and I just gave a sort of half-nod as we passed by. I am sure she fancied me!

We took our cargo to a little place just below Rotterdam. It was a small village called Scedam or Scedyke, I think that was the name. My memory is of a clean little place where we were visited in the morning by a young lady selling fresh bread and milk from a very small cart drawn by a lovely large dog. What wonderful days.

When we arrived back at London, the nephew who had fallen from the dock was waiting for us and he told us that apparently he had been lucky. There were no fractures, but he had damaged his ribs and back. The doctor had also told him he would be alright in a couple of weeks. This was good news for the nephew, but bad news for me. However, the skipper was good to me because I was only on board for sixteen days, but he gave me five pounds.

I left the barge with a heavy heart, but quite rich. Sadly, I returned to the doss house, but with a little better outlook towards life. I could afford to go out in the evening for fish and chips or sausage or egg and chips and I was feeling at this time far more optimistic about my chances of finding another ship.

My luck changed one afternoon on my return from another fruitless tour of the docks, I chanced to meet another lad who had been at Gravesend with me. This lad had been the envy of the other boys who were waiting for ships because he had gone to a plum job, a ship of the Furness Withy Company, a subsidiary of the Cunard Line. The Furness Withy ships were reputed to be on par with the Blue Funnel Line, one of the top shipping lines of the day.

We stood talking of various things — where we had both been, the school, and some of our pals who were at that moment in the far corners of the world. Then he told me that he was on his way down to one of the 'Rangi' ships, as we called them. In fact it was the *Rangitiki*, one of the New Zealand Shipping Co. vessels, where his brother, who was one of the junior officers, had arranged for him to see the chief officer about the job of ordinary seaman on board. If he was successful, this would enable him to receive tuition from his brother on the voyage to New Zealand and back, which was three or four months in total. I asked him what he thought my chances were of getting his billet on his existing ship .

The outcome of our talk was that I walked to the *Rangatiki* with him and waited on the docks until his interview was over. It seemed hours as I walked up and down with my fingers crossed, but eventually he came down the gangway, literally beaming with delight and he promised to sing my praises to the chief officer of the ship he was about to leave. We arranged to meet next morning at his ship, which was in the docks at Millwall.

I hardly slept a wink that night and as soon as I knew it was daylight I was up and away. I tried to be careful up to a point with my spending money and as it was early, I decided to walk to Millwall.

I found the dock and the ship, the *London Corporation* — also my friend who was waiting with his kit and he told me where to find the chief's cabin. We shook hands and he was gone and I never heard from him again. Nervously, I made my way to the chief's cabin, paused, took a deep breath, knocked on the door and was invited in. I asked him about the vacant position on his ship and he replied, 'From your accent you are from Plymouth or thereabouts.' I said that I was and was then informed that he was from the West Country also.

He questioned me at length about my last ship and why I had left, so I told him the truth about everything, what I had done and how I had lived since. It was then I discovered that the school at Gravesend would have taken me back and found another ship for me. He said I should have done this instead of staying at the doss house and added that the job was mine and I should go and get my gear from the doss house. At that moment I was determined to hang on to this particular ship until she went to the breakers.

CHAPTER 7

The *London Corporation* was a general cargo ship which also carried about five passengers who lived with the officers. She traded between London and North America, taking out mainly china clay, scrap metal and rope, returning to Dagenham with Ford products from their plant in Philadelphia, plus other various goods. Instead of the two pounds per month which I had been paid on the *Tamoroa*, I received three pounds, twelve shillings and sixpence, plus better food, and instead of sharing a room with the other 'Peggy' and four ratings I shared a cabin with just one ordinary seaman, a right 'weirdo'.

Our first port of call, and a place which had been the top of my list ever since I had been a young lad, was to be New York. I just could not believe it was happening, it seemed years since I returned dejected from New Zealand, but within a couple of months I was on top of the world heading for America.

I settled down on board quite quickly, chipping, painting and keeping watch on the bridge where I was allowed to take the wheel occasionally. Also, on occasions I was the lookout from the crows nest on the foremast, or at the stern of the ship. I hated this job in bad weather as I frequently got soaked with freezing sea water which swept over the fo'c's'le.

We were due to arrive in New York early in the morning and when off-watch the night before our arrival I just could not get to sleep, I tossed and turned in my bunk waiting for daybreak, thinking about the skyline which I had seen many times in the movies and which was only hours away. I will never forget the moment we passed the Statue of Liberty and entered the harbour.

We docked on 34th street, the street on which had recently been built the worlds tallest building — the Empire State — and if my memory is correct, the Hotel New Yorker was in the process of being built on the opposite side of the street, but a little further down. I also remember an airship being moored to the mast at the top of the Empire State, I think it was called the *Acron*.

Before any of the crew were allowed ashore, we were interviewed by immigration officers and very tough interviews they were. The one who dealt with me warned me to make sure that I did not harbour any thoughts about deserting the ship to stay in America as they had enough problems without me adding to them. This was made quite plain to me when I finally got ashore. There I saw the 'breadline', unemployed destitute men and women, queuing at the soup kitchens for a free meal of soup and bread and young children, black and white, busking outside large department stores singing and dancing like professionals for just a few cents.

This was the time of prohibition with its attendant bootlegging and gangland warfare. I recall on one occasion after a shooting, I raced to the scene only to see the bullet marks on the wall of the building where it had taken place.

Another of my memories is of the notices at Madison Square Garden to the effect that Britain's Kid Berg was fighting Tony Cozoneiri for the world boxing championship. Incidentally, my own home town produced some great fighters around this period — one of whom I knew quite well — Frankie Ash, who went to America and fought the world champion, Pancho Villa, in a non-title bout — going the distance, but losing on points. He was feted on his return home, but died a few years ago in an old people's home, penniless, almost friendless and practically forgotten.

I walked around New York with a permanent crick in my neck caused by continually looking up at the tall buildings. Whilst I was there I sent a picture postcard of the Empire State to Marian telling her that I was at the top of the building, looking out to sea towards her.

It had been my experience throughout life that one is continually meeting or working with smart boys, 'wide boys' or mini entrepreneurs, call them what you will. On the *Tamaroa* in New Zealand we had a couple dealing in currency. These two would take out a couple of hundred pounds and immediately exchange it into silver when we arrived in Wellington, where they received twenty-six shillings for each pound, the official rate of exchange. At that time, roughly eighty percent of all silver coins circulating in New Zealand were English, so these lads would end up with a heavy load of coins, all English. They would unload them on to other members of the crew when we received our channel money. When you consider that an able seaman's wages was eight pounds and two shillings per month, these lads did quite well, at least sixty pounds profit.

With prohibition being in force in America, the 'wide boys' on my ship in New York had a very profitable business venture. They bought cases of Johnny Walker whisky in London, at ten shillings a bottle, then in New York during their lunch break, sold it to stevedores outside their cabin at a dollar a shot. The dollar then was worth five shillings and seven pence. Although there was mass unemployment in America at the time, the stevedores belonged to a powerful union and were well paid, plus the Johnny Walker was a lot better than their bootleg hooch. With the profit from the whisky they bought second-hand dungarees from Sing-Sing prison. These overalls and trousers, although cheap, were in very good condition and they sold them to other members of the crew, or dockers and stevedores back in London, for a big profit.

We left New York for Philadelphia, an eight hour run up the River Delaware, as I recall. The flies would land on you to remain undetected until they bit with a kick like a mule.

On the port side we passed the huge factory of the Ford Motor Company and on the starboard side the shipyard where the transatlantic liner *Manhattan* was being built. I don't ever recall seeing her when she was actually in commission, but she was a great ship judging from the pictures I saw of her.

My run ashore in Philadelphia did not do a thing for me, I was just struck by the apparent poverty of the people living around the dock area who seemed to be predominantly coloured. The streets hadn't seen a road sweeper for months, and the whole place was depressing. I was, however, very impressed with the Ford plant and was surprised to see that they had ships of their own. It was at this plant that we took on the majority of our cargo for the Ford factory at Dagenham.

Whilst I was there, I was told a little story by one of the dockers. Apparently the shop-floor workers wore different coloured overalls and were continually watched by a foreman who, on seeing a different colour overall amongst his work force, would immediately check up on this person in order to find out if they were shirking or fiddling.

We had earlier in New York emptied and cleaned out our ballast tanks and they were then refilled with paper back magazines, which were very popular in those days, on both sides of the Atlantic. Books with titles such as, *True Confessions* and *True Detectives*. We loaded these books by the thousand and the 'weirdo' with whom I shared a cabin would pinch them by the hundred. He could not possibly have read or looked at them all, but I do know that our cabin was full of them. He would stuff them under both his mattress and mine, they were everywhere.

The ship called in at Halifax, Novia Scotia and after a run ashore I crossed this town off my list of places which I would love to visit again. I met a nice girl ashore and after a pleasant evening we were having a final cuddle outside her house, which was near a railway good's yard, close to the docks. Suddenly, I noticed a number of young men stealing some wooden cases from one of the railway trucks. I suggested to the girl that we should report it to the Police, but the girl said, 'If I were you I would keep my mouth shut, they hate the English around here.' That finished me with Halifax.

Our next port of call was Boston, which I remember as a lovely clean place, and while we were in the harbour a Royal Navy cruiser, HMS *Capetown,* from the West Indies Squadron, berthed in front of us. Just looking at this lovely clean warship fascinated me — all the sailors wore lovely white uniforms, even when polishing the guns and cleaning up in general. I never saw anyone wearing dirty overalls.

The Royal Navy seemed to finish work for the day at lunchtime. Bugles would be blown, men would muster on deck and then disappear ashore. Some were met by lovely ladies arriving in private cars and others were taken off for coach tours.

On our ship there were a number of seamen in their fifties and sixties. A typical remark made by these men regarding the RN sailors would be, 'Look at those lucky so and so's, and they get a pension when they are forty!'

Although I had failed the medical for the Royal Navy, I thought at the time that I might try the Canadian or American Navy, but my eighteenth birthday was approaching and I decided to wait and see what happened back home.

I celebrated my birthday in New York and the next day we loaded the last items of cargo and sailed for home. I believe that in 1932 it must have been mainly assembly work at Dagenham, because our cargo was engines, chassis and body panels. We unloaded at Fords and proceeded to Millwall to discharge the rest of the cargo. I then took off to Plymouth because the ship went in to dry dock for a couple of weeks and I was feeling homesick.

I could not let anyone at home know I was coming at such short notice, especially Marian — the most important one as far as I was concerned. It would have been too late to write and I couldn't telephone anyone in Plymouth in those days, so I just had to surprise everyone.

My younger sister, who now had a small son, had moved with her husband into a house of their own and my father now lived with my eldest sister and it was here that I went to live.

I cleaned myself up after arriving home and decided to go to Marian's house. It was then early evening, but purely by chance I bumped into her as she came skipping around the corner into Old Town Street when on her way to meet her parents who were returning from holiday at Sidmouth. We just looked at each other, it was incredible, but we knew that this was it. No more fooling around, we had to get down to serious courting. This was another occasion when some good advice would have been useful to me.

Jobs were not easy to come by ashore and I needed a steady job that would allow me to save so I decided to try and join the Royal Navy again, convinced they wouldn't have any record of my previous application. At the recruiting office, after a short test and a medical, I was accepted. Not a word was said about my feet and I was informed that I would be sent for in a month or so.

I was foolish enough to join as a stoker after listening to one of the recruiting officers who told me stokers received more money than seamen and the job was a lot warmer. This I well knew, but there was also the writing and supply branches which nobody told me about. On reflection, I was a fool because I loved the seamanship side and would probably have advanced much better in that branch, perhaps even making officer.

A telegram arrived from the shipping line in London advising me of the date for signing on for the next trip, but I wired back to the effect that I was joining the Royal Navy. Did I do right? I will never know.

PART TWO - STOKER

CHAPTER 8

Marian and I went from strength to strength with our courtship. We were together every evening after she finished her work at a local clothing factory. However, the day of reckoning came on 3rd October 1932 when I received the telegram from the Royal Navy. I was instructed to report to the recruiting office where, in the company of several other lads, we marched off to HMS *VIVID*. The name was later changed to HMS *DRAKE,* apparently to honour Sir Francis Drake.

We were only allowed out of the barracks at weekends and had to return Sunday night by 10 pm — my courting was going to suffer, of that I was sure.

My pay was seventeen shillings and sixpence per week, plus one shilling and sixpence clothing pay. Only the initial issue of uniform, bedding and other items of kit were free — after this all replacements had to be purchased by yourself. The lads who joined as ordinary seamen received a total of seventeen shillings and sixpence, so you can see that I was a foolish mercenary idiot. I never really enjoyed the stoker side of the Navy. I was trained to be a seaman and loved that side of life which probably explains why I was so happy with the Levant Schooner Flotilla under the command of Adrian Seligman as you will read later.

So, here I was in the Navy for the next twelve years. We were all given a uniform and the rest of the kit that goes with being a sailor, and a hammock to sleep in. The issue of uniforms were of the 'Fitzherbert' type, you know, if it fits Herbert it will fit you! The only items of kit which fitted the majority of new recruits were the boots and caps. I was fortunate, being of standard size, so I didn't look a total idiot as did some of my colleagues when we were finally declared ready for inspection.

The hammocks were a different kettle of fish and until one finally learnt all about these versatile and most important items of a sailor's possessions, it was wise to treat them with great respect. I said versatile because in theory not only are they expected to provide a sailor with a sheltered comfortable nights sleep, they also are supposed to be able to support a sailor in the sea. All the rough ends of the ropes, which were part and parcel of the hammock had to be finished off neatly and we were instructed how to deal with these ends in order that they would not fray out and this was quite a performance.

One's name was also very important to a recruit because every article of clothing, kit and bedding had to have your name plainly upon it. You were issued with a wooden type-stamp about one foot in length with your name carved on it. This was used to stamp your name in paint upon various items of your kit. This was where we found out why one of the instructors remarked to one of our lads, who had a long name, 'You'll be sorry,' because new recruits, such as ourselves, were required to sew their names into certain articles of their kit. In our early days of training we were continually being called out for kit inspection, which entailed laying out one's total possessions in a certain order and in a particular manner.

I became friends with three others in my class and was with them for about the first four years of my naval service. One was Dicky Burden, whom I last saw in 1936 and have never heard from since. Another was Jack Cunningham, whom you will read about briefly later on. Then there was dear old Bill Lane, I say old because Bill was four or five years older than the rest of us.

He had been one of the young lads who had been conned into going to work on a farm in Canada with promises of riches. This same carrot was dangled in front of most young lads leaving school in the late twenties. Anyway, Bill returned to England much the wiser. When we joined the Navy he was a regular 'Charles Atlas', but was a very sorry sight when he died at the age of sixty. He was taken prisoner by the Japanese when HMS *Exeter* was sunk in the Far East. He suffered some terrible beatings in the prison camp, his back was like a venetian blind because of the lashes from bamboo canes, the ends of which had been deliberately split. The end result of the privations he suffered was the cause of his early death through liver and kidney failure.

But back to our induction, after being kitted out and deemed able to put our left leg in front of the right, we were marched off to the 'White City' for our initial basic training — nothing whatever to do with our stoker training which would come later. The 'White City' was a nickname given to a former naval prison and was situated at the highest part of the Plymouth suburb of St. Budeaux where it overlooked both the dockyard and naval barracks. Shades of Gravesend, would I never learn?

This was the time of year when it started to get a bit nippy early in the morning when one was required to 'show a leg' and 'get cracking.' The bugle would sound-off and then around would come the duty petty officer shouting, 'Rise and shine, hands off cocks, on with your socks!'

Out we would scramble after having probably fallen out a couple of times during the night — funny things hammocks — it comes as quite a shock when you are hanging up in a ruddy great bag about five feet from the floor and breaking your neck for a pee, but half asleep you step out as if you were at home in a normal bed.

Every morning after successfully lashing our hammocks, which would have sunk instantly had they been dropped into the sea, we would race off for a wash and shave, not quite as bad as Gravesend as we didn't have to queue naked single file for a bath.

After breakfast we had to fall in on the parade ground in two ranks for 'Colours' — the raising of the White Ensign to the mast head. In front of each class of about sixteen men there would be an instructor, ours was 'Splash' O'Halloran, who everyone agreed was a right bastard, but he wasn't really and we all willingly subscribed to a present for him when we were released from his loving care. His nickname came about because he was wont to spray us all when barking out his orders.

In our class we had three lads named Dove, Parrot and Lynch and they used to come in for some stick from the instructor who continually yelled at them, 'You three bloody birds, get your wings tucked in.' Would you believe that in almost every class there was always one and sometimes two lads who marched swinging their left arm in time with their left leg? This used to drive the instructors crazy. In our class, it was Dove and I am sure he did it on purpose because he was a crafty 'scouser' who knew what it was all about when off duty.

Our training consisted of drills and more drills, boat pulling, cross country runs, PT and shooting .303 rifles on the range. Everyone was required to undergo this training, cooks, writers, sick berth attendants, etc., until eventually the powers that be decided that we knew how to obey orders and were quite safe to be allowed to move freely amongst proper sailors.

We eventually returned to the main naval barracks to begin our stoker training. We were taught the functions of a ship's boiler and how it was the base of all power required by a ship because it supplied the steam to drive the engines, the very powerful dynamos and the evaporators which converted salt water into fresh.

Before we could produce steam from the boiler, we had to have a fire in the furnace and this fire either had to be coal or oil fuel which was where we stokers came in. We were first taught how to build a fire correctly, priming and topping and when it was burning good and strong, we had to spread it evenly over the furnace and shovel in more coal, but not too much at once as this would kill the fire we had just spread.

Now fuel oil was a different operation entirely. The fire in the furnace was produced by forcing heated oil through sprayers protruding through cones in the front of the boiler.

When I completed my basic training I waited to be drafted to a ship, but in the meantime I was in one of the many working parties which set off each morning from the barracks to one of the ships in the dockyard. Ships of every description, battleships, aircraft carriers, large and small cruisers and many destroyers. Which one of these would be mine I wondered?

I was allowed ashore two nights out of three, in uniform of course and I went straight to Marian. Our week was made up of perhaps one night at the pictures and the other nights — if it was dry — were spent cuddling upon a vacant seat, upon Plymouth Hoe. Our favourite spot would be just below the Aquarium where we could look out over the sea and make our plans for the future.

Back to reality, on the table of our mess one morning I discovered the expected draft chit informing me that I was to join HMS *Beaufort*, a survey ship, but would you believe it — it was a coal ship. I thanked God that three other lads from my training class were coming with me.

However, before we joined this man-of-war, we had to report for a medical examination to a place which in these days would be condemned. It was a large hall or room with a stone floor. Around the walls were wooden benches with clothing hooks on the wall above them. This room would be packed with hundreds of sailors, naked from the waist up, walking up and down waiting for their ship and names to be called, as there would always be more than one ship being commissioned. At one end of this inspection room there was a screened off section, behind which was the medical officer and his assistants.

When your name was called, you stepped smartly behind this screen and faced the 'quack' who ordered you to 'Drop em' — you then let your trousers drop to the floor and were asked a number of questions regarding your health. He then looked down your throat, in your ears and eyes, up your backside and then got hold of your 'pecker' and said 'Cough!' And that was it. You were then told to get your bag and hammock and report to the drill shed.

The drill shed at Devonport was the building adjoining the parade ground from where one could see the dockyard and ships, but it was also the farthest point from our mess. Everyone at some time or another has watched two columns of ants at their labours, one line carrying eggs or food and the other line scurrying back empty handed to the source of supply. Well, this is how we sailors must have appeared to someone on high, as we stumbled from the mess to the drill shed with a great big kit bag on our shoulder, then returned back to the mess for our hammocks.

The interior of the drill shed, which was enormous, would be piled high with bags and hammocks in their designated areas, roped off and indicated by the names of the ships — commissioning names such as, HMS *Malaya* and *Courageous*. How the devil we ever got sorted out was a miracle, but I did several times. After we were all mustered and found to be correct, we were then required to load our bags and hammocks onto lorries or trucks for them to be taken to and dumped alongside our various ships. We were then marched to the dockyard and our ships.

On arrival we were required to find our kit again, then carry it on board to our mess. If it was a battleship or an aircraft carrier, it was just your hard luck as it would take you quite some time to find your way about. Fortunately for me, my ship was a small vessel which was moored alongside the south yard.

HMS *Beaufort* was painted white with a yellow funnel, this seemed to me to be rather strange especially for a coal-burning ship, but it appeared that all survey ships were painted this way and we were indeed off to survey Scottish lochs. I was one of four second-class stokers joining this ship. We were the lowest form of animal life aboard, but I was determined to make it.

The chief stoker was not a bad chap and after we had stowed our kit away, he took us on tour of the ship with special attention to our domain, the engine room and boiler rooms. The two boiler rooms, we were informed, were where we would be keeping our watches — the engine room was for more experienced stokers.

I remember my first watch in the forward boiler room with the 'killick' or leading stoker in charge. He was a Liverpudlian 'scouse' named Hudson, a real character and who I was to serve with for the next three years.

During this watch the chief stoker sent an experienced stoker down with me to show me the ropes and help me until I settled down. Quite frankly, even with all my training, I would literally have been lost without his help. The coal had to be raked from the bunkers on each side of the boiler room and not just from one side only which would affect the trim of the ship. This coal then had to be shovelled into the furnace through two or three doors which were opened by your watch mate who pulled down on the handles of the doors which shut automatically when the handles were released. All very simple in calm weather, but when the ship was rolling in a rough sea, your shovel full of coal could miss the open furnace door when thrown and hit the front of the boiler. I often wondered if the captain on the bridge knew this?

There was more to keeping up steam than just chucking coal into a fire and letting it burn. Underneath the furnace were the ash pans filled with water, the surface of which should be bright with the reflection of the burning coals above, so if any parts were seen to be dull, one had to suspect clinker on the fire bars. This had to be removed by a long tool weighing about fifty pounds and which was known as a slice and it was normally suspended precariously above our heads in company with other tools of the trade, rakes etc. This slice was pushed into the furnace along the bars beneath the burning coals where the suspected clinker was and if you had guessed correctly, you would bring this clinker to the surface of the burning coals by leaning down on your end of the slice. It could then be removed by using a rake and was then loaded into large metal buckets together with ashes which were continually being raked from the pans. These buckets were hauled to the upper deck through special chutes and emptied over the side, nothing to it! So you see a stoker's life was not all beer and 'baccy' and being asked out to tea.

Off we went to bonny Scotland to almost the furthest point — Scourie in Sutherland — but our main base was at Oban where we took on coal. Nobody from the skipper down was excused from this task. This was the one day on which you were allowed to wear anything you wished, it didn't make any difference though as we all looked like black minstrels within half an hour, although our songs were not quite the same. The majority of the stokers were down in the bunkers trimming the coal as it was shot down from above working practically blind.

When all the coal was on board, the ship had to be washed down from stem to stern — just remember, this was a white ship with a yellow funnel. What a performance this was with half of us playing the role of firemen with hoses and water everywhere, then after this, we had to try to clean ourselves. It was two or three days before it could be removed entirely from our eyelids and you could not risk going ashore in case someone suspected that you were one of the boys from the chorus of *Hello Sailor*.

I really enjoyed this life, simply because the stokers helped out with the surveying, rowing the dinghies, climbing the hills with all the equipment and building cairns on top of some of the hills. The cairns had plaques embedded in them stating HMS *Beaufort* 1933. I have often wondered if they are still there.

I remember on one occasion when we were on our way to Stornoway and were having difficulty making headway, the bearings were running hot and we in the forward boiler room were working like slaves maintaining the required steam.

There appeared to be no rational explanation for this state of affairs, but someone happened to look over the side of the ship and observed something wrapped around our bows just below the surface. The skipper was informed and he put the ship astern and a ruddy great whale shot to the surface. We had probably hit it whilst it was asleep or something. Fortunately for me I had been relieved in order to have a spell on deck and was just in time to see it slide past on our port side and I remember thinking that it looked like an overturned yacht.

After a short period at Stornoway, we proceeded to Liverpool where half the ship's company were given a weeks leave, then on their return the other half had their leave. From Liverpool the ship went to Belfast for a short period of survey work in and around the loch. It was here that I first became entitled to all-night leave, instead of having to return on board by 11 pm each time I was granted shore leave.

Belfast in those days was a really nice place to have a good time, in more ways than one, as I will relate. On one occasion, during a carnival or celebration, we were dancing in the street to the sound of fiddles and accordions and a couple of women brought out a large oval tin bath full of cooked pigs trotters. We matelots were dancing with our sleeves rolled up, holding a trotter in one hand and our partners with the other.

My other memory of this city is quite different and ninety-nine percent accurate, it is firmly imprinted on my mind, but you would not believe that a travelled young man with my early training could be so naive and surprised by what took place. What an event it turned out to be!

Another more experienced stoker than myself, chap named 'Wiggy' Bennett, persuaded me to go ashore with him on a blind date he had arranged, for me that is. The previous day he had met a girl who asked him to bring ashore another stoker to accompany her friend, thus making up a foursome. We went to meet these girls — myself with mixed feelings about what was in store for me. When we were within about ten to fifteen yards of this pair, 'Wiggy' says 'Blimey, just look at yours,' indicating the girl who was to be my partner.

Look, I most certainly did, she was just about the loveliest girl I had ever seen, ravishing in fact, with a great pair of legs like Alice Marble, the tennis player. I just could not believe my luck when I saw this blonde creature standing there in a lovely little short summer dress. I soon recovered and it was decided that we would take a bus to a little place named Hollywood and stroll over the rifle ranges which were not in use.

We arrived at this place then started walking down a country lane with hedges on each side, my friend and his girl were about thirty yards ahead of us. We were talking, mostly small talk, when suddenly my girl who must remain nameless, said to me, 'I thought you sailors knew what it was all about.'

I asked her what she meant and she came straight out and said 'How much further do we have to walk before we go over the hedge and have it away?'

After the initial shock, I caught on in a flash, you don't have to pee on my boots to tell me I am on fire! So over the hedge we went like a pair of antelopes and 'Wiggy' shouted back, 'Where are you going?'

'Bird nesting' I shouted back. Our ship was in Belfast for another ten days and during that time I managed four or five outings with my 'bird nesting' friend.

We returned to Oban to begin surveying the far end of Lock Linnhe. HMS *Beaufort* was equipped with two self-contained surveying launches, named the *Herald* and *Alert* and with their attendant dinghies they were able to stay away from the mother ship for quite a long while. This meant being away from all the discipline on board ship for us surveying stokers.

We later proceeded around to the Moray Firth, near to the entrance of the Caledonian Canal and Loch Ness. Now this period coincided with renewed speculation regarding the existence of the famed Loch Ness Monster — all very good for the media, local hoteliers and boatmen. Consequently, from Oban to Inverness, it was the number one topic of conversation and HMS *Beaufort* was continually being singled out for attention, probably by the belief that we too were searching for the monster.

CHAPTER 9

All good things must come to an end and it was with a heavy heart that I said goodbye to Scotland and all the great people I met there in those far off days when I was oh so young.

Winter was approaching and we had to return to Devonport and payoff, about twenty five percent of the crew remained on the ship to be part of her next survey cruise the following summer, but alas I was not one of them.

We paid off on the 20th December and then it was back to 'Jago's Mansion' for me. This was the shore establishment HMS *Vivid*, but to the matelots of my era it will forever be 'Jago's Mansion'.

There are many versions regarding the origin of the nickname. I prefer the one which said that 'Jago' was a warrant officer cook who organized the general messing meals, which were unsurpassed. The finest grub I ever had anywhere during my time in the Navy. His *piece-de-resistance* was thick pea soup at lunch times. It could almost support a spoon standing on end. No wonder we had so many randy matelots around. I'm sure the soup was an aphrodisiac, because the other stuff to make you 'run' was always put in the tea.

Unknown to me at this time, I had but six short weeks with my loved one before I would have to say goodbye and this time would not see her again for two and a half years. We were making plans like mad things knowing that the odds were I would be sent abroad. One of the decisions we made was to become engaged immediately, so we went to Samuels, the jewellers, in Bedford Street, opposite St. Andrew's Church. The church where we planned to marry.

We purchased for five pounds the ring of Marian's choice before asking her parents who gave their approval to the union. We then sought advice from her eldest brother Frank and his wife Louise. Frank had named his pleasure boat *Lulu* after his wife. I can see this boat in my memory today. They had not been married long and were living in a flat in Zion Street quite near the Barbican. These two good people gave us some good advice. I well remember Frank telling me that I could not possibly think of marrying and furnishing a flat on less than a hundred pounds, a King's ransom I thought, but I would get through. A savings campaign was the answer!

I immediately made an allotment of ten shillings per week to Marian — this was from my pay of twenty-six shillings. We agreed that she would add to this if and when she could. Nothing could have been simpler we thought, it was just a matter of time. I was nineteen and Marian would have been nineteen the following January.

Five days after Marian's birthday on the 30th January, I can remember looking through the draft chits that were spread out on the mess table and found one with my name on it. I was to be drafted to HMS *Frobisher*, a cruiser bound for the West Indies, but a couple of my pals told me that they were going to HMS *Devonshire*, a three-funnel cruiser, bound for the Mediterranean and one of them said that we would all be together again, just like we were on the *Beaufort.*

When I enquired what he meant, he said that there was a *Devonshire* draft chit for me on the table. I looked again and sure enough my name was on another chit, so someone in the drafting office had definitely made a mistake. Wishing to be with my mates and knowing that the *Devonshire* would be away from England for far longer than the *Frobisher,* thus giving me a greater opportunity to save, I destroyed the chit for HMS *Frobisher.* I then reported to the medical inspection room for my inoculations, necessary because I was going overseas.

Firstly, the ships' names were called, followed by the names of the ratings detailed to join that ship. The name Matthews was called for the *Frobisher* about three times — no one stepped forward — a few chaps who knew me looked towards me, but as the name was a common surname no more was said. On this occasion there were nearly six hundred of us for HMS *Devonshire.*

It was a very cold morning on the 2nd February 1934 when I struggled to find my kit which had been dumped on the dock side with hundreds of other sailor's kit. When I found it, I carried it on board to find my locker room, then went back to the dock side to find my hammock, which had to be stowed in a special fitting in your mess. There were hundreds of us dodging one another in the passage ways and gangways, but we did get sorted out and most seemed pleasantly surprised by the spaciousness of our quarters.

The following day, we were allocated our various duties and given a tour of the places where these duties would be performed, boiler rooms, engine rooms etc. We were also informed that the ship would be sailing early on the morning tide, the following day — 4th February — therefore, all leave would expire at 11 pm that night. Anxious to get ashore as soon as possible to spend as much time as I could with Marian, I failed to take notice of the instructions given regarding the movements of the ship which was that she would be moved to the outer wall further south ready for sailing.

As I made my way dutifully back to the ship after sadly leaving my loved one whom I would not see for another two and a half years, the shock of not seeing my ship on the berth where I had left if filled me with horror. I then vaguely recalled hearing something about the ship being moved and I had not appreciated the fact there were no other sailors preceding or following me back to where the ship had been. In a state of panic I made my way back to the dockyard gate at St. Levans Road and enquired from a policeman on duty at the gate as to the whereabouts of HMS *Devonshire.* He pointed in a general direction towards the south yard on the outer wall. So off I went through the dimly lit yard and before long saw her distinctive three funnels.

I eventually climbed the gangway shortly before midnight to be informed by the officer-of-the watch that I would be in the 'Commander's Report' for defaulters the following day. This was later changed to the 'Captain's Report'.

The ship's company had already been introduced to the captain on the day we joined the ship and as I recall he was Captain Herbert Fitzherbert. He told us we were off to join the finest fleet in the world, the Mediterranean Fleet, and it was his intention to see that HMS *Devonshire* was the finest ship of that fleet. This meant bloody hard work for all of us, officers and men. He considered himself to be a fair man, but also a hard and determined man, one who had to take orders and one who had to give orders, but when he gave any of us an order, he wished it to be carried out with great speed. His actual words were, 'I don't wish to see you walk, I don't wish to see you run, I want to see you fly!' I therefore approached my confrontation with him in a state of trepidation.

When the dreaded moment arrived, I was not alone in my torment as there were other defaulters standing with me to answer various charges. The master-at-arms called us all to attention as the captain stood at his table. My name was called and I stepped smartly forward to face him. The master-at-arms ordered me to 'Off caps' then read out the charge of being adrift.

Captain Fitzherbert stared me straight in the face and said, 'What do you say to the charge?'

To my surprise at finding that I had not lost my voice, I said, 'I thought that I had allowed myself ample time to return to the ship, but when I arrived back at the dock side where I had left her, she had gone.'

I thought the captain was about to have a fit, but he seemed quite calm when he pushed his face closer to mine and said, 'I know it had gone, I moved it!

'I am the captain and it is my ship, do you think that whenever I move the ship I am going to come along to the boiler room, there to shout down to Stoker Matthews that I am going to move the ship, just to be sure that you know where I take it? Fourteen days stoppage!'

The master-at-arms barked, 'On caps, about turn, quick march, left, right, left, right!' What a way to start a two and a half year commission, but I survived.

The *Devonshire* was a lovely ship, a 10,000 ton county class cruiser identical to a number of others with such names as *Cornwall, Norfolk, London, Sussex, Dorsetshire, Shropshire* and *Kent*. In my opinion, these ships, at least as far as the crew were concerned, were about the finest ships in the Navy at this time. Accommodation was spacious for us junior ratings, one could hold a dance in the stokers' bathroom. We had plenty of room on our mess deck, which was situated on the starboard side forward, below the seamen's mess deck and two decks below 'B' turret that housed twin 8" guns.

These guns were capable of firing at a range of about twenty miles. In addition, we had 8" guns in four turrets, 'A' and 'B' turrets on the fo'c's'le and 'X' and 'Y' turrets, aft on the quarterdeck. The ship also had a 4" gun deck situated amidships, below which were torpedo tubes to port and starboard. We were also armed with multiple 'Pom Poms', these were quick firing guns for repelling aircraft. We also had a seaplane which could carry a torpedo — this plane was launched from a catapult and was recovered by landing in the sea alongside the ship and was hoisted aboard by a crane.

The *Devonshire* had lost seventeen marines killed by an explosion of 'X' turret during a previous commission and was considered to be an unlucky ship. Some superstitious members of the ship's company believed it was because we carried a replica of Sir Francis Drake's Drum which was displayed in a glass case in the officer's flats. There was some justification for their superstition as quite a few things unexpectedly happened to us during our commission. One was at the fleet's week-long regatta held at Navarin. The *Devonshire* was stationed on the finishing line of the course, our racing gig finished first in the first race on the first day and the captain ordered the drum to be brought on to the fo'c's'le where he beat it. We did not win another race.

Recreation facilities were excellent, we had a cinema show once or twice a week depending on the weather as it was operated on the upper deck. We sat on long wooden benches which had to be manhandled up the various gangways from one's mess deck. Tombola known as 'Bingo' or 'Housey-Housey' was played once or twice during the week. Junior ratings also had a spacious recreation room in the fo'c's'le which had a 'Goffer Stall' dispensing soft drinks and ice cream. It was in this room that I first learnt to play Mah Jong and Solo. Gambling was strictly forbidden, but everyone did —undercover of course.

On the deck immediately below this room we had an excellent canteen where one could purchase all sorts of goodies, for example, twenty Players or fifty Woodbines, which were the same size as Players, for a shilling. All kinds of chocolate and sweets were obtainable and varieties of biscuits and cold meats could also be purchased.

If you were still hungry after the main meal in the mess, you just went to the canteen and bought a quarter pound of ham or corned beef, took it to your mess and sliced a couple of pieces of bread from one of the loaves in the 'Bread Barge' — every mess had one — and presto, you made yourself a 'Dagwood Sandwich'. I must say that in the main our meals supplied from the ship's galley were of good quality and substantial.

Each mess of about fourteen stokers had a 'killick' or leading stoker in charge who was responsible for the running, good order and general behaviour of his mess mates. He would detail from a rota, two stokers to be 'cooks of the mess'. No cooking was involved, they would, for a week, fetch and carry for everyone else in the mess. This meant fetching all the main meals from the galley and sharing it out equally amongst us, washing up and clearing away all the dishes after the meal, scrubbing the table, benches and deck every morning, with a change of routine Saturday mornings for the customary 'Captains Rounds'. This meant that in addition to the normal scrubbing and clearing away routine, all the knives, forks, spoons and metal mess utensils had to be cleaned with metal polish.

Everyone had to scrub their personal 'ditty box' and polish the name plate. These boxes were stowed in racks along the ship's side where there was also a large metal locker which housed our plates, cups, cutlery, and condiments. All hot water had to be fetched from the galley flat and all dirty water, plus waste food was carried up to the 'gash' or rubbish chute situated on the lee side of the ship, forward. Heaven help anyone who accidentally left the scrubbing brush in the bucket to hear it go rattling down the chute and go floating away astern, lost forever.

One member of the mess was chosen as the caterer and he would be responsible for the financial state of the mess. This was necessary because such items as tea, cocoa, bread, margarine, jam and condiments had to be bought from the purser by each individual mess and paid for monthly. Each mess received a cash allowance in order to make these purchases, but naturally some messes were more extravagant than others, finding that at the end of the month they had overspent their allowance which meant that the excess had to be paid for out of their own pockets, whereas some messes received a rebate.

Evening would see four, five or six matelots sat at the table busily writing home with open 'ditty boxes' in front of them. The open 'ditty box' served two purposes in this case because whilst one was writing, it would be possible to see the photographs of one's loved ones which would be displayed on the inside of the lid. The open box also hid your writing pad from someone who might be sat opposite you — we all became experts at reading upside down. You also had to contend with someone hanging up above you in his hammock reading or sleeping. It was wonderful to look around at various expressions displayed on the faces of the writers or readers, some sad, some happy, some full of lust, others downright filthy, others very far away and almost in tears. Such was life on the mess deck.

Our 'ditty boxes' were our own little individual treasure boxes and were always locked, with your own personal key, when not in use. It had a long narrow compartment for pens and pencils, and a small square compartment which would just take a bottle of ink, there were no 'biros' in those days. I still have the ink stains in mine from a loose bottle lid. The box had a main compartment where one normally kept the 'housewife', which was a very valuable part of a sailors kit. It was a piece of tough material in the form of a roll about six inches long and perhaps two or three inches in diameter. When unrolled, this 'housewife' revealed a variety of needles, threads, darning wools and scissors. The box also contained the valuables that we did not wish to carry around with us, plus our writing pads and photos etc. The whole box measured twelve inches by eight inches with a depth of six inches.

When the last war was imminent I took my box ashore to remain at home for the duration where, unfortunately, some idiot unknown, but never forgiven, decided that it would look better with a few coats of paint. This to a matelot was sacrilege, I am still trying to remove the paint sixty years later.

CHAPTER 10

Except for two brief encounters face to face with the captain, I only had occasional glimpses of him such as at 'Captain's Rounds' or Sunday Divisions', but he and the commander, who was Rudolf Slater DSO, must have been very fair men because we turned out to be a very happy ship. This was in spite of a change to our planned commission which was caused by the Abyssinian crisis and the Spanish Civil War. Life on board for us stokers was never really dull, just boring at times.

The powers that be continually moved us around, for example, during my two and half years on board I did about five or six different duties or jobs. My first duty was as a boiler room watch-keeper, which consisted of three watches, four hours on and eight hours off. This was routine stuff once you had been instructed in how to change and clean oil sprayers. It also entailed chipping off deposits of carbon which built up around the edges of the brick cones through which the sprayers protruded into the furnace.

The main base for the Mediterranean Fleet was Malta, but before we finally left Gibraltar for this island, we had to take part in an annual event whereby the Med Fleet, which was quite formidable, opposed the Atlantic or Home Fleet, in a mock war lasting several days.

This was quite an exercise when you consider the hundreds of ships involved, at least ten battleships plus numerous aircraft carriers, battle cruisers, large and light cruisers, dozens of destroyers and two flotillas of submarines. All these, together with supply ships and oil tankers, carried out high speed manoeuvres in total darkness. The Royal Navy at that time was, in my opinion, the most efficient navy in the world and a few short years later it was called upon to display that efficiency for real.

At this period of time I never gave a single thought to the possibility of war. Everyone had heard of Hitler and Mussolini, but what we had seen of the brainwashed Italians convinced us that they couldn't fight their way out of a paper bag. As for the Germans, well, we in turn were brainwashed into assuming that they couldn't last three or four weeks of war. We were told that they were flat broke, lived on ersatz food, had cardboard tanks, no rubber for tyres and no oil. Plus there was the mighty French Army and Maginot Line against them.

Many university men of my acquaintance perhaps thought differently, by virtue of their studies and privileged information and their connections with knowledgeable people employed in various government departments. I know what I thought of the international situation, precisely nothing. I was far too busy during my working hours and too busy enjoying myself when off duty.

We went back to Gibraltar at the end of the mock war with the Home Fleet, which incidentally was painted dark grey, whilst we of the Med Fleet were painted light grey. We all assembled at Gib for the 'big nobs' to compare notes, whilst we lower mortals had a glorious booze-up in one of the many cabarets with all girl bands on Main Street, I think one of the acts was Ivy Benson and her flamenco dancers. It all happened in Gib with gambling the top of the bill, after wine and women of course. The most popular game at that time was Crown and Anchor which was more often than not played in the men's toilets.

When the Home Fleet returned to their loved ones in England the crews took with them Spanish shawls (probably made in Lancashire), first class German cameras, binoculars and lighters, bottles of 'Evening in Paris' (the scent of the period), eau-de-cologne by the bucketful, Spanish castanets, cigars, live animals or birds and in some cases a dose of the 'crabs'. We of the Med Fleet sailed off eastward to Malta.

Before we left Gib, Bill Lane, one of the stokers I had joined up with, got engaged to a girl who worked in the same factory as my own girl, Marian. He too was intending to save like mad, so naturally we were two of a kind, just being able to afford an occasional run ashore. Bill and I spent many hours each evening just walking up and down the Mole at Gib making plans and looking forward to 1936 when we would return home and get married.

Malta, at this time, was a matelot's paradise. I thought it all happened at Gib, but not a bit of it — Malta was the place to be. Whatever one wanted it could be had. There were not any recognised brothels, so the only loose women available had to be solicited from Gharri drivers, whose vehicles were horse drawn covered carriages. This was a very risky business indeed and in the main was only pursued by greenhorns or young sailors with no experience of the seamy side of life. The whole operation could be compared with riding a mountain goat on a hillside at night. The performance had to be carried out in the darkened rear seat, with a female (one assumes) of uncertain age, whilst the vehicle was in motion and with your trousers around your knees.

The capital of Malta is Valetta and when the fleet was in port, I would think the population doubled. Everywhere one looked, there would be matelots, goats and priests. There were churches everywhere and their bells would ring continuously, but it was lovely and I loved the people in more ways than one.

In my opinion, ninety percent of all matelots who love a run ashore have four things on their mind when they hit the beach, a bed for the night, big eats, a booze up and a 'bag off', the last item depending on ones financial state and so it was with the lads in Malta. There were bars and eating places everywhere, but the main thoroughfare for all this jollification was Strada Stretta, commonly known as 'The Gut.' There was also the area of Floriana, a bit more select than 'The Gut' and in one of the bars there, was Bobby on the piano, who incidentally was still playing fifty years on in Plymouth whilst I wrote my story.

But back to 'The Gut' — a sloping, narrow, traffic-free street, with restaurants, bars and cabarets on either side. Cabarets? That's a laugh, the alleged artists didn't know what the word meant, but who cared? There was a common denominator, randy and hungry sailors with money to spend on girls, restaurants, tattoo artists, photographers and lodging house keepers. They were all ready to take the money from 'Jolly Jack', what could be fairer? Basically all these good people were honest hard working folk who gave *quid pro quo*.

Now let me think of some of the bars — the *New Life, Egyptian Queen, Lucky Wheel* — so many others and whenever I could afford a run ashore, the *New Life* was my favourite. As soon as one entered the bar you were immediately joined by a girl or girls for whom you had to buy a drink, normally coloured water. The girls would get a percentage of what you spent so it was in their interest for you to buy as many drinks as possible. A small band would play and one would dance. I couldn't dance, but this didn't matter as ninety percent of the girls couldn't either.

If you were wealthy or it was pay day, or you had won tombola, you tried to fix yourself up for an 'all nighter' with a girl you fancied which would cost about ten shillings. If you couldn't afford this luxury or were not interested you booked your bed before eating and boozing. It was a bit of a laugh really to walk down the street and hear the cries of the lodging house keepers — oh how it all comes back to me, 'Here you are Jack, double beds for you and your winger.'

In the main, these lodging houses were all good clean places where one was awakened in the morning with a cup of tea and all for five pence. After a quick wash it was down to the liberty boat or dhiasa probably purchasing on the way fresh bread rolls for yourself and mess mates, then back on board, breakfast, change into boiler suit and 'turn to', which is the term used for starting work.

In Malta there was an alternative to going ashore or staying on board and this was a visit to the naval canteen at Corradina. Here one could have a few beers, egg and chips and a cinema show for about two shillings.

At this period of time I did not have many runs ashore in Malta because of my financial situation. Out of twenty six shillings, I had an allotment of ten shillings to Marian, with another of two shillings and sixpence to a naval tailor. From the remaining thirteen shillings and sixpence I bought, cigarette tobacco, known as 'Ticklers', which cost one shilling and threepence per half pound tin. I also purchased chocolate and goodies from the canteen, writing materials (I sent at least three letters a week home) and paid my mess bill. So you can see that I did not have a lot of money to spend on the delights of Malta.

My next pay rise did not come until 3rd October 1935, when I was awarded my first 'Good Conduct' badge or stripe, bringing with it the princely sum of threepence per day. Mine was a limited existence, washing my clothes, darning socks, cleaning my shoes and white cap, writing letters, reading, playing cards or Mah Jong, swimming and sun bathing in Bhighi Bay and an occasional evening at Corrodina canteen. It wasn't all 'beer and skittles', but it was my world.

When I look back I often wonder what it was like to be an officer, university educated and politically aware, it must have been frightening at times, but their whole professional life and training was geared for war. Mine was just a job for money rather than be unemployed. I was trained in a certain way and the powers that be knew or hoped that in an emergency or war, I would not panic, but just do my allotted job automatically without thinking too much about the reason for doing it.

The ships of the fleet were exercised at sea quite regularly, with all the crews at action stations. You could be called out at a minute's notice, sometimes when you had just crawled into your hammock after completing a four hour watch. The ships would dash about blacked out, portholes and hatches battened down, guns firing, laying down smoke screens and assimilating collisions with other ships.

War in peacetime can only be simulated and this is all that training can be geared to. Actual bombing, explosive destruction, death and terrible injuries and fear, cannot be assimilated. This I soon found out.

The majority of our officers were Dartmouth men who were enrolled in that college at the tender age of twelve or thirteen years. They were then taught to be as tough as hell and above all fearless. If you played against a team of them at football, rugby or hockey, you would soon get the message, they would kick you off the field. They seemed invincible — these men were the backbone of our fleets and in my opinion they were unsurpassed.

Above these officers and us lower forms of animal life, were the captains and admirals, most of whom had already been through a tremendous sea war, but not aerial bombardment which was an entirely new dimension. These men were hard task masters with their constant striving for perfection, but they were also clever men who realized that all work and no play makes 'Jack' a very dull boy. To alleviate all the blasted exercising and training we would go cruising to a port where they knew that 'Jolly Jack' could obtain plenty of beer, grub and perhaps get his leg over if he fancied it and could afford it.

Ships would visit ports individually, in pairs, or in groups, depending on the port to be visited and its ability to be able to cope with the size of the visiting ship or ships. There could be up to two thousand sailors and marines on one ship alone. In our particular case we went to Argostoli on the Greek island of Kephalonia, and they were ready for us, or at least the bars and eating houses were. Most of the bars at the harbour where we landed were brothels, all had at least half a dozen girls, probably imported 'camp' or 'fleet' followers. All these bars were festooned with banners proclaiming 'Welcome British Navy' and all that jazz.'

The first one I visited was in the company of about half a dozen other stokers, a couple of seamen and a couple of marines. One by one these lads would disappear with one of the girls into one of the cubicles or rooms adjoining the bar for a 'quickie'. Well, eventually it was noticed that all the girls, about eight or ten of them, had been well and truly served, except for one girl who incidentally was as black as the ace of spades. She was certainly no Greek that's for sure, but what a figure she had, as we soon discovered — she was quite good looking too.

After a short conference with the bar owner and the girl, it was agreed that an exhibition in the bar would be performed with one of us sailors. So we held a whip round for the young lady and the bar owner, and lookouts were posted at the entrance. After much debate and more drinks a volunteer was detailed off from amongst us to be the other half of the pantomime. This stalwart turned out to be a hairy bum stoker from my mess — guess who? For this performance three marble topped tables were pulled together, the 'Gladiators' stripped and battle commenced. I can assure you that it was indeed an epic with a great deal of back slapping and cheering from the crowd.

The young lady I might add, finished up highly delighted and with more drachmas than her companions, and I survived without catching anything! We eventually left Argostoli to sail to Navarin for the Fleet Regatta.

This was the event of the year and lasted a week with the whole fleet anchored in the wonderful harbour of Navarin and what a sight it was. I have already described our own ship's contribution to the boat races, but there were many other competitive events, gambling on the tote was permitted and greatly patronised.

When the regatta was over, we continued the cruise, many of us with much less in our pockets than when we arrived. Our ship went on to visit Split in Yugoslavia and all I can remember of our short stay in this place was an organized trip to a distillery. Can you imagine taking a bunch of sailors to a distillery.

Organized, well, the entrance by the matelots might have been, but their leaving was a very different affair. Practically everyone emerged into the warm afternoon sun as 'drunk as skunks.' Drunken matelots were lying around like rotten sheep, on the grass, on park benches or wherever the nearest clean looking spot could be found. I say clean, because above all, 'Jolly Jack' is taught that cleanliness comes before Godliness. If he hasn't got that message in his first few months in the Navy, his mess mates will soon see that he does.

I recovered fairly rapidly from the drinking spree and met a nice young girl in the town and by means of sign language we agreed to take a walk which included a visit to her home for a meal where I met her folks. Later the girl and I left the house and strolled to a park overlooking the harbour. Here we sat on a bench kissing and cuddling. It was during this pleasant pastime that the recall was sounded on the ship's siren and repeated at intervals. I explained, again by sign language, that I must return to my ship and she walked with me to the ship which was lying at anchor. Rumours were rife about a war, but I promised to write. I really should have taken her address!

It was not until we were actually all safely on board that we learnt the reason for our recall. The King of Yugoslavia had been assassinated that very afternoon in the French port of Marseilles. This of course created an international crisis, so we were obliged to sail to a neutral port which was Trieste in Italy.

It was on our itinerary, but not quite so soon and was definitely off my visiting list because I was skint — I didn't have a penny piece. We were paid monthly overseas and as I recall it was about a week to our pay day. It was extremely difficult to borrow money, as the 'wide boys' on board charged half a crown in the pound interest. Twelve shillings and sixpence of my weekly pay was already allotted so borrowing was out for me.

When we arrived in the harbour, we tied up stern first to the sea wall. Trieste was so inviting and just looking at those lucky so and so's who were going ashore I wondered where the hell they got the money. However, I knew that we would be in port for over ten days because of the Marseilles incident, so I would eventually have a run ashore, maybe two.

On our third day in Trieste, a game of Tombola was being played on the upper deck, port side forward. I was flat broke, but I sat beside 'Scouse' Hudson watching him play. 'Scouse' was my mentor, a 'killick' stoker who had been on HMS *Beaufort* with me when I was a greenhorn and he had been a great help to me. Of course being a leading stoker he was wealthy, earning ten shillings and sixpence a week more than I.

When I said I was flat broke, it was not strictly accurate because residing in the corner of my purse, which is part of a sailor's belt, was a silver threepenny piece. I had found this in the Christmas pudding at Marian's house the previous Christmas and had kept it for luck. I fingered this coin for some time before I finally succumbed to temptation convincing myself that it was a simple matter to obtain another silver threepenny piece. Accordingly, I bought myself a ticket and you can guess what happened next, yes, I won the house, but not before a few palpitations. I won on number thirty three, all the threes, and the amount was three pounds, twelve shillings and sixpence, all divisible by three. 'Come on Scouse' I said 'we can just make the liberty boat.'

Ashore at last we had a drink, then big eats. Fortified with this we decided to have a look at the government controlled brothels. Now these were something to be seen, ornate, but not tawdry, very, very clean and well run by a madam. But alas, whatever the country, they are basically all the same, buying and selling, dip your wick in and out and on your way. Italian forces seemed to have passes or ration cards for these places. I suppose they were allowed so many visits per month.

Anyway, that night ashore was one of the most embarrassing nights I ever spent in my time on that ship — the reason being I could not dance. 'Scouse' was a natural, he heard music coming from somewhere and then found its source, a dance hall no less, so he dragged me in. We were immediately surrounded by girls and 'Scouse' was away on the floor with me standing like a lemon trying to make excuses in a language they could not understand whilst I could not understand them either. I was determined from that day on that nothing would stop me from learning to dance even if I had to attend to what was termed as 'pansy dancing classes'. How I wish that same determination had stayed with me in other vital periods of my life that followed.

CHAPTER 11

As a result of some incident in Yugoslavia our intended itinerary was changed somewhat and we eventually anchored off the island of Samos — quite close to Turkish territory and where, so I was given to understand, some of the marines killed when the gun turret blew up during a previous commission were buried.

On this particular day the pilot of our plane, together with a couple of other officers, one of whom I believe was our dental surgeon, decided that they would take a sailing dinghy, have a picnic and swim from one of the numerous small islands dotted about. Unfortunately, they landed on Turkish territory and trigger happy soldiers opened fire on them killing the pilot and wounding one of the others. The uninjured officer managed to get his wounded companion into the dinghy and make it back to the ship where all hell broke loose, or so it seemed to us denizens of the lower deck. Marines were armed, guns were trained on the place where the attack had taken place and we were more or less at action stations. Nobody thought of addressing us over the 'tannoy' system, giving us at least a rough idea as to what was happening, we had to rely on third and fourth hand information coming from various junior officers.

The next day half the Med Fleet arrived together with the Flagship, *Queen Elizabeth*. Many conferences were held by senior officers who were, no doubt, under the orders of the foreign office diplomats to hold their horses and not do anything rash. But we lesser beings were kept at crisis stations with no cinema shows or tombola, all very frustrating.

Within a few days everything had been sorted out, the fleet dispersed and we settled down to normal routine and HMS *Devonshire* was allowed to pass through the Sea of Marmara to Istanbul then through the Bosphorus into the Black Sea and so to Constanza in Rumania. This was really something, quite unheard of since the war and we were looking forward to this visit with a great deal of pleasure, but little did we stokers know that we would pay for the trip in more ways than one.

It was customary for us engine room and boiler room ratings to change our boots or shoes before descending down into the bowels of the ship to the engine or boiler rooms. Our footwear was stowed in racks just inside the entrance to these places and this ensured we did not wear greasy and oily footwear when we stepped out onto the main decks after keeping our watch or working below.

At Constanza we received various hoards of visitors and later discovered that we had lost most of our working shoes and these had been replaced in some cases by weird looking Turkish Caliph's footwear. Some of these had great big horns or hooks in the toes, they were not very practical for climbing up and down ladders or sliding around on the boiler and engine room plates, were quite useful for booting your mates up the backside and saying 'How's that for a Turkish delight!'

As I recall, our visit to Constanza was a great success, but the outstanding feature was that the ship was trapped alongside the quay because the harbour froze over. We sailors were not used to such cold weather and were given every afternoon off to go ashore or get our heads down, suitably wrapped of course.

Every morning a special working party would walk around the ship chipping holes in the ice below the portholes. This was necessary because we had all been chucking our rubbish out of the portholes instead of carrying it up a couple of ladders to the upper deck then down the gangway and along the quay to the rubbish dump. Runs ashore were great, the citizens bent over backwards to help us, especially the 'ladies' of the town. Our money could be exchanged in the bars and restaurants for a great deal more than the official rate, so whilst the money lasted we were very happy, but as more and more of us became skint we began to long for a return to the comforts of Malta.

Before we arrived at Constanza, fate dealt me a cruel blow which I believe was like the blow dealt to me by the loss of my mother and which would be a vital factor in my future outlook on life, in as much as I couldn't care less about anything as long as I could enjoy myself.

I received a letter from Marian saying that she had been going out with a young fellow who worked in the same factory as herself and had decided that it was him and not myself who featured in her future plans. I do not know even today just exactly what my feelings were — stunned, furious, puzzled, punished because of my own unfaithfulness, I just did not know — but I consoled myself by thinking that there were plenty more fish in the sea and I was only twenty years old and was ten shillings a week better off — I'll survive I thought!

The loss of Marian, I believe, changed my whole outlook on life or that is the excuse I use. Mentally I had changed, but not morally. I had thought that would have changed once we were married, or would it? Since then I have had four wonderful attachments — two of them very long and two quite short, but they were oh so very different from my first love. The only explanation I can come up with is age. I wonder why boy meets girl, settles down and lives happily ever after escaped me? Surely I have not been too much of a bastard — but I suppose I must have been.

After we returned to Malta, I set about enjoying myself and my new found freedom with extra pocket money. However, it was then that a buzz or rumour began going around the ship to the effect that King George V was to hold a Jubilee Review of his Navy at Spithead. Certain units of the Med Fleet would be there and we were chosen to be one of them. The atmosphere on board was electric, everyone started saving like mad as we were sure to be given leave.

I do not recall the exact date of our arrival home, all I remember is that the crew were given a week's leave before taking part in the review.

A pal of mine on the *Devonshire* was Jack Cunningham, who I mentioned earlier joined the Navy with me. Jack was one of the brighter boys of our class and his father was a publican with an establishment in Vauxhall Street, near the

Barbican. Anyway, I met Jack one morning during our leave and asked him what he wanted to do. He had a bright idea about going to the local railway station to find out what excursions were on offer.

As we neared the station, we saw in front of us a group of about six girls and it was obvious that they were hurrying to catch a train. So Jack said ' Quick, let's find out where they are going and join them.

I galloped to the booking office and Jack made his way on to the platform in an effort to persuade the guard to hold the train for us. I asked the booking clerk for tickets to wherever the girls were going, and with them clutched in my hand made a dash for the train. The girls were hanging out of the window of their carriage waving and Jack and I just made it as the train pulled away. On enquiring as to where the girls were going they answered in unison 'Newquay'.

'That will do us,' we said, 'so let's get acquainted.' It transpired that the girls worked for a local photograher, I think it was Godfrey Stuart, and were on a day's outing. Apparently they were responsible for the developing and printing. When we eventually returned to the Med, Jack and I kept in contact with the girls and they were good to us with regards photographs we sent home to them. I had some wonderful photographs of that particular time of my life, but unfortunately they were all lost when the submarine on which I was serving was sunk in 1942.

Anyway, we had a wonderful day with the girls on the beach, swimming and generally larking about. Naturally, on the way home we paired off. Jack got the best looker (well, he could fight better than me!) and I got the next best, a lovely girl named Mary. I didn't know it at the time but she was courting and I didn't find out until I returned to England some twelve months later.

Our leave quickly came to an end and the ship went to Portsmouth to prepare for the review. Whilst there I managed to wangle a weekend leave in order to visit my brother in London. At the time he was working in repertory, as a stage manager or something similar, and he was also working for a song writer. Bert dressed me in one of his civilian suits, but his shoes nearly crippled me.

Nevertheless, off we went to Drury Lane to see Ivor Novello in *Glamorous Nights*. The show was wonderful, the first I had seen on a London stage — I still have the programme. Afterwards, we had a meal followed by a few drinks in a basement bar named *The Straw Cellar* in Picadilly. This was indeed a weekend to remember, good old brother Bert — one in a million.

At the review the dear old King steamed between the drawn up lines of his ships in the Royal Yacht, *Victoria and Albert*. He dutifully saluted and us matelots in turn dutifully cheered and waved our caps in a uniform manner shouting 'Hurrah, Hurrah, Hurrah', as he passed us by.

Later that night, when all the ships were floodlit, Lieutenant Commander Tommy Woodruff, who was well oiled, gave his famous world renowned broadcast about the 'Bloody Fleet being lit up'. He should have been knighted, but instead, the establishment 'crowned him'.

We eventually returned to the Mediterranean for another year or so, but what a wonderful break it had been. I changed my duty on our return to Malta and became a dynamo watch-keeper.

The ship had four of these dynamos, two of which were always running whilst two were rested or shut down for maintenance. They were steam turbine jobs, two were situated side by side in the after engine room and the other two were in a room of their own in the bowels of the ship, access to which was down a long metal ladder through a square chute. When one looked down into this dynamo room from the top of the ladder, all that could be seen was a small square area of metal plate decking. From the top to the bottom of the chute there was a long rope at the bottom of which was a large heavy duty metal hook which served two purposes.

The official purpose was to hoist or lower buckets etc., whilst the other was purely for the benefit of the watch-keeper on duty who attached the rope and hook in such a manner as to draw his attention to anyone descending the ladder, such as the engineer of the watch or anyone else for that matter. This precaution was very necessary for the watch-keeper's peace of mind as he could be reading or dozing off, as I have done many times.

This might seem unbelievable considering the noise these monsters made, but one becomes quite accustomed to this noise to such an extent that if one of the dynamos faltered, or stopped, one would immediately be alerted.

CHAPTER 12

Our return to the Mediterranean brought us to a far different sea from the one we had previously known as our happy exercise and playground.

Mussolini had invaded Abyssinia, a country which was populated by illiterate tribesmen, armed only with primitive guns and spears,

What a pathetic man he was, with his brainwashed, peaceful, colourful, romantic soldiers, whose only delights were to eat, drink, sing and make love. They did not wish in their hearts to fight anyone and except for a small number of very brave men during the war were quite incapable of doing so, but this pompous man lead them, albeit from the rear, into a conflict with a poor African country which a couple of British regiments could have taken in a matter of days.

As a result of their victory in Abyssinia the Italians were deluded into thinking that they were unbeatable, but a rude awakening was to be theirs when five years later they were literally chased from pillar to post by the Albanians, Greeks, Yugoslavs and ourselves, by which time probably four changes of underwear was standard issue in their kitbags.

I had heard that one could volunteer for submarine service after being in the Navy for three years, so I decided to try and join. It sounded glamorous enough, but in the first instance the attraction for me was purely mercenary because I had never been what I consider to be a brave or daring person.

When I appeared before the captain with my request I told him quite truthfully that I wanted the extra money that went with the service.

I do not believe that he recalled our first meeting when I was a defaulter, although surely it must have been written on my record which was on the table before him. I did not see my service record until I was demobbed in 1945 but would you believe that my character and work during my service on HMS *Devonshire* was rated as 'Superior'. How about that? Anyway, the captain granted my request saying that my application to join the submarine service would be forwarded through the usual channels.

In 1936, partly to relieve the boredom of our exercising on a war footing, I volunteered to be a relief fireman on the armoured train carrying supplies from Egypt to Palestine. I did have coal fired boiler experience as a result of my service on HMS *Beaufort*.

The one trip I made was quite enlightening, but except for two or three instances of sporadic firing at us by Arabs, the journey passed without any serious incident.

On my return to the *Devonshire*, we took off for the Spanish Civil War, this became a testing ground for various forms of modern warfare, particularly aerial bombardment.

Our role was basically to protect the British nationals who were caught up in the conflict. This required us to land armed parties of marines and sailors at such places as Barcelona, Valencia, Cartagena and Palma. The armed parties escorted our nationals who had taken refuge in the Consulate back to the ship for passage to Marseilles. We would then return to Spain for more evacuees. On one occasion we rescued a troop of dancing girls who gave us an impromptu performance on deck in their briefs — thank you girls!

There are about three incidents which I clearly remember, one was at Majorca where we were at anchor for a number of days. It was here that mornings and evenings, three slow-moving, low-flying aeroplanes would come over the town dropping leaflets calling upon the local garrison to surrender. These planes would be met by just sporadic machine gun and rifle fire, but unbeknown to these intrepid aviators, the garrison of the fort had acquired or resurrected an anti-aircraft gun of about three or four inch calibre.

One evening as the sun was setting and most of our crew were on deck enjoying a smoke waiting for the evening raid, by which we could more or less set our watches, along came the three biplanes, dropping their leaflets and waggling their wings. They were met by the usual small arms fire until suddenly, there was an almighty 'Bang' from the direction of the barracks. Smoke, dust and debris was flying everywhere, even into the water around us.

When the dust and smoke had cleared, we could see that the part of the wall of the barracks had collapsed, together with part of a building, two of the planes were seen disappearing towards the horizon, but there was no sign of the third. It was claimed that the third aircraft was brought down by flying debris, we never found out the true story, but suspected that the pilot had lost control of his aircraft because he was laughing so much!

Another incident occurred at Valencia where boat loads of women, including many beautiful young girls, came alongside, some completely naked, begging for food. We did throw quite a lot of food into the boats, if only we could have got our hands upon some of them, but would we have enjoyed it? I do not think so. I never enjoyed a visit to a brothel in any part of the world. I have always liked the chase or scheming which eventually leads to fulfilment.

The rumours that had been circulating around the ship became fact and Devonshire's two and a half year commission ended and we set sail for home.

We approached our home port of Devonport, passed the breakwater on our starboard side and entered Plymouth Sound.

A wonderful sight, oh how many times I had seen it in all it's glories, then yet again in all it's furies. Nevertheless, this is the place where my ashes must be spread. I have asked for this to be carried out, if it is possible, under threat of a little bit of 'naughty haunting' at vital moments if my wishes are not complied with.

The ship headed towards Plymouth Pier and we turned to pass it on our starboard side with lovely Drake's Island to our port, into the Hamoaze and the River Tamar. We then made our way to the place reserved for us on the outer wall of the dockyard.

As we passed Admiralty House at Mount Wise, we were welcomed by the saluting guns of the Commander-in-Chief, to which we replied with our own salute.

Whilst all this was going on we had been trailing from the mainmast our paying-off pennant which seemed to be swirling in the slight breeze for miles astern to the annoyance of the tug boat skippers whose job it was to shepherd us into our berth. The other person who I suspect was annoyed was our skipper who thought he probably could take the ship in at night in thick fog, blindfolded with both hands tied behind his back without the aid of tugs. His *piece-de-resistance* would probably have been stern first. I thought at the time he would definitely make admiral. (I learnt many years later that he did). Thank you sir for a wonderful maturing two and a half years, my personal disappointment was not of your making, so on with life.

Hold on there, how on earth do I expect the readers of this story to understand why a mere stoker could have been observing all this activity when he should have been deep in the bowels of the ship 'a stokering'? Well, in order to explain this strange phenomenon, I must retrace my tale by about six months.

During the previous two years I had more or less performed all the duties which were required of a stoker and performed them in a 'superior manner' according to the report which I did not see until many years later. Nevertheless, I was suddenly transferred from engine and boiler room duties to a job far removed from this type of work, but fortunately where I managed to chum-up with another stoker with whom I had never previously worked, Wilf Heppell, a wonderful pal, but who unfortunately was lost on a ship in the Far East during the war, I believe it was HMS *Exeter*. Thank you Wilf, just you keep a nice clean and sharp shovel for me when my turn comes, I'll find you that's for sure.

Anyway, the job I was appointed to was the general mess party which I regarded as a demotion, 'Not a bit of it' I was assured by the chief stoker. This general mess party were a team which consisted of two stokers, two seamen, one marine and a petty officer in charge. Well, about six hundred officers and men had to be fed daily and someone had to transport the various items of food from where it was stored to where it was prepared for consumption. This is where our team came in, we were, would you believe, the pack horses, there were no mechanical aids for us in those bygone days, only arms and legs.

Just let me give you one example, bags of flour, weighing over half a hundredweight, had to be taken to the bakery, carried on one's back from a store below the stokers' mess deck. The route was up a metal ladder, along a few yards to another metal ladder, up to the seamen's mess deck, then past the canteen flat, along a passage way past some petty officers' and chiefs' messes to the marines' mess deck, then up another metal ladder to the bakery. Well, you can believe me when I say that there wasn't time to 'loaf' about.

When not working as a team we had own individual stores to look after, mine, situated aft below the officers' quarters was the clothing store where protective clothing, which was not part of an individuals kit, was kept.

It was part of my duty to see that this area was clean and tidy with every item stored where it should be. It also provided a refuge, somewhere I could get my head down after 'tot time' or 'make and mend' days, or where I could dodge church. You would be surprised at the lengths some matelots went to in order to escape church service, even hiding in the funnel casings.

Before I leave my story of the *Devonshire* I must mention something about the entertainment aboard. Someone formed a 'ten a penny band', this was a gang of about ten ratings, stokers, seamen and marines; the ship's marine band was excluded. Roughly, the composition of the band was piano, drums, trumpet, saxophone, two banjos, clarinet, accordion and something else.

These lads were purely amateurs, but you would have to be deaf not to recognize the tune they were trying to play. Eventually, with the passage of time and many hours of hard practice and dedication on their part, they became quite good, and even played at various 'do's' on shore.

Then we had the 'concert party' which, in turn, after many dedicated hours of hard work became quite proficient comics, dancers, singers and impersonators. My favourites were two ratings, a stoker and a seaman, who did an act as two 'queer' policeman. They would dance on stage in mock police uniforms and sing a song, something like this:

We're two smart lads in blue,
We're better known as numbers twenty one and twenty two,
We don't come from the CID.
But we do a bit of knobbing round the UJC (Soliciting)
We're not cockneys and we're not from the Isle of Skye,
We're known to all the flappers,
A terror to the hatters, (Queers)
Before we go would anyone like to try.

Then there was an able seaman, a comic who did very good monologues, one of which was about the matelots run ashore. This one was great, but unfortunately I can only recall snatches of it. How this poor chap when on shore did tarry awhile and fell amongst thieves and got 'Franz Liszt'. He found a bit of spare and went home with her, but much to his regret a few days later, when suffering a pain in his pecker, was informed by the 'quack' that he was unclean and not fit to live with other men. The actual words used by the 'quack' went something like this, 'Get thee hence and abide in the cottage of Rose until such times when we will have purged thee and thou hast repented thy sins.' Rose Cottage was the sailors name for the mess in which anyone with VD was billeted.

We also had a chief stoker who gave us his version of *Eskimo Nell and the shooting of Dan Magrew*, the words were fantastic, the audience were always in tears or stitches. We had some real characters on the *Devonshire* and incidentally the costumes for both 'ten a penny band' and the 'concert party' were designed and made by one of our stokers who had acquired a treadle sewing machine from somewhere and was one of the busiest chaps on board.

Now, however, I return to our arrival in Devonport. As we approached our berth there seemed to be thousands of women, girls and children waiting to greet their husbands, fathers and sweethearts, but none for me I'm afraid. Heaving lines were thrown from the ship to the dockyard 'mateys' who were waiting to secure us alongside and that as they say was that.

CHAPTER 13

Before the majority of the ship's company were drafted into barracks, we were sent on foreign service leave of twenty eight days — half of us almost immediately and the other half on their return. I was in the first period which was quite fortunate as the weather was still good at the end of August and being a free agent I could cast my net far and wide. Of course, there was Mary from the photographers who I decided I would contact later when I had time to think about my future activities on this home front.

I had chummed up with Wilf Heppell, my mate in the general mess party. Wilf lived close to the Barbican and arranged for us to accompany a couple of lads whom we knew from our school days on a weeks trip to London. This trip was made in an open top Austin Seven with wire wheels. Let me say now what a wonderful machine this was, not a moments trouble there and back with four of us and our gear. We were driven by another good friend of mine, Jim Oats.

A few days before we went to London I had met Marian, quite by chance and was immediately captivated by her, forgetting all my thoughts about my new found freedom and how I intended to exploit it fully. I talked to her at great length, pleading with her to rethink about our relationship. She did sort of half promise to think about it and we arranged to meet in the evening on my return from London. The meeting place was to be outside St Andrew's Cross Church where we had planned to marry. The four of us went off to London where we had a great week which included a flight in an old 'string bag' of a plane from Croydon Airport.

Back to Plymouth and what a fool I was not to have arranged to meet Marian perhaps a day or two later because I was well over an hour late in getting to our meeting place. She probably thought that I couldn't care less and had left forever, so that was that.

I then contacted Mary, from the photographers, and had some lovely outings with her until suddenly one evening I was confronted by a bloke who looked capable of eating me. What is more, he more or less threatened to do just that if I didn't stop seeing Mary to whom he said he was practically engaged. Well, that was another one off my list. I should have swallowed my pride and contacted Marian.

Wilf Heppell and I decided that we must learn to dance so we enrolled for dancing classes at a little place off Princess Street, which was run by a wonderful man and wife team. A large room on the first floor was for collective instruction and on the ground floor there was a smaller room which was used for individual or private lessons for people of a more nervous disposition. One shilling per session, that was value for money I can tell you, it changed my life and I enjoyed every minute of every hour that I spent learning to dance under the guidance of this great couple.

The music came from records played on a hand wound gramophone, they were all recorded by Victor Sylvester, who else for goodness sake? I became quite an expert at the waltz and quickstep, but not very good at the tango or slow fox trot, but I knew I could survive with any partner on the dance floor.

Naturally, at these dancing classes we had our favourite partners amongst the regulars. Wilf by this time was going great guns with the girl of his choice and I had my favourite, a nice little orphan girl who lived with her foster parents. She was not a ravishing beauty, but quite good looking in a certain way, what I mean is that she was not a snappy or gaudy dresser with bags of make up to catch one's eye. We got quite attached and seemed made for each other on the dance floor and it was she who first suggested that we were good enough to venture forth into the outside world of dance. We therefore decided to give it a whirl.

For our first venue we picked Plymouth Pier and what a lovely evening it was for both of us. We took to the floor like ducks to water, growing in confidence with every dance and to a real band, not to the strict tempo of dear old Victor. We were confident that is until the ladie's 'excuse me' when my partner was excused and I suddenly found myself with a strange body later to be 'excused' by another, then yet another, later to be 'excused' by my own partner who remarked that I was very popular and appeared to be one of the best on the floor. That was her biased opinion of course, but it made my evening that's for sure.

I was now stationed in the RN barracks and enjoyed many lovely evenings with my partner, but the Navy decided that I had been enjoying 'Jago's' grub too long and that the old ritual of bag and hammock packing and humping must begin again. So I bid farewell to my dancing partner for a while and as mine was a home draft I told her I would see her again soon. We did have some romantic outings, set apart from the dancing, which we both enjoyed, but these did not develop into a serious relationship.

I lost track of this wonderful girl when I joined submarines a year or so later, but literally ran into her outside the old Theatre Royal in Plymouth just before the end of the war, she told me that she was engaged to an Australian based at Mount Batten and would be going to Australia with him after the war. Always the romantic, I felt rather sad as I kissed her good luck and goodbye. I selfishly wanted her to stay.

Dear old Wilf was drafted to a ship. I never saw him again, he was lost as I mentioned earlier, another wasted life amongst hundreds of thousands of others. Wilf never hurt anyone, but had to pay the price for some other clown's dream of power.

Anyway, I was soon off and joined HMS *Keppell*, a two funnel destroyer. My new home was moored on the outer wall at Flagstaff Steps in company with a number of other destroyers, they were there for any emergency and one was always ready for sea at a moment's notice.

I soon settled down and found my way around. The conditions were not bad I suppose, but nothing like the comforts of the *Devonshire*. I lasted three days on this ship, when without warning, to us lesser mortals that is, the whole crew were told to transfer to HMS *Broke,* an identical, or practically identical, destroyer. This was the *Broke* of World War I fame, so I was told.

I lasted there for three weeks, until someone discovered that I was using the wrong soap or something, so I had to pack my bag and go back into barracks. I remember thinking to myself, how many more times did I have to do this in the next seven and a half years, roll on my twelve!

I was drafted to HMS *Wren* — another destroyer moored in exactly the same place where I had left the *Broke*. It was practically a new crew as far as the engine branch were concerned and I was detailed as the motor boat driver. There was a small problem, I didn't know how to drive a motor boat. Sail one, scull one, steer one, yes, but I didn't know anything about motor boat engines, however it sounded like a cushy job and I decided it would do me.

HMS *Wren* was part of what was known as the Irish Patrol and although there was partition between the Republic of Ireland and Ulster, we still had commitments with regard to the South. We even had an army base on Spike Island in Queenstown, matelots were allowed ashore in uniform, but the soldiers from Spike had to wear 'civvies'. Incidentally, I believe that Jack Doyle, the famous Irish boxer and latter day film star who married Movita from the film *Mutiny on the Bounty*, was employed as a porter or something in one of the hotels in Queenstown.

Anyway, back to the *Wren*, we went off to the Emerald Isle, a little piece of heaven that dropped into the sea from the sky one day. For the benefit of all you lucky so and so's who have never been around the south coast in a rough sea, let me recount what it was like for me, a young stoker. Imagine praying for death, but then having second thoughts, trying to string your hammock up, hoping to climb in and perhaps not be there when morning came, or when it was your turn to go on watch. First let me say that the hammock is a sailors best friend. When you are in your 'Mick', after all the toils of the day or a bash ashore, you are in heaven and everyone else, mother, father, wife, girlfriend, you name it, will just have to wait!

But let me see, where was I, oh yes I was a poor old, or rather young stoker feeling old, trying to sling my hammock in a pitching destroyer in a rough sea around 'Paddy's Patch'. In between spewing my guts up over the side, trying to remember which is the lee-side, I tried to focus my mind on exactly where I might find my hammock amongst all the others in stowage on the mess deck.

This was situated, below the seamen's deck in the fo'c's'le, where the pitching of a destroyer can be felt at its worst. Up will go the bow seemingly for hundreds of feet, then down it will fall through emptiness to hit the sea below with an almighty thump leaving what remains of your stomach up where the top deck used to be.

I had to get my hammock because my very survival depended upon this one formidable act which had to be accomplished. I collected my thoughts and knowing near enough where I last saw it, I made a sudden dive into the fo'c's'le to the seamen's mess deck, scrambled down the steel ladder to the stokers' mess and dragged the hammock out to the place near where I hoped to sling it. By this time I felt the urge to be sick again so I scrambled back up the ladder onto the upper deck whilst being thrown from side to side. Eventually, I emerged out into the fresh sea-sprayed air only to find that I could not be sick as I had nothing left to bring up, but I kept trying with my head spinning.

After a quick dash down to the mess again, I found that the blasted hammock had rolled under one of the mess tables, I dragged it out onto a heaving deck and got one end secured to a hammock bar, perhaps both ends, but I couldn't stay any longer and rushed to the upper deck for another puke.

I decided to make one last supreme effort to reach my hammock. Taking a deep breath I raced down below, knocking all and sundry out of my way, unlashed the hammock, kicked my shoes off, secured them in the rack, took off my boiler suit, grabbed the hammock bar with both hands and flung myself into it. 'Sod 'em all!'

I did have quite a few good runs ashore at Queenstown and Cobh, one of which I recall quite vividly. I was escorting a young lady home after keeping her out late, far too late it appears because as we walked the last few yards to her house, we were suddenly set upon by what at the time seemed to be a large vampire, with huge black wings, screaming like a Banshee. When we recovered from this attack, we realized that the 'bat' was in fact a priest in full robes who commenced belabouring my companion with his umbrella. Deciding that this was an unequal contest, I placed a boot in a well chosen spot namely his backside and he went away with a couple of 'Hail Marys' or was it 'Hell Marys'. I never saw the lady again so cannot say whether or not there was a rematch.

As well as Cork we frequently visited Bantry Bay and Glengarrif during our time on the Irish Patrol and there are two things I must say about this part of Ireland, one is the lovely warm hospitality of its people and the other is the beautiful scenery.

I will always remember when our ship was challenged to a hockey match against a girls school. Schoolgirls? We were conned, these girls were Amazonian gladiators, armed with shillelaghs. We were torn apart, the score was immaterial, but comparable with the casualties, seven to nil. The reason that the score was so low was owing to the fact that our casualties were blocking their path to our goal.

After this match, or battle, things cut up rough again, weather wise that is, and we were unable to return to the ship. However, we were assured that it was only a squall, quite frequent in these parts, and would pass in a couple of hours. So, in the meantime we took shelter in a large farmhouse. I have never seen anything like it. The kitchen had to be seen to be believed. It had a cooking range, about ten feet in length with ovens and hot plates, upon which were various iron pots, above this were large oak beams from which hung fish, bacon, hams, game, herbs etc. and over in one corner there were about six chickens tied to a flat iron waiting their turn to be butchered.

At Queenstown one day I had a problem refuelling our motor boat. I had been having a lot of trouble with water in the petrol which was kept in five gallon drums on the upper deck of our ship. I reported to the engineer officer that I was having to strain every drop of petrol through a chamois leather. Well, on this particular day when the motor boat was hoisted inboard, I was filling the petrol tank situated in the bow and I thoughtlessly kept wringing the chamois into the bilge of the boat.

Lifting a five gallon drum of petrol just to pour a pint or two into a chamois-lined funnel was quite a chore so I had borrowed a thick calibrated glass vessel holding about three or four pints. I tilted the five gallon drum into this glass container, spilling a few drops in the process, then lifted the container and gradually poured this into the chamois-lined funnel. When I considered the tank to be nearly full, I put the cap on both the petrol tank and drum, sat back, took out a fag, lit a match and 'Boom' a sheet of flame engulfed the motor boat. An able seaman and myself leapt from the boat onto the upper deck and did not have time to reach for the solitary extinguisher situated in the small engine room of the boat.

Some sixth sense told me to chuck my fags and matches over the ships side. Almost immediately the officer of the watch rushed from the quarter deck and was at my side demanding to know what had happened. I replied that I didn't know. Not satisfied he questioned me further.

'Were either of you smoking?'

'No Sir'

'Do you smoke?'

'Yes Sir, but never on duty in the boat.' He ordered me and the able seaman aft and by this time the captain and the engineer officer were also on the scene, more questions were asked, dozens of them.

The fire was eventually extinguished and the engineer officer spotted the thick glass vessel I had been using. He questioned me about it and I confessed to him that I had occasionally shaken the chamois into the bilge of the boat. Fortunately for me, this particular day had been hot and very sunny. He ordered me to come aft with him to see the captain where he explained that in his opinion the cause of the fire was spontaneous combustion caused by the sun's rays through the glass vessel. What an escape!

Edward the Eighth abdicated in December 1936 and in the summer of 1937 the new King, George the Sixth, held a review of the Home Fleet at Portland. HMS *Wren*, therefore, returned to Devonport to have a quick paint job before joining the other ships in the review and my Irish escapades were over for a while.

CHAPTER 14

When we arrived at Devonport, the motor boat crew were ordered to take the skipper ashore. Off we went with no trouble until the coxswain gave me the order to stop and go astern, this meant that first I had to pull a long lever to disengage the forward motion and then put the engine into reverse. Well, the whole damned thing came away in my hand. The spindle at the bottom had sheared off and the only course left for me was to stop the engine, or ease it down to very slow and approach our mooring until the coxswain could judge the distance to enable me to stop the engine and glide in. After a couple of practice runs we made it much to the annoyance of the skipper. Well, it wasn't my fault, was it? As for the review, well once you have seen one you have seen them all.

Once the review was over the ships dispersed and HMS *Wren* was detailed to pay a courtesy visit to Llandudno for one week. We arrived at this holiday resort early in the morning and anchored about half a mile from the end of the pier.

The following afternoon, I went ashore on a twenty four hour pass, found a pub and managed to down a few pints before it closed. Feeling just right, I strolled back to the front and took a deck chair at the matinee performance of a summer show. After a few 'catnaps' I came to my senses with the sound of applause and a shout from the bandstand of 'That's all folks.'

I decided that it was time for big eats before the 'boozer' opened again, so I strolled to a local 'greasy spoon' and had steak, eggs and chips. Thus fortified, I strolled back to the front to await opening time or whatever. Well, as it turned out for me it was the whatever. I came upon an able seaman from our ship and he was talking to a right couple of bits of crackling, he grabbed me like a long lost brother and that was it, simple as that. We paired off, although mine was the best looker by a short head. I will not reveal her name because she was young, very young, consequently is probably still going strong and I do not wish for her to be embarrassed or identified. However, we had a lovely evening and I was on cloud nine and gave no thought as to where I would sleep that night.

I decided to escort her home and thought that with a bit of luck I would have my wicked way with her. I was certain the feeling was mutual and it was just a matter of being in the right place at the right time. We entered her back garden and the fun began. Oblivious to the outside world we were more or less there when suddenly her mother opened the back door and announced she was not going to call her again (we had ignored previous calls, this will show you how worked up we were). Her mother stated that she would remain there until we said good night to one another.

That was that, so after making arrangements to meet the next time I was ashore, I made my way back into town with the knowledge that I had probably missed the last boat back to the ship and would therefore have to get my head down on one of the long wooden benches along the pier. This is not a problem when you have had quite a few pints, but when, such as I, you are stone sober, thinking of what might have been, you can be in for quite an uncomfortable few hours until the first boat at 7 am.

It was a lovely warm summers night as I walked back to the front at Llandudno making plans for my next encounter and knowing that she was just as eager as I. When I reached the sea front opposite the pier and was halfway across the promenade I came more or less face to face with a man who was perhaps ten or fifteen years older than myself.

This fellow, well dressed and well spoken, remarked that he thought I had missed my last boat back to the ship which we could see lying at anchor. I replied that I knew that this was indeed so, but that I was making my way towards the end of the pier where there was bound to be a vacant seat. I added that we matelots were conditioned and could in fact sleep anywhere that was dry and clean only needing our cap or shoes to use for a pillow, in fact I said we were very versatile.

That word, I believe, was the trigger which set off the chain of events that followed. I didn't realise at the time just what I was letting myself in for. You might wonder how the hell a chap of my experience could be so naive, but it was so, let me assure you, I had no idea until very much later what he wanted.

All sailors, I repeat all sailors, at some time or other in the mess or pub have taken part or listened to conversations about homosexuality and the chaps who practice it. They were known to us as 'brownhatters'. I personally, like many others, have also been touched up in fun, when skylarking in the showers with other members of the crew; normally to shouts of 'You dirty old so and so', or words to that effect. It was just a bit of fun. At that period of my life I don't think I ever gave it a thought to what I might do if I found myself in a situation with a homosexual.

The fellow I met on the promenade offered me a bed for the night and assured me that being at the pier for the boat in the morning would present no problems as his flat was but a short distance from where we were. So off we went. It was about 11.30 pm and the area was deserted as we approached his place, which was indeed a short walk from the sea front. We climbed what appeared to be a fire escape or something similar at the side of a large store, cinema or some such other building then stepped onto a flat roof where my companion opened the door of what today would be described as the penthouse. We entered a very nicely furnished apartment that had a kitchen, a bathroom, a dining room and a bedroom with one large double bed.

After preliminaries I accepted a drink and remarked that I had to be up and about by 6.15 or 6.30 at the latest, so we undressed and turned into the double bed, me in my underpants and singlet and my companion in pyjamas. He had not offered to loan me any pyjamas, but would you believe I still had not caught on and the reason for this, I keep telling myself, is at no time did our conversation ever drift toward anything remotely connected with relations between men. We just lay in bed talking about things in general, where I had been, where I hoped to go to, my ambitions, whether I was married or courting. I understood that he was a manager of some company in the town. I told him of my frustrating evening.

After a while I thought to myself 'will he never stop', because I was drowsy and then his left hand brushed against my right leg, well I didn't move or say a word, but then a hand came onto my right thigh. This, believe it or not, was the first indication of what my companion had in mind when he invited me to share his bed. I in turn offered no resistance to the next move he made.

Here, let me say that I make no excuses for the part I played in this episode of my life which no doubt a lot of people would condemn as disgusting, unnatural, filthy, and odious. I could not blame them for thinking this way.

I have had a great deal of time to think about this event to which at the time I did not deliberate over long. I have also thought or wondered about the state of mind of my companion. He had got into bed fully dressed in a suit of pyjamas, and he did not suggest at any time that we should sleep naked. I do not believe this was a regular occurrence for him and it is probable that he had only dabbled in this sort of thing on rare occasions. He might have been successful or perhaps disappointed, but on seeing a young sailor all alone without a bed for the night thought that here was a golden opportunity and so it proved to be. His mind must have been in a turmoil, perhaps wondering whether or not I would beat him up if he made just one provocative move.

What a decision he had to make compared with mine, all I had to do was comply with his action or dress and depart to the pier, which had been my original intention. However, as you have read, he decided to throw caution to the wind and made the first intimate move.

In the morning I was awakened with a nice cup of tea and a biscuit. I quietly washed and dressed, bid my farewell and assured him that he had indeed made a friend for life and I would see him again. These promises cost me nothing because within days I knew I would be a hundred miles from there.

The next day it was my turn to drive the motor boat to the pier with the liberty men. As we approached the landing stage I saw my female companion and started waving frantically at her. Imagine my horror when I spotted my male companion on the steps behind her waving frantically back. As the boat docked and the men dispersed I managed a few quick words with my young lady, whilst at the same time I received a look of understanding from my male friend, who then turned and walked away. I thought that was the last I would see of him.

The following day I was on the first liberty boat ashore and she was waiting for me. I could have been arrested for what I was thinking! We spent a wonderful afternoon and evening before we trekked back to her house in Deganwy where a shock awaited me. I was invited in to meet the family and have supper and was informed I could stay the night. I could have cried because at no time from then on was I able to lay a finger on her.

The next day I was on motor boat duty and to my horror both my companions were waiting again on the landing stage. This time, however, my male friend gave me a very puzzled look as the liberty men dispersed.

Well, the following morning before I went ashore, my head was in turmoil, mostly I have to say about how I was going to seduce my girl friend, but what is that old saying about 'The best laid plans of mice and men'.

As we met I could hardly keep myself from throwing her onto a bench there and then, I was so pent up inside. But I could see a very odd look on her face and there was a certain hesitancy in her voice. We walked along the pier and her first full sentence brought all my dreams crashing about my ears, 'I've come on. My periods shouldn't be till next week, must be all the excitement says mum.'

I must have looked crest fallen because she went on to say, 'I've gone and spoilt our evening haven't I?' I told her not to worry and there would be plenty of other times.

Anyway I revised my plans, glad the ship was leaving the following day, because I doubt whether I had ever had to do so much thinking, planning and decision making in such a short period of time as those last few days. However, my young lady and I spent a pleasant evening together, although I decided that she should return home a little earlier than planned. This, I told her, would enable me to return to the ship by the 10 pm boat, thus giving me more time to prepare for the ship to sail. A feeble excuse, but I thought it might also enable me to dodge my male friend who might possibly be waiting at the pier. I was really taken with my young lady fully intending to take up the invitation that had been extended to me of spending my next leave or part of it at their home.

As I approached the pier he was waiting for me. I was greeted with the words, 'Where were you on Wednesday night?' I explained to him about staying at the girls house. He then said, 'What about tonight, were you going on board without one thought for me and so early?' I then went into a detailed explanation as to the circumstances, saying that I felt so upset by everything that seemed to be against me that I just wanted to climb into my hammock and forget everything and everybody.

Well, he was very persuasive and I agreed to go home with him. This time, however, there was no tension and pure animal instincts were sufficient to satisfy both our needs. We hurt no other person and I told nobody of what had happened, until now. I most certainly did not at any time regret my actions and I never repeated the experience. I do not have any strong thoughts about the morals or ethics of what I did or homosexuality. Who am I to pass judgement?

The following morning I bid my friend farewell with promises to write and visit him. I must add that both my companions had my full name, rank and ship, but I never saw either of them again.

After a weeks leave for both watches, we set off once more to resume the Irish Patrol. During my service on the *Wren* I chummed up with an able seaman, a super character and a good pal, his name was Francis Northcott.

Frank was without doubt what I would imagine to be everyone's idea as to what a young sailor should look like, good looking, not too tall, average build and a neat and snappy dresser. Girls would stand in line just to touch his 'Dicky' collar for luck.

He was my 'boozing' companion when in Devonport, we lived quite close to one another and knew most of the pubs in our neck of the woods; our favourites being the *Farmers Home, Posada* and *Westwell Street Vaults*. We had some great times together indulging in our favourite pastime of chatting up the barmaids.

Until a few years ago, I regularly saw him around town and we would chat about old times. Usually it was only a brief yarn, with him always saying, 'You are always in a hurry when I see you,' and he was so right. The reason being that I do not drive any more and therefore have to rely on catching a bus, which runs hourly. It is quite coincidental that when I met Frank it was invariably about five or ten minutes before my bus was due to leave. In my minds eye I still see him as I did fifty years ago, but alas, dear old Francis has now departed to higher service. Oh how I wish I had spent more time talking to him and caught the later bus.

Incidentally, Frank was our 'Tanky' on HMS *Wren,* and was responsible for dishing out all the perishable food to the cooks of the mess, meat, spuds, etc. On HMS *Wren* the caterer of the mess decided what we would have for a main meal and the two cooks (stokers) would prepare everything and take it to the galley to be cooked.

For example, if we were going to have a 'straight rush', that is a roast dinner, the meat and veg would have to be fetched from the 'Tanky' who knew how many men there were in your mess. The spuds would be peeled and arranged around the meat in a large dish or dishes with a liberal dollop of dripping or fat, then the other vegetables would be prepared. Sometimes we would have a stew, a 'pot mess' as we knew it, this was dead easy to prepare, we just cut the stewing beef into chunks, added chopped onions, carrots, swede, parsnips etc., bunged it all into the cooking pot with gravy powder and water and that was it. The spuds for boiling would be peeled and placed into a net suitably identified with a mess label and placed in the galley boiler.

Sometimes we might get someone in the mess to knock up a 'spotted dick' or suet pudding, neatly wrapped in a cloth and tied with string to resemble a small hammock. On one occasion some clever sod decided to tie up a rugby ball bladder to resemble a 'spotted dick' and the cook couldn't understand why the thing wouldn't sink when he chucked it in the boiler.

In November the *Wren* was recalled to Devonport and I was drafted back into the barracks. Although the barracks were not quite as friendly as a destroyer, I didn't really mind, as the weather had turned and the barracks offered lovely grub, warmth and a chance to get ashore.

t was the 10th December 1937 when I entered the barracks and I heard, unofficially through the grapevine, that I had been called in to 'go through the school'. This is a term used when leading stokers and stokers who have qualified to become leading stokers, are put through a three month course in the mechanical training establishment situated in the dockyard. At the end of the course they are tested in order to determine whether or not they are petty officer material.

I joined a new class for instruction which began immediately after the Christmas and New Year leaves had finished. The instruction was dull, routine stuff, connected naturally with the boiler, engine and other machine rooms on board ship, how to cope with various emergencies and how to carry out minor repairs etc.

I must tell you about our Friday afternoon routine when instruction for the week finished. At about 4 pm we would form up outside the mechanical training establishment in the dockyard ready to march off to the barracks. At the head of our column would be 'Jago's Band'. This was a full band of drums and instruments all played by sailors (not marines), and known as the 'blue jacket' band. I might add that they were very good indeed. When we were all ready to march off we would be brought to attention and turned into line and the band would be ordered, 'Band ready!' The bandmaster, a petty officer, normally a gunnery rating, would say 'Now come on lads, taking your time by the dockyard clock and swinging your brawny little arms across your hairy little chests, January, February, MARCH!' The band would strike up and off we would go singing our own words to whichever march was being played, for example:

Tight as a drum, never been done, I'm the queen of the fairies.
All of a sudden a bloody great pudding came flying through the air,
it landed beside me, petrified me, didn't half give me a scare etc.

These words were sung I believe to the tune of *Blaze Away*. Nobody minded or cared, we were all off for the weekend.

At the end of March 1938 I completed my course, which had been on the whole quite pleasant. I suppose the standard I achieved was about average and I was eventually assessed as petty officer material even though I was not yet a leading stoker. This in a way was fortunate as I was hoping to go to the submarine service where I understood, although I am not sure whether or not it was true, that leading stokers could not join the submarine service.

At the beginning of May I was sent to one of the Navy's old 'wooden walls', HMS *Defiance*, which looked something like Nelson's *Victory* and was secured on the Cornwall side of the River Tamar, just opposite the dockyard. This establishment was where the electricians and torpedo men or LTOs were trained, but I was there for a HPE course — High Powered Electricity. This was because quite a few of the electrical systems in the boiler and engine rooms were maintained by the stoker branch. I believe the course lasted about three weeks.

I wasn't very excited about it, but went along and learnt the essentials. There was though one particular person on *Defiance* who will always remain in my memory, the chaplain. It was a well known fact that ninety-nine percent of all matelots at that time went to ridiculous lengths in order to dodge church parade.

They would hide in the spud locker, funnel casings, toilets, paint and cable lockers, anywhere in fact, including some of the dirtiest places on board in spite of the fact that they could be wearing their lovely white number six suits, but all this was quite different on *Defiance.*

Although an agnostic, I in company with many of the other chaps on this ship never dreamt of dodging church when our particular chaplain was taking the service. The magnetism of this fellow was something that had to be seen and heard. I am ill-equipped to describe the effect he had upon his congregation but he held us in his grip, sometimes giving us hell and when he paused to change gear, one could hear a pin drop. I cannot unfortunately remember his name and I have made many enquiries to the Navy, but without success.

I must point out that despite the esteem we had for this dear person, when it came to the hymns, it was back to square one because as with the marches we had our own words to fit the tunes, for example it was, 'Onward Christian Soldier's, not too fast in front.' The rest of the words are unprintable. Another favourite was sung to the tune of *Oh come all ye faithful*, the words went something like this:

> The King was in his counting house, counting out his money,
> The Queen was in the parlour eating bread and honey,
> The maid was in the garden hanging out the dhobi-ing
> When down came a bloody great shite hawk,
> When down came a bloody great shite hawk,
> When down came a bloody great shite hawk, etc.etc.

On completion of the course I returned to the barracks and general working parties. Ashore I met up again with my dancing partner and we spent some wonderful evenings and outings together on the grassy slopes overlooking Plymouth Sound at Jennycliffe.

On the 4th July 1938 — which was the birthday of my older sisters, Gladys and Irene, I received a draft chit which made it my birthday also. I was drafted to the shore establishment HMS *Dolphin* at Gosport for submarine training and I just couldn't wait to get there.

CHAPTER 16

I arrived at the harbour station in Pompey, in company with about a dozen other sailors. I was the only stoker so naturally I did not know any of the other lads with me. Here we were met by a petty officer who told us that his duty was to get us to HMS *Vernon,* a short distance away, from where we would be transported across the harbour by service launch to Fort Blockhouse, HMS *Dolphin,* on the Gosport side. From then on we were the responsibility of the submarine depot.

As we approached the *Dolphin* we could see a sleek looking submarine, *L23,* lying alongside the jetty and further up the creek was a small floating dock bearing one of Navy's smallest submarines, *H49.*

As we came alongside the jetty I did not know that the steps would take me to a different kind of Navy to that I had known. In the years to come I would mix with men like David Wanklyn VC DSO, Commander 'Tubby' Linton VC of the *Turbulent,* a gentleman and officer, in that order, 'Tomkinson' DSO of the *Urge,* the boat on which one of my mates, Stoker PO Bill Ashford, was lost. There are so many, many others, far too numerous to mention unfortunately. They were all comrades in arms, young in heart and age, whose sole aim was to live life to the full whilst respecting other peoples way of living theirs.

On the jetty a petty officer was waiting for us and ordered us to stack our bags and hammocks, saying that we could collect them later when we had been allocated and shown the location of our various messes. We were then marched to the guardroom a short distance away where we were given a brief summary of the do's and don'ts of the base, allocated our messes and instructed to read the notice boards in the mess.

The stokers' messes were situated right above the church which is still in the same place today, but alas the messes have long gone to far more glamorous surroundings — quite a distance away too because HMS *Dolphin* must today be twice the size it was in 1938. I wondered if some of the ghosts of my many long lost shipmates were at my side last year in 1994, when I looked at our old abandoned messes, now derelict and thought to myself 'How did we put up with this?' But we did, wasn't this the new adventure for which we volunteered, every single one of us? This was our chosen way of life and every man jack of us were hoping that we would successfully pass the medical and course.

I suppose the two most important things to the majority of us new entries was the immediate pay rise of two shillings per day, a fifty per cent rise for me, and the change to one's cap ribbon from HMS *Drake* to HM Submarines. The latter was guaranteed to get the girls, or so I thought!

The base was very compact in 1938, the only modern building was situated just inside the main gate and was known to everyone as the *Grand Hotel.* It was for the use of boats' crews only, that is the crews of submarines which were in commission based at *Dolphin* or visiting boats, all very posh, the messes even had single iron beds for one's hammock. The canteens, wet and dry, barber shop and tailor shop, were all within a stone's throw of our messes, in fact the wet canteen was just down a few steps from our mess and into the ground floor of the next building opposite the barbers.

This canteen was where I was first introduced to Hammerton's Brown Ale, sixpence a pint and my favourite. None of your 'cold fours' for me, which was ordinary mild Brickwoods at fourpence a pint. I was now a rich man and even bought on occasions Player's No I's instead of Woodbines, but I was soon to learn that life was not all 'beer and skittles'.

A submarine can travel on the surface or dive to its chosen depth, even take a rest on the bottom remaining quite quiet provided the bottom is within the diving depth for which a particular submarine has been designed. When on the surface she is driven by large diesel engines and when submerged, powerful electric motors take over. The batteries to power these motors just have to be seen to be believed.

Except for emergencies, it is normally the 'Number One', the first lieutenant, who dives or surfaces the boat, this is because the skipper is usually on his way down through the conning tower when the boat is diving, or on his way up when she is surfacing. The skipper is the one who gives the first order, for example when about to dive, he would sound the klaxon three times and shout 'Dive! Dive! Dive!' The lookouts and signalman would then scramble down the conning tower followed by the captain who would then clip down the upper lid or hatch by which time the boat would be almost under as a result of the orders from "Number One"'

To surface, the skipper would normally enter the conning tower and quietly say 'Take her up "Number One"' and he would practically have the upper lid open as the submarine broke the surface, he would then quickly scramble out, followed by lookouts. There is also the lower lid or hatch between the conning tower and the control room which is shut after the boat has dived and opened before surfacing. The word closed was never used in submarines; doors, hatches, valves, etc. were either open or shut. Submarines were also referred to as boats not ships.

Before we new entrants experienced any of the operations described we had to spend many weeks under instruction in classrooms and other places. We had to learn that a submarine dives and surfaces because it is fitted with external ballast tanks which contain air when the boat is on the surface. This air is allowed to escape from the top of the tanks when the boat dives to be replaced by sea entering the bottom of the tanks. It is as simple as that, but is it so very simple? Not a bit of it as we were soon to learn.

These main ballast tanks were situated outside the submarine proper, that is outside the pressure hull. Inside the boat we had many other tanks. Quick diving tanks which would allow us to take in extra water quickly, perhaps in a crash dive. Trimming tanks to take in sea water to replace the weight of food supplies used. Compensating tanks which came into use when torpedoes were fired allowing the equivalent weight in sea water to be taken in thus keeping the boat steady and stopping it from rising. Every gallon of fuel that was used was replaced by sea water. Tanks, tanks and more tanks, even our main batteries for the motors were in tanks.

We were taught about the importance of stowage of all movable objects, the food, kit, spare gear, and any passengers who were not part of crew. The whole safety of the boat and crew depended upon the correct distribution of weight of everything the boat was carrying. The 'Number One' was also the man who ensured before anything else, that everything was stowed and distributed correctly.

One of the first actions of a boat on leaving harbour was to do a trial dive in order to 'catch a trim', whereby the 'Number One' could judge whether or not his calculations were correct, not too heavy forward or aft, port or starboard. Neutral buoyancy is the aim of the first lieutenant so that the boat could dive and maintain its depth without rising or falling.

Back in the classroom we had to learn about our own particular branch; the engine room with diesel engines instead of boilers and turbines and air compressors, a very vital part of a boat's equipment. Finally, it was time to 'go through the tank' which I approached with excitement and a little apprehension.

This tank is where we had to learn how to use the Davis Submarine Escape Apparatus and carry out a simulated escape from the chamber of a sunken submarine. My classmates and I were all stood around the top of the circular deep tank wearing our escape sets and were told to breathe correctly in and out through the mouth, not through the nostrils, which were held together by a clip. Apart from our instructor there were a couple more already swimming about in the tank, purely to keep an eye on us and to ensure our safety in case of accidents.

One at a time we were ordered to descend the ladder into the tank and go under. I didn't like it one little bit, me a chap who had been swimming all his life, practically born in the water and able to swim like a fish under it. So what was all the fuss — well for one thing it was not natural to breathe that way. Just remember, this was in the days before the advent of people diving for pleasure. Anyway, back to me standing on the ladder with the water up to my chin. The instructor tapped me on the head and pointed downward with his finger. It was when the water came up to my forehead that I felt apprehensive, but I had reached the point of no return. There was also an instructor beneath me with one hand on my ankle, so down I went. Inwardly, I was panicking a bit, but I tried to settle down for a minute or two before continuing.

Eventually I did settle down and performed equally as well as all the other newcomers. We were confronted by the antics of the instructors who seemed able to remain suspended halfway up the tank where they even performed somersaults in the water.

The final exercise in our tank training came when we were placed two or three at a time in a special chamber at the bottom of the tank where we were called upon to assume that we were trapped in a sunken submarine and that it was necessary for us to make our escape. Into the chamber I went with two others, we were wearing our escape sets and the chamber was dry. Above our heads was the escape hatch which was shut with the sea above it which in this case was the water in the tank.

We shut the chamber door, adjusted our seats then commenced to flood the chamber from the 'sea' outside. The water came creeping around our ankles, then up to our knees, on to our chests and so to our mouths. I remember now trying to stand on tip toe — silly fool! Up went the water level until the pressure equalised with the water outside. The first chap climbed the ladder and opened a valve in the centre of the hatch and released the air which was trapped in the chamber. He then opened the hatch quite easily and climbed out to make his ascent to the surface, which in this case was the top of the tank. It was now my turn and I climbed the ladder out of the chamber, eager to get to the fresh air and daylight. I was not panicking or flapping, I was sure that I did exactly as I had been instructed to do, I climbed away from the chamber and any obstruction, partially inflated my escape set to take me to the surface, then unrolled the rubber apron and held it in front of my body to retard my ascent.

Two of the lads I teamed up with in my class were Bill Smith DSM, a cockney, and Fred Topping, who unfortunately was later lost in the *Upholder*. Fred was a smashing bloke and I'll see him again one day if my beliefs are proved wrong. I do hedge my bets, don't I?

We all successfully completed the course and were issued with our white submarine sweaters. As proud as peacocks, we were taken down to the submarine *L23* for our first dive and were instructed to keep out of the way of the regular crew going about their duties and keep our eyes and ears wide open.

The *L23* had been completed at HM Dockyard, Chatham in 1919 and was about 235ft long and 14ft across her widest part. She normally had a crew of about thirty six.

So off I went to sea in a real submarine, with mixed emotions. I remember feeling that I was in the way of everyone. The first thing that hit me was the penetrating smell of diesel oil and the noise of the twin engines when they were started up. Everywhere you looked in the submarine there were pipes, electrical cables, valves, gauges and machinery of all descriptions. To a novice it looked as though the boat had been designed without allowing any room for the crew. It was cramped, damp, smelly and noisy, but somehow it felt like home.

For a moment though, consider the significance of all the extra bodies on board the submarine, something to which I doubt any of us gave thought. We additional people were not only taking up room, but also valuable space which would normally contain fresh air. To cap it all we would be breathing air which belonged to the crew, thereby leaving them short if ever they needed it in an emergency. The submarine *Thetis* sank in Liverpool Bay with 103 men on board, almost twice her normal complement and only four were rescued.

I have often wondered how many of her crew would have lived longer with more air and perhaps, who knows, got to the surface. Nowadays, of course, a submarine can replenish its air supply.

But back to my first dive, I was situated just inside the engine room immediately aft of the control room when one of the officers told me in a whisper we had reached the diving area near the Isle of Wight. Suddenly the main diesel engines stopped and I could hear muffled orders being given in the control room. There was a hum as the main electrical motors took over and apparently we were already beneath the waves, I didn't feel a thing, what a let down. When I enquired from a crew member, he told me the depth gauge showed we were at a depth of 90ft.

My first trip to sea in a submarine turned out to be something of an anticlimax. We were shown around the boat in small groups with the permission of the first lieutenant, who had to consider his 'trim'. We saw many things in action which were difficult to explain in a classroom. The toilet for example, now there was a wonderful piece of engineering you would not believe the number of people who have got their own back when operating this infernal machine. I will not bore you with examples, suffice to say that after my first experience I approached this damned 'thunder box' with a great deal of caution, but after a lot of trial and error, I let it know who was in charge and from then on had no trouble at all. On the whole this trip was invaluable, perhaps it was just the diving and surfacing which disappointed me. I was expecting something more spectacular.

We returned to harbour to say farewell to our instructors, dispersed to our messes and then awaited our first draft to a submarine as a real member of a crew.

1921 — SCHOOL PHOTOGRAPH.
The author is fourth from the ~~right~~ *LEFT* on the bottom row and Bill Glanville is seated just behind him.

1928 — THE FLAT IN WHIMPLE STREET, PLYMOUTH
(Looking straight on)

1928 — PLAYING THE LEAD IN THE DOGS OF DEVON

1931 — GRAVESEND SEA SCHOOL.
The author is far left in the back row

W. TURPIN & SONS,

GOVERNMENT & CORPORATION CONTRACTORS

SIVE YARDS
NG OVER 2 ACRES
GROUND FOR
RAGE PURPOSES
AT LOW RATES.

FURNITURE
STORED
IN DRY
AND
COMMODIOUS
WAREHOUSES

GENERAL CARRIERS

REMOVAL CONTRACTORS

COXSIDE, PLYMOUTH.

February 12th. 19 31.

The Sea School Selection Officer
II. Hart Str
London. E.C. 3.

Dear Sir,   re Fred. A.Matthews.

　　　　I have employed the above named
boy since leaving School. as help in our
Office etc. and have always found him
Honest.. willing and industrious.

　　　　His inclination is for the Sea
and should you accept him, you would no doubt
find him suitable, and eager to learn.

　　　　Yours faithfully.

W   TURPIN & SONS, Ltd
For and on behalf of the Company.

A. Collings

MANAGING DIRECTOR.

1931— REFERENCE FOR THE SEA SELECTION OFFICER

ISSUED BY THE BOARD OF TRADE, In pursuance of 57 & 58 Vict. ch 60.

ACCOUNT OF WAGES. F.

Name of Ship	Official Number	Description of Voyage or Employment
TAMAROA 144805 ABERDEEN		NEW ZEALAND

Name of Seaman	Refr.No. in Agreement	Date and Port of Engagement	Date of Discharge	Rate of Wages
F. Matthews	33	28 JAN 1932 LONDON.	11 MAY 1932	£2

Earnings		Amount			Deductions	Amount		
Wages at £ 2 per month, for 3 Months 14 days		6	18	8	*Reduction of Wages on disrating by £ per month for months days			
*Increase of wages on promotion by £ per month for months days					Advance on joining	1	·	·
					Allotments			
Overtime 21 Hours at 6d		·	10	6	Fines			
					Forfeitures			
		4	9	2	Cash	1	3	·
					Tobacco			
					Slops			
					Channel Money	2	·	·
					Insurance 16 Weeks			
Deductions as per Contra		5	1	8	Health & Pensions	·	6	8
					Unemployment	·	12	·
Balance due .... £		2	4	6	Total Deductions £	5	1	8

Dated at the Port of _____ LONDON

this_____day of_____ 11 MAY 1932 19____

Signature of Master.

NOTICE TO MASTERS.—One of these Accounts must be filled up and delivered to each Member of the Crew, or if he is paid off at the Mercantile Marine Office, to the Superintendent of that Office, at least Twenty-four Hours before he is paid off, under a penalty not exceeding £5, and no deductions will be allowed unless duly inserted. (Secs. 132 & 133, Merchant Shipping Act, 1894.)

* When a Seaman is promoted, or disrated, wages should be calculated for the whole period of the voyage at the rate per month originally fixed, and the amount of the increase, or decrease, for the period subsequent to the promotion or disrating should then be added or subtracted. The wages for the two parts of the period should not be calculated separately and added together. (See Sec. 59, Merchant Shipping Act, 1906.)

31305 Wt. 21258/8804 600,000 1/31—B.P. Ltd.—E.51-2002

[Turn over.

1932 — SS TAMAROA WAGE SLIP

.1932 — SHORTLY BEFORE LEAVING FOR THE USA

1932 — ROYAL NAVY CLASS MATES
L to R. Dicky Burden, Bill Lane, Jack Lynch , Fred Matthews

1934 — THE AUTHOR IN MALTA

1939 — THE AUTHOR IN STOKE'S BAY, GOSPORT

30th JUNE1942 — THE DRAMATIC END OF HMS MEDWAY

1943 — BEIRUT. THE AUTHOR, FAR LEFT, WITH TWO LSF FRIENDS

1943 — LS 1 THE FIRST OPERATIONAL CAIQUE

1944 — GUNNERS PERRY AND MacCORMACK

1944 — ZAHLE, BEIRUT. The SBS REST CAMP
L to R. 'Tanky' Rowlands, 'Monty' Banks, the author, 'Jock' Andrews and
PO Bevan.

1944 — THE TURKISH OFFICERS' CLUB
L to R. Turkish officer, Gunner Perry, Carpenter, 3 Turks, Andre Londos, Capt Chevalier, Turkish capt (Mengul), 'Lofty' Miller, The RN coxwain, the author.

The author, with beard, seated to the right behind the table.

1944 — THE AUTHOR ON LS 3

1944 — MEMBERS OF THE LSF ON KHIOS

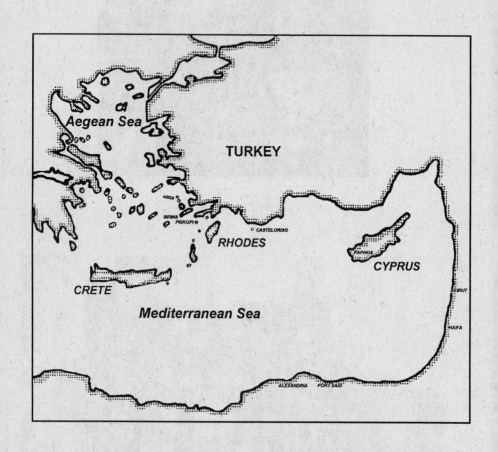

1944 — THE OPERATIONAL AREA OF THE LSF

My social life at this time was simply great, I loved every minute of it. Invariably Sunday evenings would find me at South Parade Pier, Southsea, where the top bands of the day would be making a one night stand. I saw and heard most of them in my time, names to conjure with, 'Jacks' Hylton, Payne and Jackson, Bert Ambrose, 'Snake Hips' Johnson, Billy Cotton, Harry Roy, Henry Hall, Roy Fox, Sydney Lipton and Debroy Sommers. I saw all of these and some of their vocalists, Al Bowlly, Sam Costa, Denny Dennis, Eve Beck, George Elrick, Sam Brown and many others whilst ashore during 1938 and 1939. Wonderful stuff, sheer magic, and what wonderful memories I have of them all.

Occasionally, some of us would catch the excursion train from Portsmouth harbour station to Waterloo, have a meal, a few pints or see a show, then return on the midnight or mail train.

One Friday evening, another stoker asked me if I fancied a run ashore. I can't for the life of me remember his name, which is perhaps for the best, but our first port of call was the *Black Bear* in North Cross Street. It was early evening and the lounge bar was empty, we got a couple of pints and sat at a small table and tried to decide where we would go next.

Within a few minutes, two women entered and it was obvious that they had been shopping because they were each carrying a couple of full shopping bags. One of them was about twenty-five and the other about thirty-two or thirty-three. Having bought themselves a drink they sat at another table near us and one of them said, 'That's a relief', whereupon my companion asked them if they were worn out after all that wandering around the shops. Well, one remark led to another until we asked whether we could join them at their table and they said we could.

After we bought them another drink and more talk, we were asked if we would like to come to a going away party. We said we would and asked who was going away, only to be dumbfounded when the younger of the two ladies replied that it was her husband. We were further shaken when we asked when he was going away, to be told that he had gone late that afternoon. Also, they had been down to the harbour to wave goodbye to his ship as she set sail. They had then gone shopping and had called into this pub for a drink and a rest before returning home.

My companion and I had each decided that we would be alright, especially after the eldest lady told us that her husband had been away for the last eighteen months and would not be home for another year or so. We were also informed that they were glad to see the back of the younger girls husband as he was horrible to both of them.

So we loaded up with bottles of beer and took off for their home in Queens Road where they shared a house — the elder of the two had a daughter about ten years old. All four of us, plus the little girl were hungry, but rather than have the ladies busy themselves with cooking a meal my companion and I said that we would go to the fish and chip shop for five helpings. So off we went armed with a couple of shopping bags.

During our walk, we decided who would pair off with whom, but I rather suspected that my friend had decided this long since, he being bigger and better looking than I.

However, on reflection, I am sure that I got the better of the deal, you know the old saying about 'The older the fiddle, the better the tune'. Anyway, we were sure that we were in for a long night so we collected a few more bottles of beer on the way home from the fish and chip shop.

After our meal we boozed and played cards until the young daughter went to bed. We then paired off with a cuddle in between drinks until it was decided that it was bedtime. It just seemed a natural progression, there was no discussion about it at all. Upstairs we all went, stripped off completely, then into bed; different bedrooms of course.

My partner was a right 'goer', probably because she had been without for about eighteen months. Come the morning I was shattered, but duty called and my friend and I crawled back to Blockhouse after promising to see the girls that evening.

Except for an occasional duty evening which prevented us from going ashore, we kept up our love-ins for about three weeks and I was enjoying it more and more as the days went by. I got quite used to going without sleep at night as long as I could get in half an hour during the day somehow, but all good things come to an end, don't they?

Suddenly, all leave was stopped and the reserves were called up; all we heard were rumours. The Munich crisis was upon us and there was one hell of a flap on. We lesser mortals, only read the tabloids, the *Daily Mirror* with 'Pip, Squeak and Wilfred', and 'Jane' with her dachshund, or the *Daily Sketch* with 'Dagwood Bumstead' and his wonderful sandwiches. What the hell did we young randy matelots know or care about politics and current world affairs, we were only there for the beer and crumpet.

One evening, our ladies turned up at the gates asking to see us urgently. Remember, in those days it was not just a case of picking up a telephone to say 'Not tonight Josephine.' We went to the gates to explain to our 'darlings' that there was some sort of emergency and as soon as it was all over we would be ashore for you know what. Suitably assured our girls returned home whilst we retired to the canteen to await the next move from higher up, which was not long in coming.

The following morning I was ordered with a number of others to report to the submarine depot ship *Titania* at Blyth, a submarine base on the north east coast. What do I remember of this period? Not a great deal except for some wonderful runs ashore amongst the great 'Geordie' people, lovely strong beer and a visit down a pit where I was informed I was further out to sea than where my submarine was moored.

Almost as soon as the flap had started so it finished. Neville Chamberlain, the Prime Minister, had flown back to Croydon to leave the aircraft waving his famous piece of paper, declaring 'Peace in our time.' He had just returned from the historic meeting at Bertchesgarden with Adolf Hitler, who had been supported by his lap dog, Mussolini. They had signed a worthless agreement which conned most of us younger people and I would suspect the majority of the older working class people who had already been through a useless war. A war in which almost every family had been deprived of a loved one or two.

On reflection, I would say that Neville Chamberlain had not been conned by Adolf Hitler, but had indeed gained for this nation a valuable twelve months grace before the reckoning. One precious year during which plans were made for the evacuation from large cities and towns of children.

Air raid precautions were organised and gas masks were issued to everyone. Portable air raid shelters were made and issued to every household. Various support services were formed, such as the fire service, the ambulance service, air raid wardens and fire watchers, auxiliary policemen and lots of others. So, by 1939 some sort of order was in place, just in case things turned out for the worst.

I returned to *Dolphin* to work and play, but I did not try to renew my acquaintanceship with the lady in Queens Road. My friend with whom I had started the adventure did not return to *Dolphin* as he had joined one of the newer 'S' class submarines. If he had done so, no doubt we would have tried to continue where we had left off. It did seem rather odd that my lady friend had not contacted me, but I assumed that her husband had returned home because of the crisis.

At the end of October 1938 I was drafted to 'Reserve Group A'. This was a group of three submarines used for training purposes, their names were *Otway, Oberon and Oxley*. There was just one crew, which manned the boat that was operational, invariably the *Otway* because although she was far from being mechanically fit she was more reliable than the other two.

Our role was to make daily trips to sea in order to give new entrants to the submarine service their first experience of a dive, also to give budding commanding officers their first experience of command, although we did have our own permanent commanding officer, Lieutenant Commander Cumberbatch.

This draft for me meant that I moved to the *Grand Hotel*, which was reserved for boats' crews, so instead of slinging my hammock I was now able to lay it out on an iron bed. Incidentally, we were still canteen messing where we all had to take turns in preparing the meals.

A couple of things spring to mind, making the 'clacker' or pastry for the top of the pie and mixing the batter for the Yorkshire pudding. This latter task proved a good source of fun because invariably a fork was left in the pudding pan after the batter was poured in, much to the consternation of the chap who had to cut the cooked pudding into equal portions.

The only noticeable difference between the three boats was their outline or silhouette, the bow of both *Otway* and *Oxley* sloped inwards toward the conning tower at an angle of about thirty degrees. Internally the three boats were more or less identical except for the stoker's mess in the *Otway,* which was named 'The Bear Pit'.

This mess was a converted fuel tank situated below the ERAs (Engine Room Artificers) mess and the galley just forward of the engine room and was reached by descending a perpendicular steel ladder through a very small hatch.

In November, much to my surprise, I was promoted to acting leading stoker and became 'Outside Tiffy's Mate', which, as the name suggests, is the dogsbody for the outside ERA who is responsible for all machinery outside the engine room. At diving stations this ERA manned the main diving panel and I operated both periscopes for the skipper. Heaven help me if I did not raise or lower them quick enough, I would be in for a right tongue lashing. Seconds were vital in this game and lives depended on it.

One of our stokers was Bill Haines, an ex-president of the senior rates' mess in *Dolphin,* in those days he was something of a joker. One of his tricks was to wait for the ERAs to sit down for a meal then blow the slop drain from our sink which vented into the mess above thus showering them with our waste water.

To be honest I was living the 'life of Riley' with not enough hours in the day. This was partly because Tom King, another stoker, persuaded me to share some lodgings with him in Palmyra Road, Gosport. The house was owned by a childless couple in their forties, the husband being ex-Navy. We were able to wear civilian clothes ashore as we had somewhere to keep and change into them, something which was not allowed for us in *Dolphin,* only officers had that privilege. The good lady of the house did our laundry and provided us with a light breakfast each morning. I was not a particular pal of Toms, so we went our separate ways when off duty.

I joined the Gosport branch of the National Society of Amateur Dancers, as I had been a member in Plymouth. As a club we could hold a dance on Sunday evenings, public dances were not allowed then. A couple of other stokers I knew decided to get digs ashore and I started going around with one of them, a chap named Waters, who unfortunately was lost on the *Oxley* just three days after war was declared, torpedoed by one of our own submarines because of a misunderstanding with recognition signals.

About this time I started to receive letters redirected from HMS *Wren* and *Drake.* These were coming from my two acquaintances in Llandudno (male and female). I must admit I was confused and worried and did not know what to do for the best. I eventually came clean and wrote to both of them and explained everything. I didn't receive any more letters.

One day my brother-in-law, Albert, an able seaman, arrived in Pompey on the aircraft carrier *Courageous.* He came over to *Dolphin* to visit my submarine and the following day we both travelled to London to visit my brother Bert who was then working for a song writer. We spent one hell of an evening with him, mainly in a boozer called *The Horse and Groom.*

By the end of the evening we were as drunk as newts, but Bert managed to get us on to a circus train which was transporting all the animals and their attendants from Waterloo to Pompey, albeit almost at walking pace. How he managed to persuade whoever was in charge to accept two drunken matelots besides the lions, tigers and elephants etc. I will never know. I vaguely remember being mixed up with this circus and arriving in the early hours at Pompey more or less sober, but with a splitting headache. Albert returned to his ship and me to mine, not able to meet again until 1942.

Life went on, I made two or three trips to sea per week then went ashore to live it up. I will never forget the Whitsun weekend, I met a lovely girl whom I fell for hook, line and sinker, she was beautiful and down on holiday from Radford, Coventry. We met at a dance on South Parade Pier and I couldn't bear to say goodbye to her.

When she returned home, I just could not settle down, in fact I thought seriously of trying to get out of the Navy and go to her. I had some lovely photographs of us both taken in a vending machine, but these were lost during the war. We corresponded until I was forced, by circumstances, to end it all, but thank goodness I had been given the privilege of spending a few wonderful days with her. Her name, imprinted forever in my memory, was Margo. I wonder if she is still around somewhere, I feel sure that she is and I would like to think she has thought of me at times.

I was like a fish out of water, I just could not get Margo out of my mind and it was in this state of mind that I met my future wife. It was early summer and I was on one of the evening coach trips to Southampton which was organised by our club. I knew quite a number of the girls including my favourite dancing partner at the club, Joan Ball. Joan had with her a friend named Martha, a good looking girl who unfortunately couldn't dance.

Nevertheless, I was taken with her and persuaded her to let me take her home. After that day we had a number of outings and evenings together until one night, both of us got a bit excited after a few drinks and nature took control.

CHAPTER 18

In August all reservists were recalled, as with the year before nobody knew what was happening, but we believed it wouldn't last long in any case.

We were wrong and war was declared on September 3rd. I can't really remember what my thoughts were at the time, I was probably a bit peeved that my social life was going to be interrupted for a while.

Anyway, here we were with three submarines and only one crew. We were assembled on the jetty at *Dolphin* and divided into three, one third were posted to *Otway*, one third to *Oberon* and the rest to *Oxley*. In my case I was the odd man out as there were four leading stokers, but because I was the 'Outside Tiffy's Mate' and periscope operator, I was posted to *Otway*, which as I have explained was the better of the three boats. With this all settled the complete crews for the three boats were made up with the reservists as they arrived at *Dolphin,* still in their 'civvies.'

We in the *Otway* found that except for Lieutenant Engineer McDermott our officers were changed. The skipper was now Commander (Granny) Conway, a smashing bloke, and the first lieutenant was David Wanklyn, later to win the VC and two DSOs as skipper of the submarine *Upholder*.

Without warning, after loading stores and live torpedoes, we put to sea, quite unable to tell anyone on shore where we were going and when we would return. A couple of hours later, after a trial dive to 'catch a trim', we surfaced and proceeded south westerly to be informed by the skipper that we were on our way to the Mediterranean, via Gibraltar. We should have guessed something like this, as we all had our full kits with us stowed in the fore-ends. The officers knew because they had to acquire the necessary charts, but not one word reached us lot.

What did all this mean to us young men, non-students of foreign affairs? The most important thing was that all letters we wrote were censored which meant being read by one of the officers with whom we lived in close contact, unlike a large surface ship where one was practically unknown. I was writing to both Margo and Martha at that time.

We arrived at Gib after travelling on the surface the whole way and there I found, to my surprise, secured alongside our parent ship, HMS *Maidstone*, my brother Bert's ship. He had wangled a job as assistant purser on board the P & 0 liner *Strathaird* and arrived in Gib at the same time as me en-route to Australia. I was unable to have a run ashore with him to find out how he managed it and it was just a case of hello and goodbye.

The mail arrived after a few days in Gib and with it came a bombshell, Martha suspected that she was in the family way. I must have been the biggest rat bag on the face of the earth, because I did not know what the hell I was going to do. I do not recall exactly what I promised to do in my letters, always mindful of the fact that they were being read by someone who knew me intimately. I wrote to Margo in Coventry to say that because of the flap, censorship and all that carry on, letters would be few and far between, although I hoped things would be back to normal in a month or so. I genuinely believed this to be the truth as I saw it then.

I was not quite the spendthrift you might have imagined, at the time I was sending my eldest sister money on occasions to save for me. This money was now to come in very handy and I wrote to my sister explaining the situation and asked her to send the accumulated money to Martha to help her out. At the same time I made an allotment from my pay for a weekly allowance to be paid to her. I had still not formulated any plans regarding the outcome of this unfortunate affair. We were both young, she didn't know anything at all about me really and we had not been together long enough to know and attune to one another's temperament. She was a sweet, good looking girl — that was all I knew. What on earth did she know of me, but everything was taken out of my hands by my sisters at home in Plymouth.

After a short period in Gibraltar we set off for Malta. We fully expected that Italy would join Germany and were pleasantly surprised when this did not happen. It made life just a little bit easier for us in the Med, although we knew that the situation could change overnight. The war had hardly started for us, unlike our submarines in home waters.

Deliveries of mail were very erratic and beginning to leapfrog so that any continuity was hopeless. My life was in one hell of a mess. I found out that my sisters had decided, without any consultation with me, which I agree was probably impossible at that time, to invite Martha to live with my sister Gladys in Plymouth until after the baby was born.

The *Otway* moved between Malta and Alexandria to carry out some useful exercises. We hadn't a clue really about what was happening to our pals in other boats although rumours based on fact were beginning to seep through. Most of the more modern 'S' class submarines were leaving the Med to fight at home and some of the China Flotilla were on their way from the Far East to take up stations in the Med.

The skipper had hinted to us around Christmas that it would not be long before we would be returning to Britain so I was more or less able to tell them at home about this. The result was that a marriage was arranged for February at the Registry Office in Plymouth.

It was now becoming obvious that this wasn't going to be the short conflict that we seemed to think it would be. Germany had completely overrun Poland in a matter of days and we were now shoulder to shoulder with France.

Towards the end of January 1940, we headed for home and arrived at Blockhouse to find a very different place to the one we had left the previous August. There were blackouts, sentries everywhere, road blocks and hardly a familiar face to be seen, except for the civilian staff of the base. The mood of the place had changed as three submarines, *Seahorse, Starfish and Undine* had failed to return to their base at Blyth during January and were subsequently confirmed as being sunk in the Heligoland Bight. The lads from the *Starfish* and *Undine* were captured and interned for over five years by the Germans, but the *Seahorse* was never heard of again. The submarine service was a very close knit affair and we all knew members of the respective crews who had been lost or were now prisoners of war.

Our boat was due for the dry dock in Pompey for a mini refit and the crew were given leave in two spells, mine was in the second half. During the first period of leave I exchanged letters with my family in Plymouth which enabled them to make final arrangements for me to be married on the 16th February.

Before I left for Plymouth I paid a visit to Martha's mother who was living alone and was divorced. Her husband had left her for reasons unknown to me. I thought that she was as good as gold, a plain and simple country woman who was hard working with the added distinction of being a darned good cook. Attributes which she had passed on to her daughter which was my gain. I foolishly let her go later in life, but that's another story.

Anyway to Plymouth, marriage and fourteen days to get organized. To-date fourteen hours would be roughly the sum total of the time we had previously spent together. Was I ready for marriage? Well, of course I was, I had a lovely young, good looking girl who had taken me on trust and given herself to me. I would have been stark raving mad not to have accepted her. I just wished that my sisters had let her stay in Gosport until I had returned home from the Med and let the two of us sort it out together, unaided. The end result would probably have been the same but there was a very good reason for my wishing that she had not gone to Plymouth.

When I first met Martha she had quarrelled with her boyfriend and I had probably caught her on the rebound. Being in Plymouth and having everything arranged for her was a lot different to being in her own environment. In Portsmouth she could have thought things through on her own, amongst her own friends and relatives, instead of suddenly being thrust among total strangers however kind and well intentioned they undoubtedly were. Anyway, we spent many, many lovely years together and produced two daughters who would be a credit to anyone, thanks to her.

But back to early 1940, where it seemed that the only real war was the one at sea. I had to return to Gosport whilst Martha remained at Plymouth until after the baby was born. At the end of April, Martha gave birth to a lovely baby girl, later to be christened Gladys Irene. I suppose this was out of loyalty to my sisters who had been a great help to her.

Because of the possibility of an invasion, which was expected at any time, Martha and the baby, as soon as they were well enough to travel, returned to her mother in Gosport, which in the circumstances was only natural.

The 'Phoney War' was still on in France with the newspapers doing their best to make minor skirmishes into major battles, but the main front remained exactly in the same place and state. Top of the hit parade then was that famous song, sung by that wonderful duo, Flanagan and Allen, *We're going to hang out the washing on the Seigfried line*. Another of their songs famous at this time was *Run rabbit run*; a bit of sarcasm really because of a German air raid in Scotland where the only casualties were one or two rabbits. But our phoney war of uneasy peacefulness was soon to be shattered.

Although the war on land in Europe had been more or less at a standstill the Navy had been very active and we had lost about eight of our submarines. But, suddenly, all hell broke loose, Adolf decided the time had come to make his big push and a new frightening word came into use, 'Blitzkrieg'.

I will return for one brief moment to the mobilisation of the reservists in July 1939 when the Reserve Fleet, of which HMS *Otway* was part, was reviewed off Weymouth by the King. Our submarine was chosen for a visit by the King accompanied by the First Sea Lord and Admiral Darlan, who was C-in-C of the French Navy. When the launch bearing these eminent personages came alongside it was quite choppy, with the result that the King, held both sides by members of our crew, suddenly found himself up to his waist in the sea as he stood on our saddle tanks. Consequently, he was compelled to borrow a dry pair of trousers from one of our officers. The funny side of this exercise was that as the King and his party entered the forward hatch to walk through the boat, members of the crew were coming out of the after hatch carrying all the rubbish, buckets, and brooms etc. They walked along the casing, around the conning tower and back down the forward hatch to where they started from, all clever stuff.

The Germans cheated and ignored the Maginot Line and went round it through the low countries. Further resistance by the Dutch and Belgians became pointless and the result was that the British Expeditionary Force was then right in the path of the steam rolling German Army. They simply galloped through the countryside wiping out everything in their path, finally pinning the British into a small area surrounding Dunkirk. So much for their cardboard tanks!

During the evacuation, the *Otway* and several other submarines were patrolling a position between the French coast and our own shores. Our task was to protect the evacuation of our forces from Dunkirk against possible attacks by German naval forces making a quick thrust down the Channel.

We remained dived during the day and patrolled up and down the coast keeping a constant watch through the periscope for hostile forces. All the while we observed the wonderful Armada of rescue ships, ranging from destroyers down to minesweepers, trawlers, pleasure steamers, yachts and motor boats. In fact anything that could be propelled and could carry men was used. The officers manning the periscope gave us a running commentary and occasionally members of the crew were able to have a quick look at the scene. Our station was quite close to the shore, so we were constantly in busy areas. At night we would surface to charge the batteries, get some fresh air in the boat and take the opportunity to have a good cook-up.

In submarine patrols during war it was the norm to turn night into day and vice-versa. Therefore, immediately after surfacing at dusk, breakfast was prepared, then sometime after midnight, lunch was eaten, to be followed by supper shortly before we dived at dawn. The reason for this change of routine was in order to ensure that all the cooking was done while we were on the surface and fresh air was being drawn through the boat by the powerful diesel engines. When we dived for night routine, two thirds or more of the crew rested with the consequent conservation of our precious air supply which could only be replenished when we were able to surface again.

Whilst on patrol during the evacuation at Dunkirk, a couple of us at a time were allowed to the top of the conning tower at night. As well as witnessing some of the frightening events that were taking place on the french coast I also witnessed several German bombers crashing into the Channel, trying desperately to reach their bases after being badly damaged over England. I just wonder how many of these went unclaimed by our anti-aircraft gun batteries and our night fighting aircraft.

When the evacuation came to an end, the last of the small boats returned home and we put into Devonport to refuel. My brother-in-law, an engine fitter there, came on board for a tot and a yarn telling me that I must be raving mad to be on such a vessel, but I was, yesterday was just a memory, — who knows what would happen tomorrow? Anyway, my brother-in-law was able to smuggle an uncensored letter ashore for Martha, not that I could tell her anything vital to the boats movements, I just didn't know. We in the crew were sure that the skipper was receiving orders which changed within the hour.

The cream of the British Army in Europe had been rescued, albeit without their equipment guns and trucks, the majority of them without their personal rifles. They were badly shaken, tired, bewildered and all in need of a long rest after being without a good sleep for days on end.

These troops were despatched to various depots and camps throughout England to be regrouped, others were sent on leave, very many to hospitals. The result of all this was that our home defence was very badly stretched to meet an expected German invasion of these islands.

Naval ratings, which included my brother-in-law Albert, were called upon to man the heavy guns of the Army's coastal batteries. 'Dads Army', the Local Defence Volunteers, LDVs, were organized to take up their posts, civilians were roped in to dig trenches, place obstacles on beaches and open spaces where the enemy might land. Even my old dad at seventy years plus was doing his bit as a fire-watcher on the roof of an engineering works.

The *Otway* put to sea without us being given shore leave and we were suddenly ordered into port at Fowey in Cornwall. Rumours were rife, especially as we had to take on all the fuel, water and food we could find room for.

This fuelled speculation that as the German invasion was expected to be launched against England at any time we apparently had to get out into the Channel in order that we could help to prevent some of their craft from reaching our shores. The strongest of the rumours, however, was that if the invasion was successful and Britain became occupied, we in the Navy would proceed to Canada to continue the struggle from there.

At Fowey we tied up in midstream and used our collapsible dinghy for minor trips to and from shore. This dinghy was also used for unofficial trips by

Messrs. Williams and Jones. 'Bungy' Williams, a 'killick' stoker and 'Scouse' Jones, a stoker, were reservists who had already completed twelve years in the Navy, they were great boozing mates and inseparable.

These two stalwarts decided that besides the boat being stocked up with fuel, water and food, it also had to have an unofficial supply of booze, primarily scrumpy or cider which was easy to come by in this part of the country. Well, 'Bungy' and 'Scouse' filled up every container they could lay their hands on. It was stowed in nearly every compartment, cans of it, jars of it, odd bottles of it, in washing-up buckets and even in spare tea kettles. Not satisfied with this, they managed to acquire a few dozen bottles of beer, no doubt in exchange for some contraband of sorts. This beer was then stowed in sacks outside the pressure hull, aft of the conning tower amongst the fuel lines.

Loading completed we put to sea. I don't believe any of us considered the fact that we might never see our beloved country again. We considered that the German forces might have been able to wipe their feet on the French, Belgian and Dutch forces, but the might of the Royal Navy and RAF would be a different kettle of fish.

The first thing we did, when we were at a safe distance from the harbour at Fowey, was to 'catch a trim', in order that the first lieutenant could try to achieve neutral buoyancy for the submarine after taking on board all the extra cargo. After a while the trim became satisfactory and the skipper ordered his 'Number One' to take her down to 90ft, where the fun began.

'Bang! Bang!' A couple of minor explosions were heard, seemingly right alongside of us. 'Take her up to periscope depth "Number One,"' said the skipper.

As we started to come up he ordered me to raise the periscope. So I put it up, watching both the skipper and the depth gauge at the same time in order that I did not raise it too far out of the water. The skipper had a quick look around and reported nothing in sight except the coastline and a couple of small inshore fishing craft.

'Funny,' said the skipper, 'Those bangs were like practice charges and very close' (these were small charges which were dropped by surface craft when they were carrying out exercises with you). 'Take her down again' said the skipper and down we went to 90ft. Once again a couple of 'explosions' were heard as the submarine descended.

At this point most of the crew knew what the explosions were. Those bloody beer bottles were exploding, set off by the water pressure as we dived. With every explosion 'Scouse' and 'Bungy' got more and more upset as they realised that they had lost the lot. We guessed that the skipper knew what the answer to the bangs was, but he never said a word to us, although I bet that he had a good laugh afterwards with his officers.

Prior to and after Dunkirk we made many clandestine trips to the French coast, under the cover of darkness, to land and pick up secret agents and members of the resistance. Down in the engine room we didn't really know what was going on, but it was quite unnerving to surface so close to shore, hoping that the Germans were not waiting for us.

Amongst the people we picked up or took out were some very odd characters indeed, but they tended to keep themselves to themselves. However, on the bright side we collected some lovely fish on these trips, as most of the people we were collecting or landing were transferred to and from small fishing boats.

We put into Blockhouse for a few days and found everything geared up for the expected invasion. Rolls of barbed wire etc. all the way along the sea wall and road. The football field between *Dolphin* and Haslar hospital was practically impassable with spikes and obstacles protruding from its surface.

The threat of invasion subsided and eventually we were given a few days leave and a number of changes were made amongst the crew and officers. We were more or less told that as the submarine training and exercising area off the Isle of Wight had become untenable, we in *Otway* would be going to Scotland to become the nucleus of a new training flotilla.

We left Blockhouse and went to the beautiful Kyle of Bute, there to start a base at Rothesay in the Firth of Clyde, which was the main holiday resort for Glaswegians. There were no naval facilities there until the arrival, sometime later of a parent ship, HMS *Cyclops*. Meanwhile, our crew were billeted ashore and, would you believe it, in a temperance hotel. Matelots in a temperance hotel! I wonder which practical joker thought that one up? Have you ever seen bottles of beer being pulled up the outside wall of a small hotel by a matelot in a bedroom, the bottles being tied on a cord in the garden below by one of the chambermaids he had been out with. All clever stuff and a wonderful memory.

Our skipper, Commander Conway, had left us by this time, he was soon to be promoted to Captain 'S', and was replaced by a succession of new skippers enjoying their first feel of command after completing their COs' course. Our first lieutenant, David Wanklyn, had left us before we returned from the Med. Amongst the new officers who joined *Otway* was Jimmy Jewell, later to take command of the submarine *Seraph,* famous for landing Mark Clark and his team of negotiators in French North Africa. Another of their exploits inspired the film *The man that never was*. Another officer to join us was a Lieutenant Andrew, later to be appointed to the ill-fated *Thetis* which had been raised from Liverpool Bay, refitted and recommissioned as HMS *Thunderbolt* only to be lost in the Med in March 1943.

It was quite by chance that I happened to be alone in the very small remembrance chapel of HMS *Dolphin* last year. I was looking through the book which records the names of everyone lost in our submarines during the last war when the door of the chapel opened and in walked a tall distinguished looking chap with a sort of Van Dyke beard. We began talking about people we both knew and he then introduced himself as Commander Andrew. I thought that his face was vaguely familiar, even after more than forty years. He then told me that he too had been lucky as he had left the *Thunderbolt* in order to take the COs' course shortly before she sailed on her last patrol. All in all 162 lives were lost in the *Thetis-Thunderbolt*.

During the period from our arrival at Rothesay in June until October, I was very selfishly having a whale of a time. We hardly knew that there was a war on, that is except for a few minor restrictions. We were out during the day training new officers and ratings and carried out dummy attacks on various types of surface ships, which had newly been fitted with Asdic. They would be steaming around above us searching and we would be trying to dodge them. Occasionally a small practice charge would be dropped to indicate that we had perhaps been located and when the exercises had been completed, we would fire two or three smoke candles from our small underwater gun to indicate our surfacing course. All very nice and cosy except that because of their superior speed, the surface ships would be secured in harbour long before we came in to clean up and get ashore.

Rothesay was a lovely holiday resort for the Scots, situated on the Isle of Bute and served from Glasgow by large ferries. Incidentally, the Marquis of Bute was a Naval officer and served on our parent ship, HMS *Cyclops*.

However, the town provided a temptation that I found impossible to resist. I was ashore every minute possible, lovely grub, lovely beer and lovely girls, not necessarily in that order. Situated along the front was a great dance hall, the name of which escapes me, but I would be there practically every night I had shore leave. Just a couple of pints to get into the swing of things and I would be tripping the light fantastic, never short of a partner. It could have been the uniform that did it because I was always a 'tiddly' sailor in bell bottoms.

One evening myself and two others met three girls, two would be in their early twenties, the other in her early thirties. We paired off, I with the older one who, being an elder sister of one of the younger girls was also a chaperone for the other two. Well, I had been set-up before with the second best (in this case third best), but I was not unduly worried as I have always come out on top, literally speaking.

Fortunately, it happened to be the first evening of their two week holiday, they had only arrived that afternoon from Glasgow. They had checked into a private house for bed and breakfast, sharing a very large front room containing a couple of easy chairs, a table with four upright chairs, plus in one corner a very large bed which could have accommodated four people. The girls had a very understanding landlady because with the help of a few bottles of beer from us, the dear old soul would allow us all to go into the room for tea and games. We spent a wonderful two weeks with the girls, no awkward questions were asked and no promises were made. Not that I was in a position to make any!

I sometimes went to the dance with another killick stoker who was a right 'Jack the Lad', as good as gold and he simply oozed with confidence. He would pull a right trick on some of the girls in the dance hall. A lot of the girls waiting for partners would stand around the edge of the dance floor looking inwards at the dancers, they would stand there tapping one foot with their hands behind their backs. That is, until my pal walked around behind them and slipped a dirty great uncooked 'Pusser's' sausage into their palm. Their reactions were wonderful to see, some feigned shock and disgust, others giggled, whilst some examined the sausage with some feeling, but it was all good fun.

Letters from Martha revealed that they were getting a right hammering from the nightly German air raids, so a stoker friend of mine, dear old Reg

Moore, suggested that we rented a flat or house on the edge of town at Rothesay and install our wives. This we did, as by now the holiday season was over and there was plenty of accommodation available. Martha and I, with the baby, had previously spent a weekend with Reg and his wife, Eileen, at their house in Hounslow, so we all knew one another.

Unfortunately, Martha had to travel up alone from Gosport with the baby and a large suitcase, plus various other packages. I am sure she could write a book about that journey alone. She fully deserved a medal. Martha was subjected to the usual terrible journey to Scotland, which was almost normal in those days. Crowded into often unheated trains, with many stops, delays and changes en-route, plus she had to change the baby and breast feed her whilst being screened by a very considerate soldier. I now realise that I did not appreciate her fortitude at this time. She was met in Glasgow by the wife of another of our leading stokers and brought safely to Rothesay for a rest which she badly needed. The baby's pram had been forwarded separately and surprisingly arrived within a day or two.

The house we rented at Ardbeg, on the outskirts of Rothesay, was a large detached house at the end of a drive surrounded by gardens covering what must have been about one third or half an acre. The inside was very well furnished with good solid upper middle class furniture, far too expensive for people of my background to acquire. There were large oil paintings everywhere with about five or six large beds in the bedrooms, with another in the huge kitchen. The house was a little overpowering to the girls at first, but they soon settled in with the help of the very friendly locals.

Of course the arrival of Martha and the baby in Rothesay put a stop to my fun and games. We spent some wonderful months in this lovely environment, with the baby getting bags of attention, especially from the local tradesmen which was very helpful in view of rationing.

Life was very tranquil for us during this period, we would be out to sea Monday to Friday, but we would be home to our wives each evening. Except for one particular instance, when our slow moving submarine got tangled up with some uncharted wreckage, our routine was the same from one week to another until January 1941. It was then decided that the *Otway* would proceed to the Swan Hunter Yard at Wallsend-on-Tyne for a long overdue refit lasting several months as the threat of the invasion by the Germans had receded.

Martha and I thought that it would be better if she returned to her mother in Gosport and it was decided she could travel down as far as London with Eileen. So we packed the girls' belongings and waved them off on their journey. Our submarine eventually left Rothesay and made a quiet passage around the north tip of Scotland and entered the River Tyne to witness a hive of industry.

All around us, from the yards on both sides of the river, came the continual chatter of riveting guns. Over on the Hebburn side were a couple of destroyers being built and in the yard just downstream from us, a battleship was under construction. Everywhere one could see, ships were either being repaired or built.

We could not enter the dry dock at Wallsend for a few days so we had to tie up alongside a destroyer engaged in the last few days of her refit. This was a good thing for us because we were able to make purchases from her canteen.

We did not have a parent ship so the crew had to be billeted ashore, the officers in private hotels or houses of their own choice whilst we lesser mortals were lodged in a one star doss house. Apart from living in a dump, life was very easy for the crew indeed, with only general maintenance duties to perform on the submarine.

CHAPTER 19

My memories of Wallsend are very vivid and I will dispose of the amusing one first in order that I might concentrate on the main wonderful memory I have of my stay there.

Two of our stalwarts from the stoker branch acquired a small side of smoked bacon. I believe they had managed to get this from someone on our parent ship the *Cyclops* in Rothesay. They had hidden it in our cold cupboard on board the *Otway*, this cupboard was situated across the passage way from the wardroom so they had been very clever. However, we were due to enter the dry dock and de-store, so removing all food stuffs etc. from the boat. We had lost our friendly destroyer with their useful canteen so consequently we were compelled to buy all our fags, if we could get them, from the local tradespeople.

Well, our two lads did a deal with a local tobacconist or wholesaler to swap our bacon for 'baccy'. The only problem was how to get it out of the shipyard; as it turned out it was dead easy. The wall surrounding the yard was about 10ft high, but on the inside it had been banked up and concreted to provide air raid shelters, with the top about 3ft from the top of the wall. So the plan was for our two lads to climb to the top of the banked shelter at a point about twenty yards from the main gate, sling the bacon over, then nip around through the gate to retrieve it.

Outside the yard at intervals of about 30ft or so along the pavement there were 50 gallon drums, in which a mixture was burnt on clear evenings. This was in order to provide a smoke screen to hide the yard from enemy bombers and this operation was in full force on the night of the flying bacon caper.

Our two lads duly climbed to the top of the bank and with one on the foreleg and the other on the hind, they counted 'one, two, three' and threw the bacon over the wall where it landed smack bang upon the shoulders of a dear old air raid warden doing his rounds, knocking him to the ground. The lads nipped around to discover this poor old fellow in a dazed state mumbling something about being jumped on by a parachutist. After assuring themselves that he was quite alright they promptly galloped off with the spoils of war to an accompaniment of shouts and whistles being blown by the warden and an auxiliary policemen who was patrolling the dock area.

Our route from the shipyard gate to the lodging house took us past a friendly working class pub, approximately two hundred yards from the dock gate and about five minute's walk from our digs. Our crew adopted this pub, and the landlord and regulars adopted us, to such an extent that we were on first name terms with everyone, young and old.

Surrounding the yard were rows of terraced houses, they were identical and typical of the working class house in which I lived in Gosport. They had two rooms upstairs, two downstairs and a small scullery fitted with a gas stove and an all-purpose stone sink with one cold water tap. This tap constituted the entire indoor plumbing system of the house. To the back of the house there would be what was known as the back yard, approximately 25ft to 30ft in length. In this yard there was normally a small section of earth or garden, then attached to the scullery, invariably a coal shed. Adjoining this was the one and only toilet for the house.

In most of these houses you could find, hanging up on the wall just outside the scullery, a galvanized bath. This would be taken into the kitchen or scullery on bath days and filled with hot water which had been heated in saucepans and kettles on top of the gas stove. Emptying it after one had bathed was always something of a chore, my method was to partially empty it by pouring saucepans full of the water down the sink, then emptying the rest in the back yard.

The two rooms upstairs were naturally bedrooms and downstairs the room at the front was normally known as the 'best room' and was only used on special occasions. The other room between the best room and the scullery was the kitchen-cum-dining room where most of the leisure hours were spent.

Our pub, was very plain with no frills, except for a few upholstered benches around the sides and an upright piano. There was one bar with the usual brass rail and upright stools, and in front of the benches there were wooden tables and chairs. Friday and Saturday evenings were the highlights of the week simply because there would always be a number of the younger members of the community present. In particular one young lady with a very good voice indeed who would always delight us with her rendering of a very popular song of that period, *If I only had wings*, this was a great favourite, we loved it and her. Sunday to Thursday was very different indeed and one could almost predict who would be in the pub on these evenings.

On one particular evening I sat down to talk to a couple of regulars, George and Dorothy. A fair bit of small talk ensued and I eventually asked Dorothy about her parents, Doris and Alf, who normally accompanied her to the pub. She explained however that they were not her parents, but her neighbours, also that they were not at home when she called for them. I apologised, she accepted this and went on to explain that her dad had passed away in 1937 and that she had lost her mother shortly before last Christmas since which time she had come to the pub with Doris and Alf purely for companionship.

Simply to change the subject and to keep the conversation going, I remarked how quiet it was on Thursday as compared to Friday and Saturday. George replied it was always the same just before pay day. I then said that I was at a loose end and had only dropped in for a couple of pints and perhaps might wander off to the dance.

That evening remains firmly imprinted in my memory, it never grows dimmer and I can remember practically every word that was spoken. It started out so ordinary yet finished so completely wonderful. Now more than fifty years on I recall it with such happiness. Dot and I became lovers, and such lovers. But why? Heaven only knows. I have never been able to explain it, was it fate?

She was about thirty-five years old, very slim, about my own height, with very thick dark hair and her eyes were dark brown as are my own. Her hair, which was quite long, was always made up into a bun at the top rear part of her head. She always appeared to wear plain dark outfits buttoned up to the neck which gave her the appearance of a rather stern school mistress, this was emphasized by the thick dark glasses she wore and until that evening I do not believe I had given any thought as to what she might be in life.

Our small talk had begun to wane so I asked old George whether or not I could buy him a pint but he explained that he had drunk his usual two pints and was now off home to listen to the wireless. With that he got up and left, leaving me alone with Dorothy. I was quite taken aback with his departure and I began to wonder how I could leave. I thought at the time it would appear rude if I left as well, so I decided to have another drink hoping that perhaps in the meantime Doris and Alf might come in. I replenished our drinks and settled down to talk.

Our conversation began to develop into personal details. Was I married? Did I have any children? What rank was I? Where had I joined? Was I going to stay in the Navy? Were submarines dangerous? I replied truthfully to all these questions, especially regarding my marriage.

It was then my turn to find out all about her. It seemed she was quite alone, she did have a younger brother, a sergeant in the regular Army, but he had been taken prisoner fighting a rearguard action at Dunkirk. Since losing her mother she had taken to coming to the pub with Doris and Alf just to break the monotony of staying at home.

She went on to tell me that she was in charge of the ladies department of a fairly large ladies and gents outfitters, that was privately owned by a distant relative. She explained that there was a chance of her owning or being left the business. However, she added that she was not unduly concerned if these expectations did not materialize because her house belonged to her and she was financially secure, in a modest way. I began to be impressed, not by this revelation, but by the way she spoke about herself, her attitude to others and life itself in general, I gathered that she was very well read.

I do not believe it was the strong 'Geordie' beer, but in a certain way I began to warm to her. When my glass was about two thirds empty, I excused myself for a pee. This was to collect my thoughts about whether to shove off to the dance or to hang on with her. When I returned my mind had been made up for me because she had bought me another pint and we continued our conversation. I now began to really take stock of her, she was a very attractive woman and a great conversationalist as well.

But even good conversation under these circumstances needs fuelling, so for a change I remarked that I was starving and asked if she would like to come to the fish and chip shop with me. She thought it a great idea so we finished our drinks and left.

On the way to the shop she suggested we took the food, if they had any, home to eat as it would be more comfortable. Well, we were in luck, fish, chips and peas it was, so we set off for her house and I suggested that she should keep it warm whilst I returned to the pub to scrounge some bottles of beer. On the promise to Tom, the landlord, that I would safeguard the empties, because he returned them to the brewers on a one for one basis, I managed to get from him two large and four small bottles of beer.

After our supper, we sat in the easy chairs with our drinks and began to talk once more, we also had the wireless set tuned in low for news items etc. Suddenly Dot, who I thought had been on edge for the last half hour or so, said, 'Well Fred it's getting late and we both have to be up for work in the morning.' Hell I thought, these are my marching orders, just when I was beginning to have other plans for the remainder of the night. Still sitting in her chair opposite me she handed me a bombshell by saying 'Can I ask you a personal favour?'

'Certainly' I replied 'What is it?'

'Will you stay with me tonight?'

'Do you mean sleep with you?'

'Yes' she replied.

Well, to say that I was dumbfounded would be to put it very mildly indeed, I was momentarily speechless. The shock must have shown on my face because I could see her reaction however, recovering I stood up and told her to come to me, then taking her into my arms, I kissed her in a way that I am sure she had never been kissed before. I just said to her 'I have been wanting to do that ever since we left the pub.'

She went on to say that as I had not made any move towards her all that evening she feared that I was just taking pity on her, that I had wanted to leave her company but did not know what excuse to make. I pointed out that it was rather difficult to make a move towards her whilst we were sat in opposite chairs, especially as our conversation had been strictly about formal or worldly affairs, plus the fact that I had not received any encouragement from her - wondering whether or not she might reject any advance from me. She then said 'Let us not waste any more valuable time, just give me about ten minutes to brush my hair and get myself ready and then I will call you.'

I then went to the toilet in the back yard, relocked the back door and returned to the kitchen. The wireless station had closed down and I began reading the latest war reports in the evening paper. After ten or fifteen minutes Dot called out, 'Fred will you put out the light and come to bed.' This I did and climbed the stairs in semidarkness. I could have done it blindfold, it was just like our house in Gosport, or rather my mother-in-laws house. I undressed and slid between the sheets. After several minutes she slid in beside me and removed her nightdress.

Both nude, we lay on our backs motionless for a minute or so then she handed me bombshell number two by saying, 'Would you believe me if I told you that I have never been with a man before.' I did not have a chance to reply, even if I could have done so immediately, because she rambled on about having read books on the subject, knew exactly what to do and what was required of her.

Speechless, I just put my forefinger to her lips to just whisper, 'Sh... Sh!' Here let me say that she was the classic example of the lady who thought that erogenous zones were somewhere near the equator, she was as green as grass, for all the books she had read about sexual matters, including the act itself, she knew absolutely nothing about the preliminaries to lovemaking.

With my mind in a turmoil and my body as randy as a butchers dog, I eased myself on to her. Suddenly she froze rigid, just like a warm statue, but callous devil that I am I continued. I didn't care if she cried for me to stop, I was too far gone for that. She would not be kissed and just clenched her teeth and let me get on with it, no cooperation in any way whatever, just whimpering. Thoroughly drained, exhausted both physically and mentally, I eased myself off her and rolled over to fall asleep immediately.

I awoke during the night breaking my neck for a pee and it must have taken a minute or two for me to adjust to my surroundings, but donning just my trousers and shoes I found my way down the stairs, through the kitchen and scullery to the back yard. Sitting there with great relief I started thinking about my behaviour. I was now stone cold sober. I thought about the morning, how should I behave after subjecting her to such torture, for the first time in my life I was quite remorseful. Should I dress quickly and leave quietly, or what?

With nothing resolved and feeling quite cold by now, I returned to the bedroom to be greeted by her sitting up in bed. She asked me where I had been and pulled back the bedclothes. I slid into the bed and she cuddled up to me and I knew I was forgiven.

In the morning I was awakened by her, she had placed a cup of tea for me on the small bedside table, the night light was out but there was light of some kind filtering through the partially drawn curtains. She stood there looking down on me having donned her dressing gown, she was holding her glasses in one hand and her lovely hair was hanging loosely on her shoulders. Quite instinctively, simply out of the blue, I said, 'Dorothy you look beautiful.' The effect of my saying this was electric, her eyes simply lit up and she bent to kiss me.

I pleaded with her to return to bed, but being the practical person that she was, she pointed out that the world did not belong to us and there were many thousand of others in the wheel and we were just a small cog, so we had better get out to join them or face the consequences. She also said there would be many other days and nights for us. Unfortunately, this was not to be, but we did have a few. Before I left the house that morning, she gave me a key so that I could let myself in that evening before she came home from work.

That evening I was a little on edge, and was trying to read the evening paper and listen to the wireless when she arrived. We talked whilst she prepared something to eat for herself as I had already eaten at the base. After she had cleared the dishes away we sat down to decide whether or not we should go to the pub, it being Friday. This was one of the best nights, but Dorothy in her wisdom, did not think we should go. She then explained that if we went we would probably have to remain until closing time before walking out, then give some explanation as to why we were together.

However, I thought I should return the empties to Tom as promised and perhaps obtain some replacements. I did not go directly to the bar, but to the small 'bottle and jug' bar alongside.

On my return, we settled down to talk and we certainly did have a great deal to talk over. I was hooked, bowled over by her, wishing for time to stand still. Dorothy told me that I had hurt her terribly, but that she fully understood this might happen although she did not realize how painful it could be, going on to say she also knew from her readings that it would become easier. I remarked that perhaps we should not do anything that night, but she would have none of it and said that practice makes perfect.

Now came another revelation from this lady who never ceased to surprise me in one way or another. She began telling me about the previous day, before and after she had met me in the pub. It appears that she had been feeling odd all day, a feeling that she was unable to explain. She had been unable to concentrate, with a certain premonition that something quite extraordinary was about to happen. Searching for an answer she concluded that it must be something to do with her brother, a prisoner of war. However, the moment she saw me she knew there and then that her odd feeling and me were connected in some strange way. She went on to explain that although she had seen me many times before, something was now different. Suddenly she said it came to her, she wanted me, it was as simple as that.

We decided on our plan for the morrow and went to bed. We lay there for a while on our backs with just an occasional movement for a quick kiss on the cheek. I really felt that I should not attempt to make love even though I was in a terrible state physically, however, she made the decision by easing me onto her. Even though she was not quite so rigid as the previous night, it was not really enjoyable. I was feeling guilty and she was not relaxed. So I rolled over, said good night and went to sleep, I am sure that she was in the same state within seconds.

The following day, Saturday, I finished work at midday, taking the bull by the horns I moved all my belongings into her house, assuming that this would be alright with her and so it was. As she said, it was the natural thing to do whilst we were together.

At around 7.30 pm there was a knock on the front door, which I answered, it was Doris and Alf who didn't bat an eyelid on seeing me. What an understanding couple they were. I invited them in, Dorothy came downstairs to say that she was ready and off we went to the local. I walked in front with Alf whilst the two women brought up the rear. It was only a few minutes walk so there was no time for awkward questions.

Entering the pub I ordered the drinks whilst the two women went to a vacant table, there were not many people in as yet so there were no odd looks from anyone. Eventually, the pub began filling up, the piano was going and everyone appeared to be happy. The two women sat between us men so it was difficult to talk with Alf. However, when he asked me a specific question, I walked around to his side of the table in order to hear him more clearly.

His question was 'What the hell have you done to Dot, I haven't seen her since Wednesday, but she looks ten years younger?'

I replied with two words, which were all I could think of at that moment 'She's gorgeous' and I returned to my seat.

Let me say that Dorothy had dressed exactly as she had always done, so any observant change must surely have been facially or in her manner. The evening went off as normal with a good old sing song and Dorothy and I did not invoke a second glance, we stayed until closing time and left together happy as birds in spring off to their nest.

On Sunday morning, I said to Dorothy that I would try to scrounge a ration card from our first lieutenant even if I had to tell him the truth that I had moved out of the lodging house.

Dorothy decided that she would like a bath so we got the wash boiler lit up and full of water, plus saucepans and the kettle. It was like a sauna in the scullery even with the one window open and the back door partially ajar, it seemed to take ages for the water to be ready. I brought the galvanized bath into the scullery, but she said she would bath in the kitchen. When the water was ready, I filled the bath for her and said that I would go into the front room to read the Sunday newspaper. But she would have none of it and told me stay and wash her back. She then just simply stripped off with no hesitation whatsoever, it was me, would you believe, that felt embarrassed. However, this soon passed and it seemed the most natural thing in the world to be there together. This was the first occasion that I had seen her naked in the full light of day. I have seen dozens of women this way during my life, but to me she was perfection.

The next day I saw the first lieutenant and asked him if I could have a word with him off the record, to which he agreed. I did not lie to him, I just simply laid all my cards on the table. After listening to my story he told me that a lodging allowance was out of the question, but he would do what he could about a ration card.

Just before we packed up for the day he called me and handed me a ration card saying, 'You are prepared to swear that you can't stand the grub in the lodging house.'

'Yes sir' I replied. With that he smiled mischievously and handed me a second card, adding that he did not know where the other card had come from.

Well, I was like a dog with two tails and just could not wait for Dorothy to arrive home. When I told her, she was simply over the moon and we went to the pub for an hour or so just to celebrate.

On the Thursday, the first lieutenant asked me to go the wardroom with him as he had some important news for me. He told me I had been promoted to acting petty officer, but had to leave for Blockhouse on the following Monday. I could have cried, just couldn't take it in, but there was nothing I could do about it. Even if I had refused promotion the chances were that the boat would only be there for another eight or ten weeks at the most before we would be off again, so that was that.

That evening I gave her time to get indoors and settle down with a cup of tea, then I broke the news to her. She was silent for about a minute, although it seemed an age before she spoke. 'We knew it would happen one day,' she said, but added, 'I had been hoping that we would have had a few weeks together before you left me though.' Then in her wisdom, she remarked that perhaps it was just as well before we got too involved and upset other people's lives, I knew exactly to what she was referring, *Che sera,* that was Dorothy's motto.

Being both a little subdued that evening we explained to Doris and Alf that we would not be going to the pub and we just sat quietly listening to the wireless, then went early to bed, each with our own thoughts.

When Dorothy arrived home the following evening, Friday, I gave her time to settle down before saying, 'I don't think we should go to the pub tonight either because we have so much to discuss about the future, we have been going at it a bit strong you know, supposing you become pregnant.'

It was then for the first time since we met that she began to get very cross with me, her cheeks became a little flushed and her voice raised above its normal — not a great deal — but speaking angrily she said, 'I do not wish to discuss the future, my future or your future, I am going to live for today which is all that matters, when tomorrow comes, I will deal with it

'If by any remote chance I do become pregnant it will be the most wonderful present I have ever received, it will be treasured with the memory of you. Fate will decide the future, so let us have no more talk of plans, we will just have a wonderful weekend with extra rations and I will see you off at Newcastle on Monday.'

She went on to say that we would find a way somehow of keeping in touch. During our all too brief romance there were times when her philosophy, her down to earth practical way of dealing with things, came very near to exasperating me, leaving me at a loss for words.

The weekend just flew by with us two going at it as if love were to be rationed. She decided that it must be her way or not at all as to how we would keep in touch, she would only write to me provided it was to a safe address whereby the letter could be destroyed if for some reason I was unable to receive it. She asked me to write as often as I could, but only when I was able to post it myself ashore somewhere. She added that she would never put her address or sign any letter or card she sent me. Here I must explain that any letters written and posted on board any boat by crew members had to be left open in order to be read and perhaps censored by an officer, then they are sealed and posted.

Well, that was that and we decided on a quick couple of drinks at the pub to say goodbye to the regulars then it was home to bed where we certainly made it a night to remember.

CHAPTER 20

On Monday morning I was up early because I had to be at Newcastle Station by 9.30 am. Dorothy had arranged to have the morning off, although I had begged her not to do so. I had already taken my kit to the station on the Saturday afternoon so with breakfast over, I had one last look around, a quick cuddle and off we both went.

At the station, I reported to the RT officer and was informed that the train would be at least an hour late so I asked if I could leave the station. 'It's up to you' he said, then I saw some other matelots who were travelling down to Pompey and I asked them if they would take care of my kit for an hour or until the train arrived.

This being arranged, I grabbed Dorothy by the arm and said, 'Quick, don't ask any questions.' Close to the station I had spotted a photographer's shop and I led her towards the place.

When she saw it she said 'Fred, do you mean for us to be taken together.' 'No other way' I replied. So we had our photographs taken and Dorothy promised to send me one when it was safe to do so. I then said to Dorothy that I would never take my copy home, but always keep it in an envelope with my other things in the boat, and on the envelope I would write that it must be destroyed and not sent to my home if anything happened to me.

We went back to the station where the train was already in and loaded, the other matelots had put my kit on board and reserved a window seat for me. Within minutes the guard was shouting out, 'All aboard', doors were being shut and there was just time for me to grab Dorothy in an embrace and it was all over in seconds.

The train was moving and I could hardly see her through my tears, but we waved continually until long after we had lost sight of one another. The other occupants of my compartment must have thought that I was crazy because the train must have been a mile out before I came in from the window, unable to hold back the flood of tears.

After a while the other lads and myself began talking about where we were going in Pompey. One couldn't tell by looking at their cap-ribbons which either read HM Ships, or like my own, HM Submarines. Two were for Pompey barracks, one for the Gunnery School, Whale Island, one for HMS *Vernon,* the Torpedo School and the other chap was coming with me to Blockhouse. He was joining submarines for the first time, so naturally most of my conversation was with him. After an hour or so, we all more or less settled down to reading or dozing.

For me it was a time for reflection about what could I do about the situation I found myself in. So many solutions entered my head, some quite desperate, but I had been warned about not doing anything rash. It seemed that I must take things as they came and not try to make them happen, but I would go back to Wallsend one way or another, of that I was sure. It was now back to reality and I was on my way home to Martha and the baby. Incidentally, she was pregnant again with a baby due at the end of the year — it happened during my last leave in March. What manner of man was I to be carrying on in this way? I did not believe that I was some callous individual taking pleasure, not caring who I hurt. I haven't consciously hurt anyone in my life, quite the reverse, therefore, was I simply a romantic, in love with love itself?

The boy who meets girl and simply goes through life with her alone is to be envied, not for him the heartbreaks such as the one I had just experienced, not knowing whether or not I would ever see this wonderful girl again, not for him the turmoil of the mind, just peace of mind for him, but is he to be envied? I would only answer yes if he were with someone who could compare with Dorothy, he would then be the luckiest man on earth.

But back to this miserable journey south, we made many official and unofficial stops and the heating system in the train was continually being switched on and off. We rattled on further and further away from my love. Eventually, we arrived in cheerless Pompey at 3 am. I was feeling dead miserable.

My companions split up with myself and the other chap for Blockhouse as they were taken the short distance to HMS *Vernon* by a small van. The petty officer of the watch at the guard room informed us that the earliest we would be able to get a launch for Blockhouse would be 7 am. In the meantime, he offered us the use of some camp beds in a small room behind his office where we could get our heads down for a couple of hours and this we did. In the morning the other chap, an able seaman, asked me whether we should go down for the launch, but I told him we should go to the mess for breakfast first. So scruffy, unwashed and unshaven we went to our respective messes and then caught a launch at 8.30 am.

Arriving alongside the familiar jetty at Blockhouse, I said to my companion that we could take our kit up to the parade ground, leave it by the post office and walk up to the guard room to report in. So following me, we both set off. I didn't see the other chap again, but I was told to settle into the mess and report to the regulating chief stoker the following morning.

Martha knew that I was leaving Newcastle on Monday, but of course could only guess that I might be home on Tuesday. There were no domestic telephones such as there are today, it was only times such as these that we needed them anyway. I checked into the mess, bathed and shaved, waited for my 'tot' of rum and lunch, then walked ashore to Martha and home. She was actually at the front door looking down the street as I turned the corner, she hurried towards me having left our little daughter of eighteen months with her mother inside the house. We embraced and arm in arm walked to the house and she asked questions about how long would I be home etc., questions to which naturally I was unable to supply answers.

We soon settled in again as a happy family and I was not feeling at all guilty, but during all my waking hours my thoughts were miles away.

Martha was expecting our second child which was due about the end of the year and I told her I wanted a boy this time as one of each would be nice and would also continue my family name. I must have been an awful person.

I settled down to a very ordinary routine, two nights at home, with one night on duty at Blockhouse where I was just doing humdrum jobs. The evenings at home were spent listening to the wireless and visiting our two local pubs, *The Five Alls,* and opposite, *The White Swan* — which I preferred.

I was secretly writing to Dorothy and in return received two of our photographs from her, signed 'To my darling from Dorothy.' The other photograph was for me to sign and return to her. This I did, posting my letters to her at the main post office in Gosport.

I had been hoping, with a ninety per cent chance of being correct, to be sent to Barrow-in-Furness, or perhaps Birkenhead, to stand-by a new submarine which was being built. This was quite a normal procedure in order that the more senior ratings could learn all about their respective jobs.

All these thoughts of standing by a new boat had been continually in my mind and I had rather foolishly mentioned it to Dorothy, thereby raising her hopes. You see I had been thinking that if I were up north standing by a boat, I would be able to wangle weekends with her, this was not an unreasonable supposition for a stoker petty officer who was spare crew in Blockhouse. As I have said, it was a ninety percent certainty.

Fate decided, however, that I had received my share of luck for a while, because quite suddenly I was dealt what I considered to be a dirty trick. It occurred on Sunday 14th December 1941, I had been duty petty officer all Saturday afternoon, evening and night and was due to go ashore. Foolishly, I decided to wait for my 'tot' at 11 am and also have lunch. As I recall, I was dressed in my 'No I' suit sitting in an armchair in the petty officers mess reading the News of the World. A messenger came in and somehow I knew that he wanted me. He went to one petty officer who shook his head to a question which was probably, 'Do you know PO Matthews?' However, this same petty officer stood up to call my name loudly. I could not possibly ignore this, so I raised my hand, the messenger came to me told me the chief stoker wanted to see me. It was not yet 12 noon, my official time for going ashore so I just had to go and see him. He told me that *P36* had just come in and her stoker petty officer has gone to the sick bay to have his boils lanced. The boat had got to be refuelled, so he wanted me to nip down and do it. I moaned that I had been on duty all night, but he assured me it would not take long and that he would make it up to me.

Well, that was it. I changed into overalls and went down to the boat to be greeted by the first lieutenant, a Royal Navy Reserve officer.

'Are you the stoker PO?'

'Yes sir' I replied, 'I've just come down to refuel the boat that's all,' but I added that I hadn't a clue as to where I should start simply because I had never seen that class of submarine before.

'See the 'Chief Tiffy' (Chief ERA) he barked and added 'It's bloody easy a monkey could do it.' Well, why the hell didn't he get one, I thought. I then saw the chief and explained to him that I did not have a clue, but he assured me that everything would be okay and proceeded to give me the run down of everything. Indeed it was quite simple and straightforward. This task completed I reported back to him then went to the chief stoker in his office who told me to shove off ashore. So I left, arrived home and apologised to Martha for being late and that was that so I thought.

The following day I reported to the chief stoker in his office who informed me that the petty officer of *P36* was still in the sick bay and that I had better get down to the boat to see what I could do. In the meantime he, the chief, would try to find out more about the stoker PO in the sick bay, one Tom Pepper, he would then let me know. I changed into overalls and went down to the boat where I was met by the skipper, Lieutenant Edmonds, who asked me if I had fuelled the boat the day before.

'Yes sir,' I replied. He then asked where I had been and I told him that I had just come off shore, that I was spare crew, working twenty four hours on and twenty four hours off. I went on to explain that after finishing my duty the previous day, instead of going ashore I had been sent down to fuel his boat, thereby losing part of my time off.

Well, this didn't seem to satisfy him at all. I was told that I should have reported to him or the first lieutenant, I replied that I did tell his chief after which I went to my regulating chief stoker who told me to carry on ashore. The skipper, still not happy, said that I had better stay with the boat until he sorted things out, it looked as though I had made a bad start with him. It was my twenty-four hours on duty anyway so I was not unduly perturbed and was actually finding my way around this class of submarine which I thought at the time was probably identical to the one to which I would eventually be drafted.

It was mid-morning the following day when the first lieutenant came along to me and said, 'You are staying with us.' It appeared that Tom Pepper's boils had developed complications and he was being moved to Haslar Hospital, just up the road.

Well, this was a blow beneath the belt, but I comforted myself by saying that probably it would only be for a few days and then Tom would be back. I was able to go ashore that evening to explain the situation to Martha. I also wrote to Dorothy saying that I could not write until the situation was clearer and asked her not to write either. Before I went ashore I had taken Tom's personal kit ashore to the sick bay and had brought on board my own. I must have had a premonition. As it happened it would be many years before I set foot on English soil again.

CHAPTER 21

The following day we went out to Spithead and did a few practice dives with three or four budding COs then returned to harbour where I was allowed to go ashore again.

On the Friday there was a burst of activity — we had to get our full kit on board, load stores and top up with fuel. We just knew that we were off to sea, there was some sort of flap on, German ships breaking out or something. There was no way I could contact Martha, I only had time to scribble a quick note, run up to the post office in the base, and that was all. I was the victim of what is known in the Navy as 'a pier head jump', in other words being posted to a ship at a moment's notice. I suppose I had a chip on my shoulder as the rest of the crew had watched the boat being built whilst taking it easy for a few months in lodgings at Birkenhead or Barrow. Now, here I was with all my worries, Martha expecting any time, thinking of Dorothy and I had to learn all about the boat from scratch.

As daylight faded we proceeded out to Spithead where we dived to 'catch a trim'. When the first lieutenant was satisfied, we surfaced and continued out to sea, it was by then completely dark and we would only dive again in an emergency or as daylight approached.

Everyone settled down to running routine, watches were set and this was the first time I realized that I would be keeping one watch in three in the engine room. Our evening meal was over and the dishes cleaned away when the skipper came through the boat to give us our destination. We were off to the Mediterranean to join the famous Tenth Flotilla operating from Malta. Well, up to this point in time we had lost seventeen of our submarines in the Med, so it appeared that we were not off on a pleasure cruise.

The passage to Gibraltar was uneventful except for the atrocious weather conditions we experienced. When we were on the surface, we had to rig a canvas bath at the bottom of the ladder from the conning tower in order to catch the sea water which continually poured into the submarine. Christmas day we spent dived, at times at periscope depth where we rolled quite a lot and conditions were generally unpleasant.

Only officers, chiefs and petty officers possessed bunks, the rest of the crew, seamen and stokers, lived in the fore-ends, between the racks of spare torpedoes. Only when the torpedoes had been loaded into the tubes to replace ones which had been fired did the crew have any additional living space. Many was the time I was compelled to climb over sleeping bodies in order to carry out my duties during my watch.

My tiny mess contained four bunks and was situated immediately aft of the fore-ends, with the bunks crossways. My own was the lower one forward and my feet occasionally stretched out into the narrow passageway where they came into contact with various bodies passing through to the forward torpedo space or to our tiny 'thunderbox' toilet and small wash basin. If ever I managed a few hours in my bunk, which occasionally I loaned out to someone else, it was always a restless sleep.

When we arrived at Gibraltar we tied-up alongside two other submarines which were secured to our parent ship, HMS *Maidstone*. One of the boats was the *Clyde*, a large submarine with two engine rooms, the smaller of which was equal to our own engine room in *P36*. The other boat was the *Thunderbolt* — formerly the *Thetis*.

We were certainly glad to arrive after our battering in the rough weather across the Bay of Biscay knowing that we would at least be able to have hot baths, good regular meals and a few nights of uninterrupted sleep before setting off on patrol again.

New Year's eve arrived, but there were no celebrations for our crew. We had already missed Christmas and were compelled to get our night's rest early owing to our departure from Gib, before dawn. This early departure was to ensure that no spying eyes could report our leaving the base on patrol. It follows that none of us had been allowed on shore to see the 'Old Year' out as we had to load the boat with all our kit again, plus piles of supplies destined for beleaguered Malta. Every little bit of food, fuel and medical supplies which could be transported was worth its weight in gold to the island. The submarine was, therefore, fully loaded and moving from one part of the boat to the other was an obstacle course.

We also had a number of passengers, together with their belongings, they included three spare submarine officers, a couple of ratings on their way to join boats in Malta, and Michael Peter Churchill, the secret agent, whom we discovered later had to be put ashore near Cannes in the South of France. Peter shared my bunk whilst he was on the *P36*

P36 was one of the Navy's smaller submarines. She was about 200ft in length and had a displacement of approximately 650 tons and proved quite a headache for the 'Number One' to keep her in trim when submerged.

Conditions within the boat were generally unpleasant due to all the boxes of supplies and kit which were occupying spaces which would normally be filled with air for us to breathe and the extra passengers on board were also breathing what air remained.

My job itself was also a nightmare, as a result of my not having a lot of sleep. I was still learning about the boat, finding out where everything was and in addition to my watch keeping, the internal ballast tank was also my responsibility. It should be pointed out that water taken on as ballast in Portsmouth can be a different colour and weight from that in the Mediterranean. Therefore the water in the ballast tanks was continually changed in order that a different type of water was not pumped out in enemy waters, where it could have been observed.

With regard to our passengers, I am indebted to Wing Commander Cooper, a nephew of our skipper, who kindly sent me extracts from Peter Churchill's book *Of Their Own Choice*.

These extracts fully confirm my story of our condition on leaving Gibraltar until we landed this very brave man on the shore near Cannes.

Peter Churchill gives a graphic account of his trip in *P36* and also states that he spent much of his time in the petty officers mess, where fortunately I was able to have many a conversation with him and I have to say I have nothing but admiration for his bravery and devotion to duty.

Our skipper experienced great difficulty in trying to land Peter near the place he had chosen, mainly because of adverse weather conditions. However, after many farewells, he was put down about eight hundred yards from shore, from where the hotels, houses and motor vehicles were easily discernible from our position.

Peter had spent nine days in our company and we were all sorry to see him go, but we too had an essential job to do. So it was on with the patrol and passage to Malta with our valuable supplies for the base and island.

The difficult part of our passage was through the narrows between Cap Bon Tunis and Sicily. This was always a dangerous route because situated between these two points was the heavily fortified Island of Pantellaria. The whole area was continually patrolled by Italian destroyers, torpedo boats and other anti-submarine craft. Also, there were many mine fields to negotiate before reaching our own swept channel at the approach to Malta and even here Italian mines were continually being dropped. These mines had been responsible for a number of submarine losses, but we arrived without incident and secured alongside the base at Lazaretto.

What a different Malta from the one I had left in February 1940, two years before. There was a chronic shortage of everything except air raids, these were seemingly nonstop. We, in company with everyone else except the anti-aircraft gunners, were continually diving in and out of shelters. When out, we were invariably clearing away bomb damage and rescuing the belongings of boats sunk in the harbour.

Quite a lot of our food was salvaged from these ships. The tins of food we recovered had long since lost their respective labels — the only recognisable ones, because of their shape, were corned beef, herrings and sardines.

A run ashore to one of the bars was also a chancy business. Invariably it resulted in just getting a few glasses of the local brew, Ambete, which I am sure that if it had been available in sufficient quantities and heated to the correct temperature, would most surely have provided us with an alternative fuel supply.

We left harbour rather suddenly for our second patrol to take up a position between Khoms and Misurati. This was a little to the east of the port of Tripoli to which a reported convoy of enemy supply ships were heading.

Nothing was seen for a few days until our asdic operator heard the HE, the hydrophone effect, of propeller and engine noise approaching our position. This was on the 24th January. The skipper was called to the control room and after a brief look through the periscope, ordered 'Diving Stations'. Every member of the crew took up his action station, ready for our attack.

The skipper had seen two supply ships escorted by two destroyers, heading in an ideal direction for us. He decided to fire two torpedoes, followed by another two after a brief interval. The depths of them were set at 8ft, 12ft and 14ft. It was as the first of our second salvo of two torpedoes left its tube that our bow rose up rather sharply and we partially broke surface, to be seen by the destroyers who then headed in our direction. We immediately went as deep as we possibly could, changed our course and awaited the expected counter attack.

We waited quietly at our stations and could quite clearly hear the approaching destroyer with the swishing noise of its propellers churning up the sea above us. The closer it came, so the noise of the propellers increased until suddenly, she was right over the top of us. We waited for the fall of depth charges, which strangely enough did not come as she passed over. My heart eased a little, but not for long because back she came. This time she dropped a pattern of charges before reaching our position, which meant that we were thrown about a bit before she passed overhead.

After that a few more charges were dropped, but none were very near. We heard our attacker moving further away, but being a bit shaken, the skipper decided to lie 'doggo' for a while to check for damage.

We heard an explosion which could have been from one of our torpedoes hitting home, but when we surfaced there was nothing at all to be seen and no noise effect heard. The boat had suffered no material damage, there were just a few electrical faults and minor leaks of water and air here and there and after a few more days we were recalled to base.

CHAPTER 22

The 15th February found us patrolling the southern approaches to the Straits of Messina. Hydrophone Effect was heard by the asdic operator who identified the engine noise as turbines, indicating enemy warships of considerable size. Sure enough, in moderate visibility at least two cruisers were seen being escorted by destroyers, so the skipper decided to attack. We were at a position of 37° 36'N when he fired four torpedoes at the group of ships.

We did not hang around near the surface to observe the results of our attack, but immediately dived deep, shutting off all compartments to await any counter attack. This, surprisingly enough, was sporadic and not very intense. We considered ourselves very fortunate indeed. One or two of our torpedoes were heard exploding and we later found out that the Italian destroyer *Carabiniere* had been hit.

At dusk we came to the surface and as there was no sign of the enemy we set about charging our batteries, reloading the torpedo tubes and had something to eat and drink.

The following day we dived at dawn and in almost the same position as we were the day before we heard the approach of heavy ships. After a short while, the same group of ships as we had encountered the previous day came into sight. They were on a course which was ideal for us to launch an attack and the visibility was very good. So, the skipper selected a target and fired our remaining salvo of four torpedoes and as before, we immediately dived deep and shut off all compartments

This time, however, it was a very different story from the day before. The destroyers came at us seemingly from all directions, just like express trains. They seemed to be all around us and dropped depth charges everywhere. Bloody hell it was terrifying, all you could do was hang on to overhead valves or pipes for dear life or grim death. A destroyer or two would stop right overhead and send out 'pinging' impulses, that we could quite clearly hear, trying to locate us. Then they would start to move again as they were afraid to remain stationary too long in case they were hit by a torpedo.

Down would come another soul shattering pattern of depth charges some exploding quite close to us, rocking the boat from side to side, sending us tumbling in to each other. A few air lines were split and one of the hatches lifted slightly. Another destroyer was heard approaching our position and so the cat and mouse game continued. All in all, the attack lasted nearly seven hours and during this period between 250 to 300 charges were dropped near to and around us. All the while we were sustained only by sips of water and biscuits that were passed from hand to hand.

It is at times such as these when morale is called into question. I do know that I was questioning my own as I looked from face to face of my immediate companions in the subdued lighting of the control room.

The nervous stress is frightening, one's mind is in continual turmoil with wild thoughts. One of my thoughts was that I said to myself something like 'If I ever I get out of this alive and back to base, I'm going to sneak off somewhere and hope I am not missed .' Wild thoughts of course, just where in hell can one run away to in Malta, there would probably have been a waiting list anyway! However, good solid naval training, discipline and above all your boat mates get you through and you are back for the next patrol.

Here it should be explained that when our boat was under attack, as I have just described, there were only about a dozen members of the crew of thirty two who were occupied in positions requiring mind, thought and deed. The rest of us having done our job during our own attack, have in the main absolutely nothing to do except hang on to something stable and think one's own thoughts, wondering how the hell you came to be there. I would certainly not condemn anyone who cracked under such a strain, the conditions I have tried to describe have to be experienced in order to be understood and fully appreciated.

There were many times when I stood out in the open during air raids upon Malta and actually watched bombs leave the planes and then wobble momentarily before they screeched down through a clear blue sky - seemingly aimed at one's own position. I have also taken part in a fierce battle against German soldiers, but never have I been as frightened as I was when being depth charged, there is just nowhere to hide.

When our boat eventually surfaced at nightfall we had expended all our torpedoes and were in need of repair and we signalled base that we were on our way back to Malta. It was when we had settled down to passage routine that the skipper came through the boat and asked how many torpedoes we had heard explode. Remembering that they could easily be heard before our presence was detected and the depth charging commenced, practically every member of the crew who was asked replied, 'Four Sir.' He in turn thought that it was impossible to hit his target with four torpedoes, but some very strange things have occurred with torpedoes and targets. However, records later showed that the cruiser *Gotitzia* had been hit during our attack.

It was on our way back that we heard that our living quarters at the base had received a direct hit. So we were anticipating returning to Lazaretto to find out that our only possessions would be those which we had with us.

When we arrived at Malta, we managed to find our way through the swept channel to berth finally alongside our base, this in spite of an air raid which had become 'par for the course'.

With permission of the skipper, a number of us commenced to tunnel into the debris which covered what had been our living quarters in the hope that we might be able to salvage some of our personal kit which was kept in steel lockers. As luck would have it I found my own, badly distorted, but with its contents intact.

There and then I made the decision to take all my kit on board and keep it in one of the spare parts storerooms to which I had access as part of my duties. The reason being, as silly as it sounds, was, 'If my kit goes, I go and vice-versa'.

However, as fate would have it, it was not to be, did I not say that I was a born survivor? I wish I had realized at that time just how right this would be, at least it would have saved me many a change of underwear in the years to come.

Before this last patrol, as part of my duties, I made a number of trips to the dockyard in order to obtain spare machinery parts. It was during one of these trips that I arranged a swop with a dear old Maltese store man. It was strictly illegal of course. Nevertheless, in return for some rusty tins of grub, plus a Gordon's Gin bottle with about three or four 'tots' of rum, I acquired twelve 'Pusser's' torches complete with batteries. These I secured at strategic places throughout the boat which proved to have been a good swap when we were under attack and lost some of our lighting.

The situation in Malta became more precarious day by day, due to the incessant bombing and the lack of fresh food. Our living quarters ended up as any odd corner amongst the debris. Personal hygiene was a big problem, especially trying to keep one's underwear clean. Lack of sleep was a big factor, everyone was on edge, not knowing what the next day or even hour might bring and information handed down to us by our officers was also very scant, probably because they didn't know too much themselves.

The practice at this period in time was for boats in harbour to remain dived in the creeks all day, with just one boat remaining alongside the base for maintenance. This diving in harbour, in my own opinion, was a dead loss, for whilst it may have prevented the boat from damage, it did nothing for the crew's morale and it is the crew from the skipper down who have to fight, the boat itself is powerless without them.

Diving to the bottom of the creek and being dive-bombed is akin to being depth charged, except that one is unable to take evasive action and in the clear water, we could easily be seen by the enemy bombers above. The continual sound of bombs exploding all around you and being partially lifted off the bottom at times was a nightmare I could not recommend to anyone.

The strain on the commanding officers was fully recognized by Captain 'S', 'Shrimp' Simpson. He was able to rest them occasionally by letting another officer take a particular boat out on patrol in their place. Not so with the crew, the most some of us could hope for when in harbour was perhaps a few days in a rest camp at Ghain Tuffieha, whilst our colleagues dived the boat in one of the creeks. Rest camp, that was a laugh for a start, but more of that later.

The position of the Tenth Flotilla became more and more untenable; to us lesser mortals the situation could only be described as organized confusion. To be honest most of us just wanted to get back to sea where although we might have to endure a depth charge attack we would at least have some respite from the continual bombing of the island.

The *P36* had been undergoing repairs because of the hammering we had sustained on our last patrol and a great deal of welding was required to the plates on our pressure hull. One of our hydroplanes had been thrown out of line and numerous bits of internal machinery had shifted from their mountings. During this period about a third of our crew were at the supposed rest camp, but not yours truly. My body was required on board; no rest for the wicked!

At the end of February it was deemed that we were fit for sea, so we set off on patrol to take up a position to the east of Tripoli. It was a relief to go to sea on patrol which proved to be so with our present position because apart from sighting a destroyer, the one which probably sunk *P38*, the patrol proved uneventful. We had not been in a position to attack the destroyer, so all in all we managed to get some uninterrupted sleep.

On the 12th March, *P36* was berthed alongside *Upholder*. Both submarines were preparing for patrol. We were required to patrol off the port of Taranto together with one of our larger submarines from Alexandria, the *Proteus*.

I happened quite by chance, to be standing on the casing of *Upholder* talking with Fred Topping. We had joined submarines and trained together but had gone our separate ways since. It was whilst we were talking that *Upholder's* skipper came aboard, Lt Cdr Wanklyn VC DSO. David, as he was always known to his fellow officers, recognized me from the *Otway* and said 'It's Fred Matthews isn't it? And they have made you a petty officer'

I replied, 'Yes Sir' and went on to congratulate him on his award of the Victoria Cross. I also explained that Fred Topping was an old pal of mine and that he said that they expected to return to the UK shortly for leave and to join a new boat, expressing a hope that *Upholder's* crew would be together in any new boat. David Wanklyn was sort of noncommittal, but wished me good luck for the future before disappearing down the fore hatch and that was the last time I saw him.

The *Upholder* was subsequently lost with all hands, depth charged by the Italian torpedo boat, *Pegasus,* off the coast of Tripoli on 14th April 1942. The Royal Navy, therefore, lost one its most outstanding submarine officers and I lost more of my friends and drinking companions.

However, on the 14th March, both *Upholder* and *P36* set off for our positions off the port of Taranto. A convoy of supply ships were due to leave Alexandria for beleaguered Malta and it was thought that the Italians having learnt about this would send a strike force from Taranto to attack the convoy. Admiral Vian with a large task force protecting the convoy was more than ready to deal with the Italians probably looking forward to finishing them off once and for all.

On the 22nd March our asdic operator reported the HE of heavy ships heading out to sea from Taranto. The skipper was called to the control room, ordered 'Diving Stations' and all crew took up their attack stations. After observing at long range an Italian battleship with a number of cruisers and several destroyers, the skipper ordered a change of course and, poking our transmitting aerial just above the surface, we were able to signal Admiral Vian that the Italian Fleet was putting to sea.

The signal was received and proved to be vital by subsequent events. I have read Captain Roskill's official history of this event and have seen and read other versions written and compiled by various people, both naval and civilian. Apart from mentioning the fact that *P36* alerted Admiral Vian regarding the Italian Fleet movements, it is implied that no further action was taken by our boat, but nothing could be further from the truth.

I have written previously that organized confusion appeared to be the order of the day at Malta in these times and John Wingate in his book, *The Fighting Tenth* refers to the communication problem which plagued so many COs in the Mediterranean at the time. After reading *Seedies List of Submarine Awards WW 2*, I suspect that quite a few actions of boats and recommendations for officers and men were lost or shelved without being forwarded. For their devotion to duty, Lt Edmonds and the crew of *P36* went unrewarded. This I consider to be a grave injustice.

Surely it was inconceivable that having sighted the Italian Fleet and being the nearest submarine to it, the skipper would not have set about trying to manoeuvre into position to launch an attack upon such a valuable and important target. I can assure you that he certainly did just that, I WAS THERE and do not have to rely upon versions compiled by someone who was not.

Our skipper, when in position, fired a full salvo of four torpedoes at the enemy and knowing the strength of opposing destroyers, we dived to a depth that was the deepest we had dived to date, shutting off all compartments in the process. Depth charges were dropped for quite a while by the escorting destroyers before we fired our torpedoes, therefore it was difficult for us to determine whether or not any of our 'fish' had hit the enemy. We were then subjected to a fairly sustained period of depth charging, but apart from a couple of patterns which were dropped quite near, the others were way off target. Eventually the hunters lost us and we were able to steal away and set course for Malta.

Stress amongst submariners was a problem, but you just had to get on with the job. The following extract from *The Fighting Tenth*, regarding stress, is quoted with the permission of the author, John Wingate DSC.

In October 1942 Surgeon Lieutenant A. F. Crowley RNVR, a psychiatrist, was flown out to the Tenth Submarine Flotilla based at Malta. His terms of reference were to observe morale and to offer help where necessary. His presence was not unanimously appreciated nor was his speciality entirely understood. However, on the 12th October the submarine Una set off on a twelve day patrol under the command of Lieutenant C P Norman and with it went Surgeon Lieutenant Crowley. The Una at first carried out a successful operation of landing a 'folboat' party off the Catabrian coast, then on the night of the 17th/18th, having sighted a convoy of ships, Pat Norman selected a tanker as his target and was about to fire a salvo when the convoy altered course straight for him, forcing Una to go deep. Then the tankers escort of three destroyers began a fierce and very accurate counter attack with depth charges, three of which dropped unpleasantly close.

After the patrol, Surgeon Lieutenant Crowley summarised his impressions thus:

The cramped accommodation, close contact with mess mates and lack of exercise all played their part in setting up a state of nervous tension. Though this is slight at first, it increased as the days went on and proved to be the last straw' when a more severe nervous strain was superimposed.

This condition was somewhat offset by the increased amount of sleep which submarine life imposed and also by the welcome diversion which meal time provided. Again and again, I noticed how all looked forward to meals and how any default in the bill of fare was met with grumbling and general lowering of morale.

Atmospheric conditions — once the initial discomfort had been overcome, appeared to be quite adequate for the amount of work required. But considerable discomfort was caused by excessive respiration due to the raised atmospheric temperature while dived. Towards the end of the dive when oxygen content had decreased and carbon dioxide had increased, there was a noticeable slowing of mental processes together with creating irritability and shortness of temper.

During a depth charge attack, it was observed how calmly each person behaved. This was partly due to the fact that atmospheric conditions had probably slowed down the intellect. However, when the second attack followed some time later, there was a noticeable increase in excitability as evidenced by the holding onto any available fixed object in an endeavour to steel oneself for the impact and its consequences.

When the action was over, the effect was seen in the form of increased excitement and excitability and in myself at least, physical exhaustion. The result of a prolonged attack can be imagined. Submarine patrolling is probably the most exacting of all types of modern warfare. From the foregoing, it will be seen that apart from the ordinary hazards of life, the submariners chief enemy is nervous strain. This should be combated by allowing each man a complete change after patrol together with the granting of all amenities possible, e.g. good food and reading material whilst on patrol.

Surgeon Lieutenant Crowley's conclusions were taken with a good humoured pinch of salt.

CHAPTER 23

We arrived back at Malta on 29th March, two or three days after *Upholder* and were ordered to remain dived in the creek to await our turn to go alongside at Lazaretto.

April Fools day duly arrived and we surfaced and went alongside the base. At the time an air raid was in progress, but this was such a normal occurrence that it did not prevent us from docking. Arriving alongside, the skipper ordered 'Clear the boat, everyone to the shelters.'

The coxswain, 'Dixie' Dean, said 'Hang on Fred — I've got a couple of "tots" of rum here.' The bombs started dropping nearer and nearer and we were just trying to get our tots down when a particularly heavy bomb fell right alongside and lifted the boat out of the water. We could hear water rushing in and made it to the conning tower and over the side in about ten seconds flat. We didn't know at that time that just aft of the control room was the 'Outside ERA' together with our torpedo officer. These two had been ordered to remain on board during the air raid perhaps to deal with any emergency.

It transpired that we had been holed rather badly and the boat was gradually sinking. We all emerged from the shelter during a lull in the raid and the skipper ordered us to secure more ropes and wires to the pillars of the Lazaretto arches which supported the upper floor of the base. This in the vain hope that it might prevent our boat from going down involuntarily. However, it was not to be and it became obvious that our precious *P36* was going to take her final dive.

The skipper reluctantly ordered all ropes and wires to be removed, remarking that he did not wish to face a Court Martial for losing his boat and pulling down the base in the process. *P36* slowly sank to a ledge below, where she remained clearly visible for the next sixteen years until she was finally salvaged and given a burial in deeper water off Malta, together with all my kit and possessions including my very treasured photographs of loved ones. All of them!

Well what now? There I was standing with everything I owned, smelling like a pole cat. I was wearing a filthy boiler suit, singlet, socks, underpants, shoes and peak cap and I owned nothing else!

I found my way to the 'Pusser's' store, where normally new articles of clothing could be obtained. In this particular case the store contained miscellaneous heaps of an assortment of clothing, some new and some salvage, but again, all of the 'Fitzherbert' type. There were no complete uniforms to be had, one could just pick out bare essentials. So I picked up a fresh set of underclothing, a pair of khaki shorts, a shirt, towel, toothbrush, hair brush and comb and a small linen bag to keep these prized possessions in.

I then boarded a truck with a number of known and unknown naval personnel and was driven by a half mad stone deaf Maltese driver to the rest camp at Ghain Tuffieha.

The air raids continued during our hazardous journey to the camp and our route was constantly under fire from German ME 109 fighter bombers. During one attack we had to keep banging like hell on the top of the driver's cab in order to get the frightened madman of a driver to pull into a hedge and stop so that we could seek shelter. I dived out of the truck and crawled underneath, on emerging I found that in my panic I had sought shelter beneath the petrol tank!

Arriving at the camp we were told by a person in authority to find a vacant hut and make ourselves at home, whereupon a dozen or so of us made for a hut and luckily found it unoccupied. It was a long dormitory affair with roughly twenty iron beds, each with two blankets and a pillow. I grabbed one at the far end, next to the bathroom containing a large bath. There were also two toilets next door to the bathroom and at the other end of the hut there was a similar arrangement.

There were only a couple of the ratings who were known to me personally. The others were from the *Pandora,* which had been sunk the same day as ourselves, and from the *P39,* which had been sunk in the harbour a few days before. Everyone acquired a bed and proceeded to lie upon it waiting for a lull in the air raids before venturing forth into the camp.

During a break from the air raids, which must have been about an hour or so after we had all arrived at the hut, a very young army lieutenant entered our hut and called out loudly, 'Who is in charge here?' Nobody answered him for a moment and we all looked at each other, hoping that somebody would speak up. It should be pointed out that we were in the main wearing somewhat odd combinations of shirts, trousers, overalls etc. with little or no distinguishing badges as to rank or rating. Probably because I happened to be the only one with a petty officers cap, all eyes finally turned in my direction.

The young lieutenant came towards me saying 'It appears that you are the senior man here and I want you and the rest of the men here to help move an unexploded bomb which is lying just outside this hut down onto the football field.'

Quite taken aback, I replied, 'Yes Sir, but we have just arrived here and don't know where any stores are, we will need a lot of rope and tackle, probably about five hundred yards or so.'

That was my mistake because the young lieutenant asked me why I would want all that rope.

Foolishly, I answered him thus, 'Because five hundred yards is the nearest I'm going to get to that bloody bomb.' Well he went mad and shouted at me about insubordination and such like. I pleaded that I was stressed from my ordeal and he eventually calmed down a bit. Arguing with him was no good and we had to go outside with him.

What met our eyes when we all trooped out was a bomb of about 4ft in length, lying roughly 10ft from the corner of our hut. Sat astride it was an army corporal who remarked to the lieutenant that in his opinion, the bomb was not a 'dud' and what did he want to do about it? We all had our own ideas about where to stick the ruddy thing!

A suggestion was made by one of the lads from our hut, to which everyone, including the officer agreed. We got one of the iron beds from our hut then dismantled another to use as a ramp, in order to roll the bomb onto the first bed. Surprisingly enough, we managed to do this quite quickly, the difficulty was how to manoeuvre the bed over the rough paths downhill to the football field, about a quarter a mile distant, without the bomb rolling off.

Finally, the difficulty was overcome by making a number of shafts from other dismantled beds, these were firmly attached fore and aft like handles and enabled the whole of our party to use their lifting ability. With the bomb secured, we set off. As we moved over the rough ground the bomb started to roll from side to side. We all panicked and lifted our particular end of the bed up causing the bomb to roll back the other way.

But eventually we safely managed to get it to the middle of the field where we carefully tipped it off the bed and legged it back to the barrack room. I think all of us had to change our underpants! The final insult, however, was that the bomb exploded during an air raid later in the day. I did say that the term rest camp was a bit of a misnomer didn't I?

A few days later, a Maltese civilian worker at our camp, who was over the moon with two or three tins of grub I had given him, took me to his house in the nearby village. You see, I had managed to bring a small haversack of salvaged tins from Lazaretto. He presented me with my reward, a very nice young lady of about eighteen years of age and very enjoyable she was too, just the sort of therapy I needed after the previous few weeks!

Unfortunately, I was unable to repeat the visit to the young lady because suddenly after a couple more days, it was back to Lazaretto where as before, organized confusion appeared to be the order of the day.

The information that finally filtered down to us lesser mortals was to the effect that Flag Officer Submarines, Vice Admiral Sir Max Horton, himself a World War 1 submarine ace, had decided that the base at Lazaretto was no longer tenable for us all and that he had decided that we should evacuate to the First Flotilla's parent ship, HMS *Medway* at Alexandria.

His reason was that although it would take longer for the flotilla's boats to reach their patrol areas, at least when in harbour the crews would be able to enjoy good food under excellent conditions and they would also be able to sleep and relax in peace and replenish new articles of clothing.

In harbour at this time at Lazaretto was the submarine *Urge,* whose stoker PO was Bill Ashford, an old mate of mine. The *Urge* was due to leave for Alexandria shortly and Bill and I arranged that whoever arrived at *Medway* first would try to secure a kit locker and billet, on the assumption that the mess might be a little crowded with all the extra bodies turning up.

I eventually took passage to Alex on the *Porpoise,* a mine laying submarine. The night before *Porpoise* arrived at Alexandria we were preparing to surface at dusk, an action which everyone on board had been praying for.

The submarine had roughly double her compliment on board, which included the survivors from the Greek submarine, *Glukos,* which had also been sunk at Malta. The air in the boat quickly became unbearable, especially with all the foreign bodies on board who made frequent use of the few toilets. The stench itself was unbearable. The order to surface finally came and the skipper was out and on the bridge in a flash. Fresh air had just started to enter the boat when suddenly the klaxon sounded and skipper and lookouts tumbled back down into the boat and we crash dived. The engines were stopped and all compartments shut-off.

The excited chattering of our Greek passengers was unsettling to say the least, but after about fifteen minutes the compartments were opened up and news filtered through to the effect that as we had arrived on the surface, so did a U-boat just a short distance from us. This news made the babble from our passengers even worse until a voice boomed from the control room for them to keep quiet whilst our asdic operator listened all-round. The waiting itself was nerve racking as you could not help but think of the possibilities of being torpedoed or rammed by the U-boat.

Here it must be explained that before surfacing it was standard practice for the skipper to order all unnecessary machinery to be switched off and silence in the boat observed. This was in order that there would be no distraction for the asdic operator who would be listening out for the sound of any other craft in our vicinity prior to surfacing.

On this particular evening, the U-boat had been doing precisely the same as ourselves — reducing their own noise to a minimum whilst listening out for others in her area. Fortunately for us our lookouts were already on the bridge and spotted the enemy breaking surface, bow on to us. Therefore, our skipper had us diving before the U-boat lookouts could emerge from their conning tower. Only the skipper and others in the control room knew of this at the time, thank goodness, or I would suspect that there would have been quite a flap amongst our passengers had they known the truth behind our sudden dive.

At this time, during quieter moments I often contemplated as to what I should do about the tangled web I had left at home. But these thoughts faded as I began to reason that I might not live to see the next day, let alone get home to sort things out. Life was now about living for today and worrying about tomorrow if it came.

CHAPTER 24

I was glad to see our parent ship, HMS *Medway,* with her brood of submarines looking all serene alongside her. Standing on the casing of *Porpoise* I could hardly wait for the gang plank to be put in place in order to get aboard for a good bath, some new clothing, decent grub and a good night's sleep.

I first sought out the supply assistant at the clothing store and managed to secure a hammock and bedding, underclothes, shorts and a shirt. I was informed that the following day I could be measured up for a full new kit of uniform, both blues and whites.

The *Medway* was a new dimension for me, there was luxury indeed aboard her. Our mess was spacious and not as full as I anticipated. There were plenty of large lockers for one's uniform, so I grabbed a spare one and put Bill Ashford's name upon it, but alas the *Urge* never arrived and dear Bill had gone to join many of my other pals at the bottom of the Mediterranean.

After settling in, I met a number of acquaintances from the Blockhouse days, amongst them was Alfie Backers DSM, he won his award when serving on the submarine, *Spearfish,* in the North Sea .

Within a few days, I found myself kitted up with brand new uniforms and what is more, being deemed a survivor, I was sent on leave to Cairo, there to take up residence in my own cabin on a luxury floating hotel on the Nile, belonging to the Gezira Sporting Club.

There were quite a number of us, all submariners from Malta, who had been sent there to rest and recuperate, so settling down to the 'life of Riley' was no problem. We were also permitted to use the other facilities afforded by the club and these were many. So apart from one trip to the Pyramids and another into Cairo itself, I remained at the club.

However, within days it was panic stations again! Everyone had to go back to Alex immediately. Rommel had reached Alamein and was threatening Egypt so we had to pack our gear and board the train back to Alex and the *Medway.*

The flap in Alexandria was similar to ones we had experienced in Malta, organized confusion — all sorts of rumours were circulating, the main one being that the *Medway* and her brood, the First and Tenth Flotillas, would have to find a safer harbour further to the east and soon. Rommel and his Afrika Corp were supposedly only a few miles from the outskirts of the town.

This rumour proved true and at dusk on the 29th June 1942, the *Medway* slipped her moorings and proceeded to sea with an escort of destroyers. This was accompanied by loud jeers from the crews of French warships in the harbour. At that time the French ships were at their moorings, immobilized in order to prevent them from putting to sea as it was feared they may be used by our enemies against us.

The *Medway*, in addition to its normal crew and spare submarine crews, was evacuating a great number of staff from the base at Alex and also had an upper deck cargo of spare torpedoes and equipment which made moving from forward to aft something of an obstacle course.

The following day, 30th June, was beautiful with hardly a cloud in the sky and with just a slight sea running. Myself, in company with another petty officer, had helped the mess man to scrub out our mess and were just settling down to play a very popular game of that period known as 'Attack' when there was an almighty thump and the ship shuddered.

My first reaction was that we had hit a mine, within seconds the lights flickered and this was followed by another explosion. Almost immediately the ship listed to starboard and the lights went out. Stuff was falling about all over the place and I could hear the excited shouts and curses of men from all around me. The ship creaked and groaned as she started to list even further and my only thought was not to get trapped below.

I was situated two decks down from the main deck and this created some difficulty by virtue of the fact that large steel kit lockers were falling about, as were mess tables and benches. There was kit, utensils, crockery, what have you, all over the place. The ladders were by now perpendicular to us and I had to climb up from the mess through two decks, dodging all sorts of items which were either sliding about or being torn from their fittings to block our route to the upper deck.

As I climbed and scrambled my way to safety, in company with many others, the sound of thousands of gallons of water pouring into the ship could be clearly heard beneath us.

The sound of the ship breaking up as the water broke through into the holds and cabins below me was an eerie noise that I will never forget. There was no real panic only a determination not to die, trapped below decks when the ship finally went under. Upwards and upwards I climbed and with one last effort I dragged myself out onto the main deck, which was now at a sickening angle. There was no doubt the ship was going all the way over.

Exhausted, with the exertion and fear of it all, I took stock of what was happening. The order to abandon ship had obviously been given as there were hundreds, or so it seemed, in the sea and packing cases and crates were floating everywhere. Destroyers were dashing about like mad things depth charging the U-boat which had torpedoed us. I later discovered it was the U-372. I have to admit it was not a pleasant experience being on the other end of a submarine attack.

Looking about, I discovered about six others who were well known to me. One of these was Alfie Backers who, would you believe, had some daft idea about trying to get down to the mess in order to retrieve some of his personal possessions. This was very typical of Alfie, quite fearless, I doubt whether he could have made it down — he sure as hell would never have got back up.

In our little group was Phil King DSM, 'Chief Tiffy' of the *Turbulent* who was with me on *Otway* at the outbreak of war. Phil should have been pensioned in

1939 and was nearly twenty years older than the rest of us in this little group up on deck. He decided to launch himself into the sea with a large group of others who were about to take off to swim to one of the destroyers that was engaged in picking up survivors.

Our group which comprised of myself, Alfie, 'Taffy' Brooks, 'Geordie' Chariton, 'Rene' Houston and 'Geordie' McKenzie, decided to hang on for a while, for two reasons. One, it was quite congested in the sea and we were hoping that one of the rescuing destroyers would come closer to us and two, we had not smoked all our fags or finished the raft which 'Rene' Houston was trying to construct from empty diesel cans lashed together.

As we were discussing our next move, the *Medway* shuddered and went right over on her starboard side and we all made a grab for something to hang on to. It was obvious she had probably only minutes to live, so we decided that it was time for us to get away from her as quickly as we could. We all climbed onto the outer hull of the ship and quite calmly walked into the sea down the port side.

Foolishly, I had kicked off my shoes, thinking that perhaps they would be a hindrance. I immediately felt the result of my mistake as I had to walk and scramble over the razor sharp barnacles that covered the side of the ship. Each step was a painful experience, but as the ship shuddered and groaned and began to go under so I found the will to ignore the pain and eventually reached the sea.

Alfie managed to find a life-belt for one of our group who could not swim and keeping him in the middle, we took off for one of the destroyers. During our swim we could feel the impact of the depth charges which were being thrown from the destroyers, dashing about in their hunt for *U-372,* and en-route we encountered the chaplain who was paddling along on a packing case of sorts. He asked us if we were all OK and then paddled serenely on his way.

Our group duly arrived safely alongside HMS *Hero,* where serving on board, but unknown to me at this time, was my old school friend and classmate of 1921, Bill Glanville, who as I mentioned earlier became Lord Mayor of Plymouth in 1987.

After being pulled up the side of HMS *Hero* came shock number two for me. As a result of discarding my shoes, together I might add with literally hundreds of others, I was compelled to stand upon the red hot steel upper deck. My feet were already in a mess from the barnacles and I had to keep shifting from one foot to the other for some relief. Eventually, hoses were rigged and sea water was pumped over the deck, which helped a bit.

Situated as I was on the fo'c's'le, where everyone was more or less concerned for themselves, I hardly took any notice of one poor chap near to me who remarked, 'I didn't think I was going to make it, I can hardly swim.' With that he just sank to the deck and died. All of us were helpless, we knew nothing in those days about the art of mouth to mouth resuscitation.

The *Medway* gave one last groan, lurched upwards and then slid beneath the waves, stern first. The *Hero* continued to pick up men from the sea and finally took off for Port Said, which was the nearest place us survivors could be accommodated. Considering our condition, our passage was not unduly uncomfortable, until the sun went down. Most of us only had our underclothes on and had to huddle together in groups for protection from the wind created by the speed of the ship. Our underwear eventually dried off, but this was small comfort in the freezing night air.

Our arrival and greeting at Port Said was a shambles, we were treated like sheep being taken to market, except our destination was a transit camp on the edge of the desert. Here we were given one hairy blanket, not the woven variety, old soldiers will know what I mean. Also, we acquired an enamel plate with a tablespoon. Upon this plate was dumped, mashed potatoes, corned beef, beetroot, prunes, pineapple chunks, a dollop of margarine and a couple of slices of bread. Our instructions were to go and find somewhere in the sand to lie down until morning when we could be sorted out.

It was pitch dark and no lights were allowed. There we were wandering around with our grub and blanket, falling over obstacles such as guy ropes and tents, bumping into portable latrines, falling into trenches or pits, and all during an air raid in which those screaming wires on parachutes were fired up at enemy planes — this frightened the life out of me more than being torpedoed.

At dawn, we looked like the lost tribe of Israel. Some army sergeants directed us to a make shift kitchen where a breakfast of sorts was served to us. I received a couple of slices of bread and margarine, two soya link sausages, one piece of bacon and a hard boiled egg. Later, we were told by an army officer that we would be receiving emergency Red Cross clothing and also some money.

Later in the morning, a couple of lorries arrived amongst us and we were given a Red Cross bag in which was a small cloth affair containing a pair of 'Fitzherbert' pyjamas. The bag also contained a small bar of soap and flannel together with a toothbrush, powdered toothpaste and a comb. Another lorry arrived with boots and shoes and these were thrown out to us by two army lads on the reply to their shouts of ' Who wants a pair of sixes or eights or nines ?' Later on we managed to acquire socks, shorts or trousers and a shirt.

What a right shower we must have looked when we arrived at the pay tent and formed up in single file. We had to walk through to a wooden table where an army paymaster dished out £10 and this was recorded by another army chap at his side. The standard practice was to pick up your £10, march out of the tent to rejoin the queue in order to march through again. By which time you would have thought of a new identity and official number to collect another £10. Win some, lose some as the army type said on running out of cash.

Alfie and I had a couple of good runs ashore in Port Said whilst our money lasted, but we were soon on the move again, this time to Haifa, which I understood had been the intended destination of the *Medway*.

We caught one of the usual Egyptian trains where there are more passengers riding outside than in. The seats were made of solid wood and there was a constant stream of vendors passing through the train flogging their wares, shouting at the top of their voices, 'Eggs and bread, eggs or icy cold lemonade.'

Every so often the train stopped, sometimes at an official station, other times miles from anywhere. At each of these stops more people seemed to climb on to the train and it was a wonder the train could move at all. The journey was a nightmare and one that I was to repeat many times in the years that followed. Home seemed so far, far away at that particular time of my life.

CHAPTER 25

At Haifa we were based in a transit camp at the edge of the town. Submarines arriving from patrol were accommodated alongside destroyers or other ships in harbour. Here they were continually disturbed because of the movements of the ships they were secured to. We did have some workshops on shore, but in the main the majority of repairs were carried out at Port Said.

My main job was to take a working party of stokers down to the harbour base daily and to bring them back to camp and that was it. I had no other duties to perform, well, not for the Navy anyway. I was bored to tears until I discovered a small café bar along the sea front a short distance from the camp. It had a small dance floor at the side where a group of maybe three or four musicians would normally be playing.

I loved this place and frequented it almost every night. Beer was one shilling for a large glass. Well, one night at the camp, I found myself down to my last two shillings and was trying to decide whether or not to risk going down to the café, knowing that if I did dance with anyone, I could not afford to invite them for a drink.

My route to the sea front took me down a lovely tree lined avenue with houses on both sides all possessing large front gardens. I took particular note of a house about the third or fourth on my right hand side. This was because I briefly glanced towards a couple seated at a table drinking. The man, who appeared to be quite elderly, was wearing khaki shirt and shorts and the lady, a white blouse and blue shorts. They were the only people I saw as I made my way to the front. I spent an hour or so at the café and just enjoyed listening to the music and drinking my two beers. Being flat broke, I decided to return to the camp, or rather that was my intention.

On my way back, I saw a young woman come out of the front gate of the house in which I had earlier seen the couple in the garden. As she approached me, I could see that it was the same woman. She passed me on the inside because I had moved to the outer side, she smiled and walked slowly on. With thoughts racing through my head as to whether to talk to her, she turned to look towards me and paused.

Well, that was enough for me, I walked back toward her as she had stopped and I assumed correctly that it was an invitation to talk. Reaching her I asked whether she was going to the café or was just out for a walk, hoping against hope that she would not say café, with me being broke. Thinking quickly before she had time to answer my question, I said that I had just come from there and did not think it was very good that night. She then replied that she had only come out of the house for a short walk around the block, so I asked if I might accompany her. She smiled and simply said 'Yes.'

We walked and talked about generalities until we arrived back at her house where we stood and continued to talk. She enquired as to what time I had to return to camp to which I replied that as long as I was there for 7 am the following morning, my time was my own. I was then invited into the garden for a drink.

I sat alone at the table whilst she entered the house in order to fetch the drink which turned out to be a home-made concoction, similar to Sangria. My companion brought out a tray with three glasses and a large jug of the drink, which was cool, pleasant to the taste and potent, as I later discovered.

The three glasses puzzled me momentarily, but it was explained almost immediately by the appearance of an older man who came out of the house and whom I assumed incorrectly to be her father. I rose to greet him and was introduced by Sonia, my companion, as follows. 'Fred this is my husband Karl.'

Well, I was speechless at first, but quickly recovered and made the usual response of how do you do etc. and resumed my seat to a turmoil of thoughts.

We talked of a few personal details, home, status, hopes and general mundane things. At no time did they enquire into details of my job. I feel that I would have been on guard if they had. I discovered that they had got out of Austria in 1936 having realised that the situation was rapidly becoming intolerable for Jewish people such as themselves. Also, they more or less informed me that theirs was a marriage of convenience, adding that I was no doubt curious about the age gap between them, which must have been in the region of thirty years or so.

I assured them that I had read a great deal about the troubles in Austria and knew that the Jewish people were trying to reach Palestine by every means possible. The talk continued and the jug was refilled two or three times.

At some point in the conversation I felt Sonia's bare knee brush against mine beneath the table and it remained touching. Obviously, I knew then that I could have her for the asking, but how could I accomplish it?

Would it be possible to take her for a walk along the front when it was really dark. Quite suddenly the solution came from Karl himself, he announced that he had drunk sufficient and was now off to his bed, explaining that he always slept alone on the veranda at the rear of the house because of breathing difficulties, adding that he would try not to disturb anyone. Well, if that was not explaining the situation to me, why tell me?

Sonia and I remained in the garden for about another thirty minutes before she said, 'Come on, let's go to bed' — just like that!

I carried the tray indoors to the kitchen, then she immediately took me to the bedroom and got undressed in about five seconds flat. It took me about five seconds longer and she was at it before we could hit the bed. Sonia was a right 'goer' and must surely have been without for quite some time I would think, perpetual motion was her middle name.

After our first session I was breaking my neck for a pee so I went to the bathroom, when I returned, she immediately got astride me. I managed to perform and then fell asleep only to be woken up after a couple of hours to find her wanting it again. I duly obliged and shattered I fell asleep.

The following evening I returned to the house at about 6.30 pm, Karl had conveniently absented himself and Sonia was at it practically before I could get my pants off.

Fate stepped in to save me from 'Bar Mitzvah' at my mature age, because I was ordered to Beirut with the rest of my party. This was to take over a recently vacated French barracks, which we would transform into Medway 2. I had promised to keep in touch with Sonia and said I would try to visit her sometime. This I managed to do on three occasions and very nice it was too.

On my first night in the barracks at Beirut about six of us shared a room. Later, chiefs and petty officers were to share cabins, cells actually, two to each one, but on our first night the six of us in our room settled down for a good night's rest.

We were awake at daylight to a nasty shock, all our clothing had been pinched and only the chaps who had pushed their shoes under the bed still had any footwear. The local thieves were responsible, they had removed our gear through the open windows by means of fishing rods or such like, in spite of the perpendicular iron bars which ran down the whole length of the windows.

Most of my working hours as spare crew were spent assisting Petty Officer Osborne who was in charge of our oil stores. My leisure periods were spent in either playing cards, visiting the cabarets or attending French lessons. Learning the language that is, with Alfie Backers at the American University. Alfie was well in with the teacher and was also very friendly with a family who lived in the street opposite the University.

I could cry when I think of what is happening to Beirut today, because in my time during the war, it was a fabulous city surrounded by lovely little villages and resorts in the adjacent hills and mountains.

I decided at this time to try for my boiler room watch-keeping certificates, this was necessary before I could get a progressive, which would mean a little extra money. It was also needed before I could be considered for advancement, this latter point did not worry me because it was my intention to leave the Navy when I had served my twelve years, ending October 1944. With the war beginning to turn in our favour it seemed that I would stand a very good chance of being out on time, or so I thought.

Would you believe it? I was sent down to Haifa to await a suitable ship in which I would be able to do my watch-keeping course. There wasn't any immediately available, so I was billeted back in the transit camp. This suited me because I had now completely regained my strength, and felt able to do battle with Sonia.

As soon as I could on reaching Haifa I set off to Sonia's house. Quite by chance she had been looking through her window and saw me reach the front gate. I walked down the path and stepped through the partially open front door to find her standing there starkers. Sonia was fast alright, she could trip you up and be underneath you before you hit the ground. Karl, it appears, was in hospital being treated for gail stones. Much more of Sonia and I thought I would probably be joining him!

On my second day at the camp, a large notice appeared on the main notice board on the gate.

WANTED — STOKER PETTY OFFICERS AND STOKERS WITH DIESEL EXPERIENCE FOR SPECIAL DUTIES.

I didn't pay a great deal of attention to this notice until I heard it discussed in the mess that evening. It was then that some 'know it all' just out from the UK, with his knees still white, said that he knew what these volunteers were required for, adding that he wished he was experienced with diesels. He then went on to explain what was required. He said that there were thousands of landing craft being prepared in England for the invasion of Europe and they were driven by diesel engines situated in the stern of the vessel. All that would be required would be to run the vessel close to the beach, off load the vehicles and troops then return across the channel for another load. Dead easy he said for the stoker petty officers and stokers, who would be driving. I asked him if it was dangerous and he jokingly answered me by saying you couldn't get hit at the back behind the engine!

I thought about it all night long and the chance to go home was too much of an opportunity to miss so I decided that first thing the next morning I would put my name down.

PART THREE - ODDBALL

CHAPTER 26

Although the maxim is never volunteer, I did just that and this book is the result of that action. On reflection, I would do it all over again, just to meet some of the finest chaps it has ever been my privilege to know and serve with.

Within three days, I was ordered to proceed to Cairo for an interview in room 213 or similar number at the GHQ. This seemed rather odd to me somehow and I was puzzled throughout the whole of my journey on that damnable train back to Egypt.

Arriving in Cairo I reported in at the station and was taken to GHQ in a truck. I was then directed to the particular room scheduled for my interview. On entering the room I was surprised to find about twenty other servicemen — petty officers and stokers, army sergeants and privates. Talking amongst ourselves brought us no nearer to the real reason for our being there, however, we did not have to wait long to be enlightened.

We were all seated on wooden chairs in about three rows facing a small table with two chairs, behind which was a large blackboard. I had been there about fifteen minutes or so when a two-ringed Wren officer entered carrying a clipboard upon which she noted our individual names and rank. She went on to explain that in a few minutes a couple of officers would arrive to give us the details of the special operations for which we had volunteered.

This all seemed ominous to me and I was beginning to have second thoughts which were telling me that this job, whatever it was, had nothing whatever to do with going home to the UK in order to drive invasion craft for the second front.

The Wren left our list of names on the table and walked out of the room, you could have heard a pin drop. Within a few minutes a naval officer accompanied by an army officer, entered the room. I believe the army chap was a captain and the naval one a commander.

After greeting us, the naval chap went on to explain that a new force was being formed, but not yet named, to carry out reconnaissance missions in the Aegean Sea. This would involve secret landings being made on various Islands. A number of caiques, small Greek fishing or trading vessels, had been acquired and we would be required to handle them. Outwardly, they would look the same as an ordinary Greek caique, but internally they would be fitted with large fuel tanks and a powerful diesel engine. The engines would be the same as the ones which powered some of our tanks in the desert.

Before the area of operations had been disclosed to us, we had been asked whether or not we wished to opt out in which case we could return to our various units at once. When we were called upon individually, we all decided that we wanted to sign up. Don't ask me why, I have no idea. Perhaps we all wanted a change from the usual service routine and it did sound exciting swanning about the Greek islands like a group of latter day pirates.

We were given a little more information, such as our dress would be casual and nondescript whilst on operations and there would be about four or five in each crew, including one officer.

The briefing went on to explain that from time to time we would be carrying additional personnel, members of the Special Boat Squadron or Long Range Desert Group and such like, and we would be called upon to assist them in every way to help them complete their operations. It was explained that this information was all that could possibly be given to us at that point in time. When the interview was over we reported to HMS *Nile* — a shore base in Alex. This base also went under the name of *Sphinx* or *Mosquito*.

After a couple of days, I found myself on the train once more heading for Beirut — I just couldn't believe it. There were a number of us travelling together so the main topic of our conversation during the journey was naturally enough about our new job. At no time did I consider that I had volunteered for anything dangerous, after all I had previously been depth charged, bombed and torpedoed and I reasoned that this couldn't be any worse.

Arriving in Beirut, we reported to HMS *Martial,* a small ex-French depot situated in the city itself. The depot was quite close to the docks where our newly formed unit had acquired a couple of sheds with landing facilities and where we also had a mess room of sorts. We were, however, billeted in private hotels. I lasted a couple of days there with another SPO, 'Jock' Weeks and a few stokers. We were entrained once more back to Cairo in order to undergo a training course on diesel tank engines, similar to the type which were to be fitted into our boats. The course was at Abbassea, a large army barracks on the outskirts of the city and close to the airport.

We petty officers and the ERA were billeted in the sergeants' mess, but slept in one of the small huts containing about a dozen or so men. On our first morning we were woken up by the shouts of gunfire and hundreds of men rushing across the parade ground waving enamel mugs above their heads. The explanation was soon forthcoming from one of the sergeants who explained that this was the army cry for early morning tea. Subsequently, every morning thereafter, I joined the rush with my mug. We all suspected that this was how the Army administered the Epsom Salts and Bromide.

I really enjoyed the course on the tank engines and I took a number of trips over the testing ranges in both a 'General Grant' and 'Sherman' tank. Both of which had recently inflicted such havoc upon Rommel's forces at El Alamein. My admiration went out to the chaps manning them. I would much rather be in a submarine any time. With my course completed, it was back on the train to Beirut, but I did manage a few good nights out in Cairo during my stay at Abbassea.

On this occasion in Beirut, I shared a room with another chap in a different hotel, it was very fourth rate and close to both HMS *Martial* and the brothel area, just off the main square, which was naturally out of bounds. This notice was ignored by quite a few intrepid servicemen, especially the 'Aussies' who didn't give a 'monkeys' for notices of that nature. My room at the hotel had the customary french windows which opened onto a small balcony above the main thoroughfare of the brothel area. From the balcony, I could see it all happening in various rooms just across the narrow street. Sometimes I am sure that the pantomimes were staged for my benefit.

With a large fishing rod, I'm sure I could have reached the balcony opposite our room. Curtains were rarely drawn and the windows were left wide open. Some of the performances were quite stimulating, but as I have written earlier, I never did take to this buying and selling of sex, though in my opinion, it was necessary in those days as the only means of relief for some.

I was happy to leave this doss house after a few days, mainly because after dusk the floors were carpeted with cockroaches, especially the toilets where one could hear them cracking under one's feet in the dark. Invariably, someone had pinched the light bulb in the toilet, to replace the one which had gone in their own room.

Very soon I was off again on my travels, but not very far on this occasion. With a number of other lads from my outfit I travelled to a little place outside Beirut, where a detachment of the Fourth Indian Division, who specialised in the art of camouflage, were camped. Camouflage is indeed an art and these specialists made it so. I was simply amazed at some of the things these chaps concealed with so little material. I certainly learnt a great deal about the simple techniques of camouflage. For example, how to break up the outline of the object to be concealed, not to create shadows, to be very careful of things which might reflect and the use of ordinary netting with small branches of foliage and a few bamboo poles as spreaders.

An instructor took us to a hill to look down into a small valley where he explained a number of his men were concealed together with a mock-up of a caique measuring about 30ft by 7ft. He invited us to spend a few minutes trying to detect it from a distance of a couple hundred yards. Well, one or two of us thought we could see it, or some of the men. We pointed in the general direction, but we were quite wrong as we discovered when a whistle was blown and the men stood up to reveal themselves and uncovered the camouflage mock-up of the caique. There were at least twenty men and the mock-up had been laid out in roughly the shape of a caique by the use of empty petrol cans, packing cases and ordinary dull green netting.

It just had to be seen to be believed. We had been standing still whilst trying to detect it, so I would say that it would have been almost impossible to have been seen by a passing patrol vessel or spotted from the air.

Back in Beirut we found that everyone had now been found a billet in HMS *Martial*. This was good news because hygiene in the places where we had previously been billeted left a lot to be desired.

Let me mention some of my contemporaries in our newly formed outfit. Amongst the officers at this time to assist Adrian Seligman, the commanding officer, were a couple of army officers. Captain Gardner was our supplies officer and Captain Benyon-Tinker was the intelligence and gunnery officer. There was also Lieutenant Commander Andre Londos of the Royal Hellenic Navy and Lieutenant McLeod RNVR. Eventually, more officers joined us.

Captains Gardner and Benyon-Tinker were assisted by a very able and resourceful sergeant, a chap named Jones. Between the three of them, it appeared that anything was possible to obtain. Jones was a right schemer and a damned good gunnery chap to boot. We had an army sergeant fitter from the Tank Corps who was an expert with Matilda engines — he was known as 'Tanky' Rowlands. There was a carpenter shipwright, 'Chippy' Nineham, an army private who later transferred to the Royal Navy and was immediately upgraded to the rank of petty officer. Henry — such was his Christian name was a very good pal of mine and remained so until his death about ten years ago. We also had an ERA, 'Jock' Andrews, who doubled up on engines with 'Tanky' Rowlands. There was also a Scot named Weeks, an SPO like myself. He was always half-pissed in harbour, quite fluent in french, he was very friendly with a family who owned a vinery, hence his condition. He was also a very good friend in more ways than one, as he fixed me up with a few good dates.

'Jock' Weeks was unfortunately lost, together with six others, when LS 4, one of our caiques, disappeared without trace on passage from Beirut to Cyprus. She was in company with LS 3, but the two boats parted company during the night crossing. It was widely believed that LS 4 was a victim of U-boats operating in the area. This was a tragic loss to our newly formed flotilla.

Adrian Seligman soon got down to the serious business of our training once we had three boats fitted out and ready for service. You could not help but get excited at the thought of the adventures that lay ahead and I do not think for one minute I considered the dangers of our intended operations.

The base was well organized and when one considers the odd and individual characters amongst us, discipline and routine were first class. In the main, I suspect that all of us were in effect eager beavers with a zest for a complete change from our previous occupations and their strict routines. This does not suggest that we were casual in our approach to our officers or to our tasks, quite the reverse in fact, because of our longing to be part of a well trained unit. Another important factor was that we were formed into groups of about half a dozen men which relied entirely upon one another and we knew precisely what was happening, instead of taking and obeying orders without knowing why, this was a completely new dimension for all of us.

Initially, our boats were very small indeed, some ten to twenty tons. The insides were completely gutted in order that a large diesel engine could be installed together with equally large fuel tanks. This enabled us to travel to many islands in the Aegean without having to refuel. However, on many occasions, we were able to use the sail as our main means of propulsion, thus saving our essential fuel supplies.

After we had stowed our equipment, such as sleeping bags, food, our ᷉ons and camouflage gear etc., there was absolutely nowhere to shelter ᷉deck. Perhaps two could crouch together in the forward stowage space, but their heads would practically be above deck. There was room to move around the engine compartment, but even this held guns and boxes of grenades.

The crew ate and slept on the open deck, sometimes using the sail as a makeshift tent, we washed in sea water, but a drop of fresh water was permitted for teeth cleaning. If one wanted a pee or a big job, it was over the side.

We were armed to the teeth, quite capable of starting a revolution in some parts of the world. We all possessed our own .38 revolver and a tommy gun or carbine and our boats were fitted out with mountings to take .303 Vickers machine guns and .50 calibre Colt-Brownings. Even the smallest vessel could mount a 20 mm Solithurn anti-tank rifle up forward. You had to be careful firing this weapon, especially when the boat was rolling.

Apart from all this, we also had boxes of hand grenades and mills bombs. On one occasion when I was doing a trip with the intrepid duo, Gunners Perry and MacCormack, they acquired, seemingly from thin air, a I" or 2" mortar. They would sit or rather balance on the gunwale and take turns to load and fire it into the sea, in order to supply everyone with fresh fish, or so they said.

Everyone, irrespective of rank or rating, was taught how to handle and respect our variety of weapons and how to maintain them. My old pal Alfie Backers would have loved the life, he was of the swashbuckler type and a good man to have in one's corner.

When our first three boats and their crews were ready, Adrian started us off on our training proper. This included many night exercises just north of Beirut where the coastline afforded many small inlets, ideal for our training of stealing into the rugged coastline of the many enemy islands we would be visiting. We practised the landing and retrieving of groups of SBS (Special Boat Squadron) personnel, together with their equipment. No small feat when one takes into account the size of some of our boats which had just about enough room for the crew.

Once we landed our passengers safely, the boat then had to be secured with great care and suitably camouflaged, because although all our operations were to be carried out in total darkness, on what hopefully would be unoccupied coastlines, we might be required to remain 'doggo' during the following daylight hours to await the return of our SBS pals — hence the camouflage.

Adrian was a stickler for detail, in as much as it could be applied to our type of operations, he was also a great navigator who seemingly had eyes that could out see any cat in the dark. 'Turn in here to starboard,' he would say to whoever was manning the tiller and sure enough we would be precisely where he wanted us to be.

Having completed our training, it was decided that two boats *LS 1* and *LS 2* were ready to set sail for Paphos in Cyprus, there to carry out just a couple more exercises together before going our separate ways.

In early June 1943, at about 5 pm one evening, our two little boats quietly slipped away from the base accompanied by the good wishes and waves of our colleagues. They would shortly follow us as soon as their respective boats were ready. The two caiques rounded the end of the harbour mole, then headed for the open sea. The sun was on its way down and as we would lose all sight of land in the fast receding light, it was necessary for us to make doubly sure that everything was secured in place and ready for whatever was in front of us.

Here it should be pointed out that these two craft, *LS 1* and *LS 2,* were the pathfinders, because although caiques such as these had been sailing the open seas for perhaps hundreds of years, I would venture to suggest that they had never been equipped or loaded such as we. Heaven only knows what our true weight was when you take into account the heavy diesel engine, fuel tanks to port and starboard, together with all our arms, ammunition, food and equipment. The distribution of all these items was very important for the safety of the craft and ourselves, as yet untried over a long sea passage.

Nightfall came all too quickly and to avoid a collision our two little craft increased the distance from each other, but true to Adrian's motto, the caiques 'stood boldly on'. Next stop was Paphos and then who knows?

With Beirut many miles astern we soon found ourselves heading into a strong wind and sea. In fact, we were soon literally ploughing into it with our bows plunging up and down, throwing some large waves over us so we eased down a little because we were all getting very wet. Fortunately, it was a warm night so we did not feel too cold against the night air and I with others managed to drop off to sleep for a couple of hours.

The controls of the engine were only a matter of feet from the tiller and there were many occasions when I took my turn to steer our tiny craft by the phosphorescent glow from the compass which was an RAF type.

Sitting alone on a moonlit night, with my arm resting upon the tiller of our small caique whilst she quietly ploughed her way through a moderate sea, was one of the most wonderful experiences I ever had. Some lovely thoughts entered my head at times such as these and being the romantic that I am, I invariably emulated 'Walter Mitty'. It was perhaps just as well that two others were always awake and alert, because I am quite sure that there were occasions when I was a subject of self-hypnosis and in a world of my own.

We made landfall at Cape Gata in a rain storm at dawn, just when we were hoping for the sun to come up to dry us all out after a very wet crossing from Beirut. However, it turned out just to be a very bad squall which soon passed, so still having forty miles or so to travel along the coast to Paphos, we all stripped off and hung our sodden clothing in the rigging to catch the fair breeze which came up. Then out came our primus stoves, frying pans, bacon and eggs and beans, it was beautiful and the war seemed so far away then!

With the sail up, we reached Paphos in about five or six hours. *LS 2* arrived quite safely after us, experiencing the same wet crossing as ourselves. We were due to part company with her a few days later to become the first boat to actually set off on operations proper. I couldn't wait! We had also acquired a name, we were now known as the Levant Schooner Flotilla.

CHAPTER 27

Our final day in Paphos was taken up by us taking on maximum fuel and food, checking all our equipment, writing letters home and having a final drink ashore with the lads from *LS 2*.

We also acquired two extra crew in the shape of a couple of SBS men, Captain Chevalier and Sergeant George 'Lofty' Miller. These two chaps soon settled down to become welcome members of the crew which now numbered seven in total. We were due to leave early the next morning and make the crossing to the Turkish mainland to a point just to the east of the Italian island of Casteloriso.

It was a lovely day when little *LS 1*, with her crew of five armed to the teeth, ready to do battle with all comers and bolstered by two dauntless SBS men, set forth into the unknown. I say unknown, because our Greek commander, Andre Londos, did not divulge to any of us what his terms of reference were until we were at sea.

We reached the Turkish coast and proceeded westward along it in order to steal past Casteloriso at night. The high rugged Turkish mainland was on our starboard side and in the darkness it shielded our small craft from the Italians on the island, roughly about a half to three quarters of a mile distant.

Everything went as planned and we passed the island without any problems. Unable to take the greater risk of trying to creep past the formidable island of Rhodes, Andre decided to find a little uninhabited inlet on the Turkish coast with which he was very familiar, there to hide up under camouflage during daylight hours and go on our way at dusk.

Hidden from everyone, except wildlife, we all had a good meal and rested, then as the sun began to set we rigged our sail, hoisted the Turkish flag and headed for Rhodes with just a fair bit of apprehension. I personally didn't feel any fear as to what might happen, quite the reverse, I was elated and just couldn't wait to get to grips with whatever lay ahead, this feeling I am sure was prevalent throughout the whole crew.

During our rest-up in the little Turkish inlet Andre gave us the main outline of his orders. We were required to visit a number of the smaller islands in order to discover at first hand whether or not they were garrisoned by Italians or Germans, or if they were just visited occasionally by patrols. Our orders were also to obtain an estimate of the strength of garrisons and patrols, what facilities there were for possible landings by our forces, suitable beaches and isolated inlets that could be used and other useful information.

The plan was for Andre, who was fluent in both Italian and Turkish, to go ashore with either Captain Chevalier or Sergeant Miller as his minder. Both would be dressed in nondescript clothes, as were we all. The two of them would tour as much of the island as possible to talk with any shepherds and visit any smallholdings they encountered. Andre explained that it might be necessary for us to land in a variety of locations and that we would have to remain hidden w' his team were ashore. In actual fact, there were occasions on many of our landings when they were gone for most of the day.

But back to our approach to Rhodes, where the Germans were now firmly entrenched, the plan was to sneak quietly past, hugging the Turkish coast as we had done the previous night at Casteloriso. We had to be more alert because although Rhodes was some distance from us, perhaps some ten to fifteen miles away, the area was subjected to searching sweeps by enemy patrol boats and aircraft.

Fortunately, it was a cloudy night with not much wind or sea as we made our approach to round the northern most tip of the island. Andre decided that the two SBS men would rest and would only be called upon if an emergency arose. Consequently, he positioned himself at the bow as he always did, just aft of him was our telegraphist, Carpenter, amidships sat Gunner 'Taff' Perry, then at the stern was myself at the engine controls and within arms length of my back was our coxswain on the tiller.

About two or three hours or so before we would get to our nearest point to the island 'Taff' Perry came aft to tell me that because of our gently rolling from side to side in the swell our engine exhaust was throwing up spurts of sea water, which appeared phosphorescent and could be seen. We cured this by draping some weighted wet sacking over it.

Shortly after this incident, perhaps half an hour or so, back came 'Taff' again to say 'Fred, can you see anything away to port, or is it my imagination?' I throttled back on the engine sufficiently enough to reduce the sound without jeopardising our forward movement.

Looking through the night glasses, not only could I see something, I found that I could also hear the rhythm of powerful engines. 'Bloody hell,' I said, 'it's a German E-boat, capable of blowing us and our little craft to kingdom come.'

Andre, by this time, was also aware of the situation and had alerted our SBS men. He told us to keep as quiet as possible, cut our speed, train as many weapons as we could towards port and then wait for any command from him.

I don't remember being afraid, but I certainly remember the adrenaline pumping through my veins, the butterflies in my stomach and my mouth being as dry as sand paper.

Captain Chevalier, 'Lofty' Miller and Gunner Perry, had quietly rigged a couple of machine guns and we all had our individual arms, mine was a tommy gun, cocked and ready, I even had an open box of hand grenades at my side. With everything ready we waited for the enemy to close us.

Suddenly, the E-boat, which had been on an opposite course to ourselves, turned to starboard in a wide sweep and proceeded onwards, presumably back to where she came. If she had turned to port instead, she would have surely spotted us because we could not have been more than eight to ten hundred yards from her. Fortunately, we were low in the water against the back drop of rugged darkened Turkish coast.

We decided that was enough thrills for one night, but none of us could s there was quite some distance to go before we rounded the tip of the island. In fact it took me quite a while and in comparative safety, before I felt at ease. I felt exhausted, the tension had been electric.

The rest of the night passed without further incident, but none of us settled down at all. We remained fully anchored to our weapons, not daring to even light a cigarette. We were well safe as the first streaks of daylight entered the sky and Andre decided to find a secluded inlet on the Turkish coast for us to rest up.

Andre informed us that the part of the coast where we were hidden was alive with partridges, so whilst the others were bedded down, Sergeant Miller, 'Taff' Perry and myself went ashore to bag us a brace or two. This part of the coast, we were told, was largely uninhabited and after a scout around we managed to disturb quite a flock of birds, which took to the air. I blazed away at one with about half a magazine of bullets, but didn't hit a sausage. My two companions both had American carbines, 'Taff' brought one down, but 'Lofty' missed completely. Perhaps it was a good thing that I missed because any bird I would have hit, would surely have been torn to shreds with .45 bullets.

Suddenly, whilst we were firing, there leapt out from behind some rocks an elderly woman dressed in red pantaloons, a dark coloured jumper and a head dress of sorts. I can still see this poor old soul today jumping up into the air and waving her arms about like a demented dervish. We held up our arms as a gesture to calm her before we approached her position and it was then that we could see in the distance, some sort of dwelling. The old lady had apparently been attending to a small cultivated vegetable patch, we eventually had her smiling again when we gave her all our remaining cigarettes. We then returned to the boat with our prize of one partridge to receive a right 'rollicking' from Andre for our escapade.

Almost before the first streaks of daylight came into the sky, we had stowed everything, breakfasted and were on our way to the small island of Patmos, some hundred miles or so distant and Andre thought that this island could be garrisoned, so we must be on our toes. The island was one of a small group to the north of Kos and Leros, both of which were known to be garrisoned. It was also about twenty to thirty miles to the south west of Samos which was not only garrisoned, but also possessed an airstrip.

Our little craft was bowling along under a lovely blue sky with just a moderate sea running and we were taking things easy after checking that everything was as it should be when quite suddenly the sound of an aircraft was heard and it was becoming louder. Andre immediately shouted, 'Behave normally — and keep your guns hidden!' At the time we were flying the Turkish flag and Andre hoped that the aircraft would accept us a neutral vessel.

The aircraft, which turned out to be an Italian seaplane, approached us from the stern and could only have been a hundred feet or so above the sea. It was probably on anti-submarine patrol, however, it flew right over us and Andre shouted, 'Everyone wave' which we all did, whereupon the pilot pulled back the canopy of his cockpit, leaned out and waved back. As he disappeared into the distance I raised two fingers in his direction.

Well, that was thrill number two and the old adrenaline had arisen in us all again. With me it took quite a while to subside, but once again I felt no trace of fear, I didn't even think about the consequences of what might have been.

All the crew, including the SBS men, were by this time familiar with procedures, equipment, camouflage and the various tasks allotted to us all. In short, we were a team and a damned good one to boot! We could creep into an inlet under the cover of darkness, secure and hide the boat and ourselves practically blindfolded. I loved every minute of it and all thoughts of my private life at home receded into the far corners of my mind.

CHAPTER 28

A ndre decided to go around the southern tip of Kos in order to keep the group of islands of Kalymnos and Leros on our starboard side. There were quite a number of islands associated with these two, but by taking the course he had chosen we had a direct run to Patmos which we reached after dark without further incident. Once we located a suitable inlet we secured and camouflaged our caique and settled down to catch some sleep and await first light.

At daybreak we prepared a simple breakfast on our primus stoves and Andre outlined his plans for the day. He told us that in company with his minders, Captain Chevalier and Sergeant Miller, he would carry out a detailed reconnaissance of the area. One of them would return before sunset, but in the unlikely event neither of them returned, the rest of us must remain where we were for at least twenty four hours before attempting to leave the island and then only under the cover of darkness. The coxswain would then assume command and make whatever decisions were necessary to get us back to Cyprus.

Whilst our companions were gone, only 'Taff' ventured forth from our hiding place, this he informed us was to try and catch some fish. His normal practice was to throw a hand grenade into the sea, but the coxswain would have none of it. However, our intrepid fisherman came back with a capful of winkles and other assorted shell fish.

It was late afternoon when our three explorers returned to sighs of relief from those of us who had remained behind. Although they had been moving about the island and mixing with people, we had remained relatively hidden and that in itself was a stressful experience. You had too much time to think about the consequences if you were discovered.

After a cook-up Andre related their adventures. They had covered quite a large area and Andre had spoken with a number of shepherds whilst the two SBS men concealed themselves at a discreet distance. Andre had passed himself off either as a naturalist or someone taking preliminary surveys of the area in order to build a small house for himself. During his forays, he used many excuses for his presence and I might add that he also possessed a supply of gold sovereigns in case he needed to bribe his way out of trouble.

When our explorers settled down to rest and make plans for their next excursion, we others took turns to bathe with our cakes of salt water soap, and exercised by clambering over the rocks.

After another meal we set off for the island of Mykonos, roughly seventy miles westward. Arriving after dark, we found a suitable hiding place; we never approached a possible landing place where even the slightest glimmer of an artificial light could be seen.

Once the caique was secured and camouflaged, we settled down to await daylight. This particular visit was almost identical to our visit to Patmos, except that on this occasion Gunner Perry accompanied Captain Chevalier in place of 'Lofty' Miller. The reason being that Andre wanted everyone to gain experience in explorations.

As before our men returned quite safely, but exhausted , with the information that the island was sparsely populated by hill farmers, shepherds and fishermen and had a small garrison of Italian soldiers.

Our fuel supply was quite healthy due to our frequent use of the sail and our food supplies were also good, however, after allowing for these two factors, Andre decided that we would not venture further north.

Making our way south, or rather southeast, we visited a couple of tiny islands, the name of one I cannot recall, but the other was I believe Kinaros. There was hardly anything to report from these two visits other than that they were unpopulated except for one lonely shepherd family.

Heading further south, Andre decided to visit the small island of Sirina. We made our approach as usual at night and under a cloudy sky, there was a normal type of sea running, not rough, but quite choppy. We were all at our usual position in the boat and Andre was standing in the bows relaying orders,

'Slow.'

'Port a little.'

'Starboard a bit', suddenly without warning, there was a sickening crunch and our forward motion came to an abrupt halt.

We had been holed in the fore-peak on the starboard bow after hitting a submerged sharp reef just off shore. Within seconds the sea was pouring in, in spite of the efforts of 'Taff Perry' to plug the hole with sleeping bags. We were flooded within minutes and began to slide off the small reef we had hit. Andre shouted for us all to grab what we could, keep together and swim for the shore.

At the time I was wearing a duffle coat and had a pair of night binoculars around my neck, I was also wearing a belt with a .38 revolver in a holster together with ammunition, but would you believe it, I was again without shoes. Would I ever learn?

I had been wearing the coat because of a breeze which had got up and my bare feet had been dangling in the engine compartment over the top of the engine and my shoes were drying out on the engine. The caique finally slid below the waves and we half swam, half scrambled ashore. I remember going under as I entered the sea, due to the weight of my coat, but somehow I managed to get ashore and scrambled onto the rocks.

When we were all ashore Andre took stock of the situation and decided we would remain on the rocks until daybreak, we found a suitable location and huddled together to keep warm. Not very much floated off from the dear little craft we had all grown to love, just two or three wooden camouflage poles. Eventually, we did wring out the duffle coat and propped it up with the poles to afford a partial shield from the night breeze.

After a very long night and much to our relief, the first light of dawn enabled us to see exactly where we were. What a relief it was to be able to move about and stretch our cramped arms and legs. However, the daylight also exposed the cuts and bruises we had all sustained from clambering up over the rocks in the dark.

Without a boat to get us home things looked pretty desperate, but I never doubted that we would get back. We were all alive and together and nobody had any broken bones. Only our pride had been dented!

We looked a fairly forlorn bunch moving about on the rocks to keep warm and on top of everything else we were all desperately hungry, a feeling which was to remain with most of us for quite some time. We were all naked as we had spread what clothing we had upon the rocks to catch the first rays of the sun. Taking stock of our possessions did not take very long, which in the main was the clothing we were wearing when the caique sank, underpants, khaki shirts and shorts.

Andre was wearing sandals and Captain Chevalier and Sergeant Miller were both wearing their SBS long stockings and commando boots, whilst the remainder of us were shoe-less. We also possessed three wooden poles or staves, one .38 revolver with about ten spare rounds, one pair of night binoculars, partially flooded, and one wet duffle coat weighing a ton. As you can see, we were still a formidable force, in spirit anyway.

After our clothing had partially dried, we dressed knowing that it would air off by our exertions, a conference was then held with Andre deciding that he would sally forth together with Sergeant Miller armed with the .38 revolver. The rest of us remained on the rocks with the order that we should not venture too far from our present position.

We decided that it was reasonably safe to collect shellfish from the shore and the coxswain, the telegraphist and Perry started the search. I remained with Captain Chevalier who, as luck would have it, had with him his 'housewife kit' which consisted of an assortment of pins, needles and threads. From this he made a hook from a safety pin and was successful in catching a number of small fish, after, I would add, seemingly hours of patient effort.

Our three foragers returned with some bottles they had found which they had filled with rainwater from pools situated above the water line. They also found a few large rusty tins which did not leak. With tinder which had been gathered from the immediate area, Captain Chevalier managed to start a fire by using the bottom of one of the bottles as a magnifying glass against the very hot rays of the sun, which by then was quite strong in a cloudless sky.

By this time we had discovered that we were nowhere near any sign of habitation and consequently were not too concerned about getting a fire going and it really did cheer us up.

It was about mid-afternoon when Andre and 'Lofty' returned to say that there was just one shepherd family on the island, comprising of a man in his fifties, together with his wife, a son who was probably in his late twenties and a daughter in her early twenties. They appeared friendly and had given Andre two round loaves of bread for us, which we devoured as he was talking.

He went on to explain that they could not shelter us, but would give us food whilst we were on the island. The shepherd told Andre that it would be best if we took shelter during the night in one of the many caves scattered about the island. This seemed fair enough, so off we went to their dwelling place which was quite a slow process for those of us who were without footwear.

I had previously discovered a piece of rubber sheet washed up on the rocks and with needles and thread from Captain Chevalier's 'housewife' set about trying to make myself some sort of footwear. The completed shoes were a cross between sauce-boats and Turkish Caliph's shoes. However, they did afford a measure of protection from the sharp stones of the terrain over which we had to walk.

When we arrived at the shepherd's dwelling we discovered it to be a dry walled structure, how on earth the builders had managed to lift some of the stones, heaven only knows. There were huge boulders which must have weighed somewhere in the region of a couple of hundredweight each at the lower part of the dwelling which was split into two rooms. Between the stones there was some sort of cement or possibly clay. There were no windows as such, just one or two small openings, plus a hole in the roof which allowed the smoke from their fire to escape. The roof was made up of odd pieces of tin sheet, wood and branches etc.

The largest of the two rooms was a general purpose area where they ate, slept and spent their leisure hours, if any, and where they kept a fire burning in a stone structure in the centre of the room.

The other room was really fascinating as it contained a grinding mill, their kitchen and their stores. There were bunches of herbs, fish and meat hanging up to dry above a large stone oven and in the centre of the room was the mill, roughly 3ft high and about 3ft wide. Sunk into the centre of the platform was a thick round metal spindle, this in turn was threaded through a large round flat stone about 2ft in diameter, then set into the outer edge of this stone were a couple of small spindles. How this machine was put together was beyond my reasoning at the time, because I just cannot guess what the weight of the upper stone was. All this family had were a few small basic tools and implements, plus their bare hands. They must surely have had help from someone outside the island.

The mill was our main means of support, food wise that is, except for an occasional small fish that we would roast in the embers of the fire. 'Taff' Perry and myself used to help the mother grind the flour. She would tip the grains into a hole set into one of the stones and we would turn the other stone until the ground flour appeared at the edge.

The dear old soul would then make this flour into a dough, what on earth she used for yeast god only knows. Judging by the taste it was probably fermented fish, goat's pee or something equally as disgusting. The loaves when they were being baked smelt wonderful and when eaten hot or warm were quite good, but when they were cold, they were vile, just like sawdust.

The main meal for the family was invariably a stew prepared in a large iron pot, you name it and it was in the pot, spuds, vegetables, herbs, fish heads and bits of old goat or sheep. The family helped themselves from this pot by ladling out dollops of the stew onto their tin plates by means of a large enamel mug. Just one mouthful was enough for me, I never went near to that witches brew again, hungry or not.

I survived on hot bread, an occasional small fish and home-made cigarettes made from tobacco grown and dried by the son. We would roll the mixture in old newspaper, which was a precious commodity to the family I might add and was jealously guarded.

Our first full night was quite an experience, we had to get to our cave nearly a mile distant and over rough ground before nightfall. It was quite cold after sunset and our only protection from this was my duffle coat and three or four grotty hairy blankets which we borrowed from the family's small stock of possessions.

Huddling close together before we dropped off to sleep, we at length discussed our plight and possible outcome and unanimously decided that we must hijack the first visiting small craft to the island. Andre told us that we must be prepared to overpower the crew if they were unwilling to help us.

The dawn brought a revelation, there were sheep and goats everywhere and they had deposited their excrement all over us, we were plastered in the stuff and we smelt disgusting. Our day was spent on the beach where we had first landed, cleaning ourselves, our clothing, the blankets and my duffle coat. Everything was then rung out and spread upon the rocks to dry.

Later in the day, Andre and 'Lofty' returned to the shepherd family to explain what had happened and also to get some food for us. The coxswain and telegraphist volunteered to muck out the cave using brushes made from scrub and to find a means of securing the entrance once we were inside.

Whilst Captain Chevalier was trying to fish, 'Taff ' and myself, being good swimmers, tried to locate our ill fated craft, *LS 1*. This we did, it was easy to see her in the clear water, but she was far too deep to retrieve any salvage. We dived many times to try and reach her, but eventually exhausted by our efforts, we gave up. When we told Andre on his return, he decided to dive onto *LS I* himself and his eagerness prompted us to believe that he was after his precious cache of sovereigns. However, after carefully noting its location from landmarks, he too gave up.

With the exception of Andre, 'Lofty' Miller and Captain Chevalier, the rest of us were having foot problems. Mostly they were cuts and bruises which were eased to a certain extent by sitting on the rocks with our feet soaking in the sea for an hour or so.

It was discovered by Andre, in conversation with the family, that there were no set times for visits by people from adjacent islands. In the main the visits were made by four or five men in a small caique with the sole object of bartering with the shepherd. The normal trade, apparently, was olive oil, candles, second hand clothing, shoes, salt, tea and newspapers in return for sheep or goats. Our spirits flagged a little when Andre explained that it could be two, three or four weeks before they came. In view of this it was agreed that we would grab the first one to arrive by fair means or foul.

It was on the eighth or ninth day when Andre, on visiting the shepherd family, discovered three other men there trading goods for goats.

The father of the family had not disclosed to these men the presence of us on the island, this was left to Andre to explain after he was introduced to them. The caique they had arrived in, with two other men, was secured in a small inlet near to the house and Andre feared that if he left to inform the rest of us, the men, who incidentally were Greek, would leave the island and perhaps inform on us to some authority or the military. He, therefore, managed to persuade them to accompany him to where we were, in order he told them, to meet a very high ranking English officer, Captain Chevalier.

All our crew were within sight of one another when we saw Andre and the three men approaching and on meeting were introduced. Everything said was in Greek, so naturally Andre had to interpret for the rest of us. The gist being that Andre had promised them practically everything except the Greek throne if they would help us to escape to Cyprus or Beirut. He also told them that we were armed and if necessary would be compelled to use force. The three men questioned Andre as to how long it might be before they would be allowed to return home. Andre replied that it could be a week or two, but in the meantime he would try to get word to their families that they were safe and well. Upon hearing this, they agreed to help us, but added that the two men who were looking after the caique in their absence were young and impetuous and also at times rebellious.

Andre, therefore, decided upon the following strategy, he would approach them with 'Lofty', who would be armed with the .38 revolver, the remainder of us would stay in the background, together with the three Greek crewmen. Andre would then inform the other two men of what had been agreed between us all and ask for their cooperation. If they did not agree with our plans, he proposed to use force.

Initially, these two young men were indeed rebellious and wanted no part in helping us, but they were obviously impressed by Andre's commanding, forceful personality and eventually agreed to his plan.

We off loaded the supplies which had been brought for the shepherd family and took nothing in return. Andre assured everyone that they would all be more than compensated for their cooperation. With that we boarded the caique and set off to where, at the time, I knew not. But what a relief to be on the move once again.

CHAPTER 29

Our young Greek engineer had been persuaded to start the engine and Andre had asked me to check the fuel situation over a thirty minute run. This I did using a watch from one of the Greek crew. I came to the opinion that using the engine alone would give us an absolute maximum range of about eighty miles with a moderate sea. We were only capable of a speed of just around five knots or so.

There was a moderate breeze so the sail was set and the engine stopped Andre decided that we would only use it when absolutely necessary. He also informed us that he had decided to head for the neutral port of Marmaris on the Turkish coast where he had a few contacts. His main hope was that he would be able to obtain enough supplies of fuel and food to enable us to continue on our way without internment. Marmaris at that time was a very small unimportant place where any officialdom in Andre's opinion would be very third rate.

He told us that our journey would be hazardous and we must be continuously alert for mutiny by members of our Greek crew, who had been more or less hijacked. We had a distance of one hundred miles or so to travel as the crow flies and our approach to and beyond the German occupied islands would have to be accomplished during daylight hours. The waters around these islands were continually patrolled by the enemy and any small caiques that were discovered sneaking past at night would most certainly arouse suspicion, as it would be alien to their normal way of travelling from island to island.

It was with some trepidation that we approached the passage between Piskopi and Alimnia, the distance between the two being some ten to twelve miles. We were ready to restrain our two younger members of the crew in case they were tempted to raise the alarm if we were sighted by a patrol boat. However, with Andre continually assuring them of rewards, we passed safely through to our next hazard, the northern tip of Rhodes, some twenty five miles further on.

Andre decided to head north after passing Piskopi, because he wanted to approach Rhodes and round Cape Alupo on the Turkish mainland during the hours of darkness. By dawn we had safely reached the Turkish coast and hugged the coastline as we headed for our destination.

We eventually rounded Cape Marmaris, but as we made our approach to the small port, we came under small arms fire, seemingly from a lighthouse on shore. We immediately started to wave anything resembling white which we could find, whereupon the firing ceased. However, we were shortly met by an official launch which came alongside and escorted us into the harbour. Securing alongside the quay, we became the object of attention from seemingly most of the population. Dozens of officials and military personnel were on the boat and quayside, all talking and gesticulating at once with Andre in the thick of it. Not one word of English was spoken except by us British. All we could hear was a mixture of Greek and Turkish, sometimes heated, sometimes low key. The boat and all of us on board, both Greek and British, were thoroughly searched and we were briefly examined by a doctor. Andre, acting as an interpreter, explained that we were all going to be escorted to the public bath house to clean ourselves.

Climbing on shore we British were escorted to the baths by a couple of Turkish soldiers, one a private and another a sergeant who looked and probably was about seventy years of age. We walked for probably half a mile or so before reaching the building and this was quite an ordeal for those of us without shoes. Even with my rubber flip-flops, which were partly worn through by this time, I found the going quite uncomfortable over the roughly made road.

The bath house turned out to be a very primitive sort of affair, housing a series of raised stone benches in a large circular room that contained a number of shower fittings. The water was hot and plentiful and as we were unable to vary the temperature it was very difficult to see one another through the steam. However, it helped me to pinch a tablet of soap belonging to a rather large and fat Turkish gent who was groping around the floor looking for the soap. The attendants had only given us a couple of small tablets of soap between us. It was a lovely feeling to shower in hot fresh water after so long without such a simple pleasure.

Unfortunately, the feeling of being clean did not last, as we emerged from the bath house we were handed a very small towel each and were ordered to put on the same clothing which we arrived in. We were expecting to have at least a clean pair of shorts or trousers and could not believe our ears when being told to put our old rags back on.

Once we were dressed our escorts accompanied us back to the quay where the caique was secured. From there we were taken to a Turkish officers' club and were informed that we were going to be served with a meal, which after the treatment meted out to us, so far, seemed quite unbelievable. Before the meal, however, we had to pose for a couple of informal photographs and fortunately we were given prints of these later in our stay.

Apart from a few Turkish soldiers and a Turkish captain, who was very helpful, the rest of our companions were all in civilian clothes so it was difficult to know or decide just who were actually serving members of the Turkish forces. What was apparent was the fact that the average Turkish soldier was treated as a 'dogs body', seemingly employed at everything from loading boats to sweeping the street.

Seated at the meal table there were just twelve people, us seven from LS 1 and five retired or serving Turkish officers. The outstanding feature of the layout of the table was the absence of cutlery. Everyone seated provided their own from their pockets, so it was necessary for one of the soldiers to be ordered off somewhere to get us a knife, fork and spoon. Apparently cutlery was regarded by the Turkish soldiers as something akin to jewellery.

The meal, after all that we had been through, was in one word, tolerable. I have no idea as to it's composition, I simply 'wolfed' it down. It was supplemented with what I can only describe as fire-water or Indian snake oil. It was colourless, had a kick like a mule and was seemingly available by the bucket-full because the soldier servants made sure our glasses were continually full. It would have made a wonderful cure for a cough, simply because you were afraid to cough in case you lost control of your bowels.

After the meal, there was much coming and going with the officials and Andre advised us to stay calm and cheerful as he was going to attempt to make contact with the British Consul or someone who would help us on our way. The Turkish government and people, at that time, were sitting on the fence as far as the war was concerned, one day being pro-British, the next pro-German.

Whilst Andre went about his negotiating we were taken back to the boat to spend the night. The caique was under armed guard, the Greek crew had not been allowed to leave the boat, as we had done, although they had been given some food. They seemed genuinely surprised at our return.

The following morning, we were escorted back to the officers' club, where we sat on the verandah facing the main street and the quayside. We were given a snack of bread and cheese and endless offers of fire-water, but most of us had learnt our lesson the night before and declined. The Turkish captain who was continually with us and obviously in charge, was a great chap who made every effort to help us and when you consider his position, supposedly neutral, he deserved a medal. I have since found out his name was Menduh Eegul and from the bottom of my heart I thank him for his kindness.

The ordinary Turkish soldier appeared, by our standards, to be very poorly treated. Their uniforms and footwear were pathetic, it was no wonder that we had not been given any new clothing, they just did not have it to give as they were so poor themselves.

Andre returned later in the day with a report of his negotiations. He had pleaded that we were not strictly military as could be seen by our dress and we had just been taking supplies to some of our Greek friends, who had helped English civilians caught up in the war. He went on to explain to the authorities that we could not possibly be considered as a military unit as we only had one revolver between us. Andre again promised everyone that they would be more than compensated if they helped us and that seemed to do the trick. Within hours we were given some fuel, bread, cheese, fruit and some sort of dried meat and our caique was soon on its way.

What a relief it was to be back at sea, with a bit of luck Andre said we would make Paphos in a couple of days or so, less if we got a fair breeze. It meant a passage of some two hundred and fifty miles or more with the only foreseeable hazard, our passing the island of Rhodes once again.

Consequently, it turned out to be quite an uneventful, but fairly uncomfortable trip, by now I think we had all had enough adventure for the time being and just wanted to get home.

Entering Paphos we encountered a couple of our caiques on their way to do a few working up exercises. Andre headed towards one in order to hail it, but the caique headed away from us, however, we managed to attract the other boat by shouting out, 'LS 1 here!'

Their response was 'Bloody hell, you've grown a bit and where have you been? We thought you had been bagged!'

We entered harbour and secured alongside and within minutes the harbour master appeared. He had obviously been alerted to our approach. Andre explained our position to him, above all our need for a good bath, a change of clothing and a good meal, in that order.

'Leave everything to me,' he said to us, 'Just remain where you are whilst I arrange things, I will be back within the hour.' True to his word he did just that.

Andre went with him in order to telephone the Naval Officer-in-Charge, Cyprus Ports, and he and the harbour master returned to tell us that a truck was being sent to take us to the local army unit, the Bhopals, commanded by a British major. Andre meanwhile, took our Greek companions to a good local taverna and instructed the proprietor to take care of them, giving them anything that they wished.

Our truck duly arrived to transport us to what at one period we had thought was gone forever. The memory of that lovely relaxing soak in the tub will remain with me forever, all my aches, cares and pains went swirling down the plug-hole.

There was the sheer joy of donning fresh new clothing, that is until I came to my shoes, which although of the correct size, crippled me. My poor feet were sore and tender from their mistreatment, however, to overcome this, I was given some soft canvas shoes which did the trick.

After a good meal, I felt on top of the world. We were later joined by Andre who too had been transformed back to his former commanding self. Even his striking beard had obviously received attention. He informed us that he had arranged sleeping bags, blankets, food and fuel and we should get back to the caique, collecting our Greek companions en-route and leave for Beirut at sunset.

So we collected our friends from the taverna, by this time they were in a most agreeable mood, even the two younger ones. It appeared that they had devoured their fill of meat and drink, at Andre's expense, and were fortified further with promises of much more by Andre.

It was decided that we should set off on our passage to Beirut, some two hundred miles plus, using both the engine and sail if possible, although our young engineer, thinking of his pride and joy, suggested that we should rest his engine every two or three hours. This was most welcome because the noise and vibration was terrible.

Andre reckoned that given good weather, we could do the journey in about thirty hours. Indeed, the weather was kind and we made landfall at dawn on the second day to arrive at our own base to a tremendous welcome. Our survival had been relayed to them from Paphos so that they were ready to receive us, this after believing for a while that we had gone the way of our dear comrades in *LS 4* — lost without trace.

CHAPTER 30

After a short debriefing, Captain Chevalier and Sergeant Miller left for their base at Zahle, a beautiful little village set into the hills above Beirut. I made a number of trips there whilst in Beirut, mainly to visit SBS acquaintances, I even went skiing in the mountains on a few of the trips.

The crew of *LS 1* were told to draw some pay and get lost for a few days after reporting to the sick bay for a check-up. We were told that they would send for us when it was time to report back to our base in the harbour.

Andre told us that he would arrange for our Greek friends to return home suitably rewarded and although I do not have any details of this, I feel sure Andre would have settled for nothing less. I did hear, unofficially, that one of the two younger men became a useful recruit to our organization.

After three or four days we were all bored to tears with visiting the various bars and bordellos and we, decided to report back. What a surprise awaited us, one which we had failed to take note of on our brief visit a few days previous. The place was a hive of activity. There were so many new faces, both officers and men and new caiques were being fitted out ready for sea.

The officers at Beirut were all new to us, with the exception of Andre Londos and our base maintenance and supplies officer, Adrian Gardner.

Amongst the faces we knew were about five of our original complement, Sergeant 'Tanky' Rowlands, ERA 'Jock' Andrews and 'Chippy' Nineham, the carpenter. There was also our wizard, Sergeant Jones, the man who could charm the birds down from the trees, nothing but nothing was unobtainable to him. You name it and he could get it. Spare parts, guns, not necessarily British, fags, booze and every kind of tinned food imaginable. He was also capable of directing one to the best place for obtaining a bit of 'yo ho-ho.'

It is said that no man is indispensable, but Sergeant Jones must surely have come close to being just that. Anyone who could teach me to drive our 30 cwt. truck through the streets of Beirut from scratch must rate the tops. Horn, brakes, blind faith and skid marks in my underpants, that was me, good old Jonesy — unforgettable in every way.

The other lads who were at the base when Adrian, our CO, first began the task of licking us into shape, were now all up in the islands and by the reports which were filtering through to us, it seemed that they were having a rough time, work wise and health wise. These lads included the Stokers Wall and Osborne, Leading Seamen Hallybone and Dawes, Petty Officers Bevan, Simmonds and Banks, and Gunner MacCormack. It was decided that us experienced spare bodies should relieve our pals for a few days, to give them a rest and a chance to clean up.

At this time the Italians were on the point of collapse and Adrian Seligman, who had been anticipating this for some time, had been busy making plans to secure a forward base for our operations. He had decided that the island of Leros would be ideal, this was an Italian submarine and sea plane base with all the necessary facilities. Consequently, he had secured, by our standards, a large caique, one which could act as a mother ship to some of our smaller boats.

Adrian, with his new caique, numbered LS 8, loaded with stores, had left in company with tiny LS 3, skippered by Charles Bradbeer RNVR. With him he had taken Captain Benyon-Tinker, our gunnery officer and the rest of us were eager to follow them. News filtered back that the two caiques had reached Casteloriso, an island a few miles off the Turkish coast, and we prepared to join them.

I cannot recall the number of the caique on which I took passage to Casteloriso via Paphos, or indeed any of the names of the crew, they were all new faces to me. We spent a terrible night in wet sleeping bags en- route to Paphos, where we managed to secure a thirty-six hour drying out period before setting off for Casteloriso, which was reached without any further discomfort.

On our arrival we found that the Italians had indeed capitulated and were cooperating with us, if indeed cooperation is the word to use. Of the remaining Italian troops there, the officers were strutting about like comic opera generals, simply plastered with medals. Their uniforms were immaculate, but the common soldiers were a different kettle of fish, they were pathetically scruffy, down trodden and bewildered. Leaderless in fact and appeared only to be interested in getting away from it all, back home to their wine, women and song, but then again, didn't we all.

These were the people who under Mussolini literally stabbed us in the back when they thought that Hitler had us beaten in 1940. They were in the main too cowardly to join in the war before this, it follows therefore, that we had very little time for them, perhaps feeling that we ought to teach them a lesson, but we didn't. We more or less ignored them in order to concentrate on getting to grips with the Germans in the islands.

Adrian in LS 8, together with LS 3, had left before we arrived, carrying a number of LRDG (Long Range Desert Group) troops under the command of Captain Charlie Saxton. By the time we got to Casteloriso they were installed at Leros, together with some of our earlier caiques and the lads we knew.

Casteloriso was like a ghost town, most of the Greek population had dispersed to other islands where they had relatives and friends. Myself, with others, strolled around the harbour area and even bathed in the fresh water fountain without attracting attention. It was later reported in the press that some looting had been carried out by our people; quite ridiculous really, there was hardly any room on our caique for our own gear, let alone loot. Fortunately, with a number of others, I managed to secure a lift on a naval ML (motor launch), which was leaving that evening for Leros. I just couldn't believe it, it was luxury travel after the caique, we simply flew through the water arriving at Leros before noon the following day.

We were off loaded in the main harbour of Leros, Port Largo, and were then left to our own devices which simply meant finding out if Adrian was around or whether or not any of our caiques were in harbour.

The harbour was quite impressive, there were workshops, hangers for sea planes and also a floating dock. There was also a couple of Italian destroyers moored in the harbour. We discovered that the Senior British Naval Officer at Leros, Commander Villiers, had set up his headquarters on an Italian vessel and to this ship we made our way. There we were informed that the naval headquarters were now on shore at Navy House, a building on the other side of the harbour.

Off we trudged with our little bags containing, just one change of underwear, socks, khaki shirt and shorts, plus soap and a towel. The official buildings all appeared to have Italian sentries on the outside. When they challenged us we replied in English and they let us pass at will. At Navy House, we were informed that a couple of our caiques were at anchor in Partheni Bay, although one of our larger boats was at a workshop nearby and this turned out to be *LS 7* under the command of my old skipper, Andre Londos.

This caique was seemingly our largest to date, she had not been at Beirut I am sure. Andre must have acquired her up in the islands because he had left Beirut before I had. Adrian in *LS 8,* together with *LS 3* was away operating with Charlie Saxton and his LRDG, landing at various islands such as, Jura, Syra, and Thermia.

The German forces were beginning to realise that we were indeed a force to be reckoned with. One of the results of this was that Leros was subjected to severe air raids from them, JU 88's were mainly used, this for me was shades of Malta. The civilian population moved out of town to take shelter in caves or other makeshift places and obtaining food became very difficult indeed.

Our lads coming and going were feeling the strain, not in morale, but physically because of sea sores and boils etc. Some of the sores would eat right through almost to the bone and required immediate medical attention.

These ailments were caused by lack of sleep, no washing facilities, salt sea bathing and sleeping in the same clothing, which was often wet through and allowed to dry on oneself. Our diet of tinned food and stewed tea did not help although we did have some pills of sorts which were supposed to help, but in the order of things, these were mostly overlooked or mislaid. Plus there was no rum!

I made a number of trips in various caiques as a relief for some poor devil in need of urgent medical attention. On one occasion we were required to proceed to Serephos to pick up part of an LRDG patrol and this we did. However, we also acquired some RAF chaps who had been shot down, so naturally our small caique was packed with bodies. On our way back to base, I just happened to tell one of the RAF chaps just how bad it was for our lads at Leros, that's nothing he said, adding, 'You ought to wake up in a cave to find a ruddy great goat or sheep on top of you.'

I just laughed and murmured, 'Baah.' He was not amused, but soon calmed down when I explained about the sheep and goats on Sirina.

We, the lesser mortals in our organization, did not seem to know more than a few days in advance where we were going. I suppose this also applied more or less to our officers, as in a relatively small cloak and dagger outfit, such as ours, operations did not require weeks of planning. We could take off at a moments notice in a small boat with a crew of just five or six. It was a good life really in spite of the discomforts, one felt like a pirate at times, nondescript, armed to the teeth, with the wind and the sea in one's face, meals al fresco, literally a life on the ocean wave.

I eventually returned by ML to Beirut to join a new caique that was supposedly being fitted out. When I arrived there wasn't a boat for me as they all had their own crews, so I was spare once again.

About this time it was rumoured that Adrian was in the bag, in other words, captured. He had been dashing around everywhere in the most dangerous forward locations, as had Andre Londos to a certain extent. However, out of the blue, Adrian turned up in Beirut, this was the first time I had seen him since I left with Andre on the ill-fated *LS 1*. Adrian had been on Samos with members of the SBS, LRDG and the Greek Sacred Heart Squadron — an outfit similar to our SBS.

However, we had acquired a large schooner, large by our standards that is, which was to become our operational headquarters and base ship. The plan was to find a suitable place for her, somewhere quiet and secluded, in one of the many bays and inlets which were uninhabited along the Turkish coast.

It was necessary for us to have such a vessel as this because of the rapidly changing scene, the Germans had taken Leros so it was decided that Samos should be left to them also. The loss of both of these islands made it imperative for us to set up a forward base. Our schooner was subsequently equipped and numbered *LS 9*.

The *LS 9* was a schooner of some one hundred and fifty tons. She had a small wardroom aft, containing a couple of bunks, there was a Greek crew with their skipper in quarters forward, whilst amidships in the hold, there were a number of bunks for us serving ratings that we shared with numerous rats to whom the vessel was a home from home.

The SBS, under the command of Major Earl Jellicoe, had also acquired a large schooner named the *Tewfik*. This vessel, crammed with SBS personnel, left with *LS 9*, and three small caiques numbered 3, 5 and 10, to locate a forward base, wherever that might be.

The little armada set off on the first leg of the journey, the passage to Cyprus. Adrian, who was in command of *LS 9*, had with him the army captains, Benyon-Tinker and Gordon Hogg. Also taking passage with us were Major Earl Jellicoe and his second-in-command, Captain Tom Patterson. On board *Tewfik* at this time was Captain Anders Lassen SBS, Danish by birth, fearless and brave, later going on to win a posthumous VC.

During our passage to Cyprus, the weather deteriorated rapidly and it was quite rough. Conditions for us on *LS 9* were not all that bad and we passed a fair amount of time in our bunks amidships listening to the scurrying, squeaking rats. The rats obviously preferred our section of the vessel to the fare in the Greek quarters which was probably barbecued octopus and ouzo, the national fire water.

Our accompanying caiques, 3, 5 and 10 took a real hammering and poor little *LS 5,* the smallest by far, was quite soon in a bad way. It was decided to take her in tow and get her crew on board for rest and shelter as they were worn out with their exertions and soaked to the skin. With her in tow, we plugged on until nightfall when we lost track of the others.

The gale worsened and we knew that we would not get any shelter until we neared the coast of Cyprus, many hours away. The tow line to *LS 5* was secured to what was considered to be her strongest point, the mast. However, during the night the battle was lost, the mast parted company with the caique leaving us in *LS 9* trailing the mast at the head of the tow line. Poor little *LS 5* had gone.

On the following morning we arrived at Cyprus and entered the harbour at Famagusta where we secured alongside the *Tewfik.* Later in the day, little *LS 3* came in to join us. Subsequently, we found out that *LS 10* had broken down shortly after leaving Beirut and was forced to return to base.

On reflection we subjected these little boats to tasks for which they had not been built. Firstly, by installing a heavy diesel tank engine and large fuel tanks, then secondly loading it with all our equipment. This included a good supply of tinned food, heavy guns and ammunition and sometimes a small number of SBS personnel with their gear. Then again, a number of our smaller boats carried a 20 mm Solithurn antitank rifle. This was a terrible weight to have forward.

I do not know whether dear little *LS 5* had one or not, but her fuel tanks must have been about seventy-five percent full, which is quite a weight. My training in submarines had taught me all about the distribution of weight which affects the trim of any craft, but all in all, apart from a few tragic losses, we did yeoman service to the war effort in the Aegean with the craft at our command.

As compensation for the rough crossing, shore leave was given which coincided with the SBS also being allowed on shore. This was definitely a mistake, but probably the commanding officers of both boats had decided that it would probably be the last chance anyone would have for a booze-up for a considerable time.

A number of us from *LS 9* having eaten to the full, retired to what was known as a 'Bar-cum-Cabaret' - this is a laugh for a start because any of us sailors could have put on a better act than any of the so called performers.

One did with an impromptu rendering of *This old hat of mine*, the song which any old ex-serviceman, especially sailors, should be familiar with. The words went something like this:

> This old hat of mine, the inside is quite new, but the outside has seen some stormy weather.
> I cast this hat aside, I mean to travel wide, far across the seas I aim to wander.

These same words were repeated with every article of clothing taking the place of the hat until the singer was starkers.

On this night, everything was going well when unfortunately, or perhaps fortunately, I suddenly felt awful, it must have been something I had eaten or drunk because I felt as sick as a dog. Feeling hot and dizzy, I just had to get out into the fresh air and once out in the street I threw up everything I had eaten and drunk. I felt that I needed just to lie down for a while, so I made my way back to *LS 9.*

It was shortly after this, when all hell broke loose back at the bar. Heaven only knows what it was about, or who started it for that matter, but the place was wrecked. The noise could be heard from our schooner and as I felt a little better, I came up from my bunk to see what the commotion was about.

In the distance I could see some of our crew, together with a number of SBS lads, being shepherded back to their respective boats by an army patrol. In the vanguard of this motley crew was our own MacCormack, carrying a heavy chair from the bar to defend himself from the enemy.

It appeared that the fight was between two forces — on our side were the naval ratings and our pals from the SBS — the opposition was the local defence force which were recruited from the local population. The result of all this was that Famagusta was put out of bounds to our lads and the SBS.

The following day our depleted armada, consisting of *Tewfik, LS 9* and little *LS 3,* set forth for Casteloriso. We did not get very far before the engine of *LS 9* started acting up. I had long before sighted this infernal engine and had there and then decided that I would keep well away from it. Our Greek engineer decided that we could not proceed to Casteloriso and we returned to harbour for repairs to the fuel system.

Tewfik and *LS 3* continued with their passage north and we had to wait for three or four days for an engine part to be obtained from Limassol. This was too much for Adrian who, together with Major Earl Jellicoe and Captain Patterson, managed to obtain passage on a motor launch which was about to set off for Casteloriso. With Adrian gone, this just left us with a young sub-lieutenant to act as our naval commanding officer, although Captains Hogg and Benyon-Tinker also remained behind

After a few days the repairs were completed and we set off once more and in spite of some really nasty weather, managed to reach the Turkish coast, near Cape Annamur. From there we intended to hug the coastline for about one hundred and eighty miles or so and were well on our way when it began to cut up rough. It was blowing a gale and making things quite uncomfortable for us all.

At times we lost sight completely of the coastline and the schooner continually rolled from side to side as it tried to make headway against the pitching sea. The engine was making hard work of it, so the Greek crew partially rigged the main sail to try to help, but this was a difficult exercise and proved to be of no avail.

With the majority of us more than a little apprehensive regarding our position, the sub-lieutenant, after receiving advice from the Greek skipper, decided to turn about and return to the coast of Cyprus. The wind howled and the sea broke over us on many occasions, swamping everything below and it was a very wild journey indeed.

We had been assured by the Greek skipper that it was our best option, after all, he knew the area with its vagaries weather-wise, having made the same passage countless times. It was a very long, wet and uncomfortable night, however, the next morning we reached the coast of Cyprus, dog tired and thankful to be entering the peaceful harbour of Limassol in one piece.

Twenty four hours later, after a rest and tidy up, we set off again with the sea like glass, not a ripple disturbed it. We were approaching Paphos when a caique was spotted evidently heading straight towards us and it could be seen that an individual was standing at the bow waving, seemingly trying to attract our attention. So, we altered course towards him and were within shouting distance when he asked if we were LS 9. On being told that we were, he informed us that we were to return to Paphos to await further orders.

Entering the harbour at this time, for a schooner of our size, was a bit tricky and seemingly out of the question. So we had to anchor whilst our two officers, Captain Hogg and Captain Benyon-Tinker went ashore to confer by telephone with their superiors in Famagusta.

Our sailing orders had been cancelled because of the sighting of a U-boat in the area, consequently, we had to remain where we were for a couple of days. The weather began to deteriorate and our Greek captain decided that we must change our anchorage to the lee of a headland, which he thought would afford a certain measure of shelter for us. Having done this, we sat tight to await the expected onslaught of the approaching storm. Captains Hogg and Benyon-Tinker were trapped ashore, trapped? They were the lucky ones, because we took a real hammering. The following week was just one long nightmare, one felt so hopeless, the only way we could have got ashore was if we had been ship wrecked on the rocks.

We managed to remain at anchor only because the skipper kept the engine running slow ahead most of the time. Everything was wet through including our bunks down below. We were as miserable as sin, even the rats must have hibernated because we did not hear or see them during the whole of the storm. Although we were only a mile or so from Paphos, there were times when it was impossible to see through the curtain of driving rain.

Hour after hour, day after day, we had no respite at all, just going to the galley or the 'thunderbox' on the upper deck was worthy of a decoration.

It is said that nothing lasts forever and so the storm slowly blew itself out. We were still rolling a bit, but the sea gradually subsided and this enabled us to commence clearing up and our skipper decided to move back to our former anchorage, nearer the shore. There were times when we thought that our anchors and engine would not be sufficient to save us from disaster.

We had all been on edge, unable to sleep and had practically no hot food except soup throughout the whole ordeal. However, with everything 'Ship Shape and Bristol Fashion' once more, we set off into the wide blue yonder. This time without the Captains Hogg and Benyon-Tinker as they had managed to scrounge a lift on a fairmile which escorted us to the Turkish coast, which was reached with no trouble at all and we continued safely to Casteloriso.

The next part of our journey had everyone on their toes with apprehension, because it entailed passing the German held island of Rhodes. However the Gods of Mercy decided that it was our turn to get lucky and we were allowed to sail on unhindered to our destination, which was an anchorage at Turk Buku, situated north of the island of Kos in the Gulf of Mandelya.

En-route we rested up briefly at an anchorage named Kiervasili, leaving *Tewfik*, who strangely enough we had caught up, to proceed ahead of us to Turk Buku.

The SBS then began having a field day, raiding everywhere, striking right, left and centre, including pinching small caiques loaded with supplies destined for German garrisons on the islands. They managed to grab a good Italian launch which was put to good use and amongst their captures was a large schooner, loaded down with tons of goodies including many cases of lager beer, which was shared out.

Because of further operations which were being planned, it was decided that we would all be better off at another anchorage further south, so we moved to Port Deremen with the connivance of the Turks who were not adverse to accepting Baksheesh, whatever its form. These poor people really knew the meaning of poverty at this time.

We all settled down at this new anchorage to a steady routine, but alert at all times, with lookouts ashore at various vantage points, twenty four hours a day. One day, just for the want of trying something different for a meal, MacCormack said to me, 'You come from the West Country, what about making some pasties, we've got plenty of flour.' We decided we had nothing to lose - I had seen my mother and sisters do it hundreds of times and we had all the ingredients, including corned beef.

'Mac', who was carrying around a couple of puppies, one in each duffle coat pocket, dumped them in their box and got stuck in to chopping up all the veg into very small diced pieces whilst I started on the pastry. My rolling pin was an empty wine bottle. 'Mac' and I spent about a couple of hours creating this feast for the Gods and that is exactly what it was. The officers back aft could just not believe it, they wanted more and it was a good job that I was called upon in a day or so to take part in what for me was a bizarre operation, otherwise I would have been making pasties for evermore.

There are times when I look back at the events I am about to describe and ask myself as to whether or not it was all a dream, but let me assure you it was real enough. I was not a professional soldier, trained to fight, I was just a simple stoker who looked after engines and was only in the Navy because it was a job. However, I really liked serving with the Levant Schooner Flotilla and the thrill of being part of such a clandestine unit was difficult to ignore. It is only now that I question my sanity at this period of time and I only assure myself as to my state of mind, by saying that I was young and disciplined with perhaps no thought as to the outcome of my actions, which now I consider foolhardy for want of a better word.

CHAPTER 31

Shortly after the 'pasty' episode, which proved to be my *piece-de-resistance*, I was called to the wardroom for an interview by the SBS officer in charge and whose name I am unable to recall. I was asked whether or not I would be able to start and drive away a German landing craft. I replied that I would not be able to say yes or no until I could examine it. Asked how long I would need to do this, my answer was, 'A minimum of twenty minutes or so'.

'Right,' he said. 'tonight you will land under the cover of darkness with a detachment of SBS with the object of stealing such a craft.'

I didn't question the order or have any thoughts as to what the mission might entail. I was certainly no hero, just a well trained young man who obeyed orders from a superior. Apparently the landing craft was rigged with a mass of aerials and antenna etc. and this had aroused the curiosity of our people and they were very eager to grab the vessel.

I was selected not because of my expertise, but simply, because I was the only one available at the time who knew anything about marine engines. I received very little briefing about the trip and was told to be ready to join the crew that same evening.

I, together with a stoker, a leading seaman, who was to be our coxswain, and an able seaman, plus a detachment of SBS from *Tewfik,* boarded an ML as darkness descended. I was dressed in trousers, a black beret, khaki shirt and pullover and a battle dress jacket with a shoulder flash simply saying 'Royal Navy'.

My weapons consisted of a Thompson sub-machine gun with a spare magazine and a .38 revolver in the holster of a belt containing spare rounds. I was also carrying a haversack containing 5 lbs of plastic explosive fitted with a ten minute time pencil. I had been instructed that if I failed to start the engine, I was to plant the explosive in a vital position in the engine room and get away the best I could.

Once we were under way I entered into conversation with the SBS lads, some of whom I knew by sight, I discovered that we were on our way to the island of Piskopi. They told me the island was fairly rugged and uninhabited on the side where we were to land and the only habitation was in the small town of Piskopi itself on the outskirts of which the small German garrison had their headquarters. I was assured by my SBS companions that this would be a piece of cake, strangely enough I don't think that I was really concerned.

Piskopi is situated about 25 miles or so from Rhodes and Alimnia and it was on the latter island that six British commandoes were captured on a subsequent raid and executed by the Germans. Two of these commandoes were with me on *LS I,* one was Sgt 'Lofty' Miller and the other was Carpenter — our wireless operator.

We approached the island in complete silence under a cloudy night sky, we closed to within roughly half a mile from shore, then manning our folboats, two man collapsible canoes, we paddled our way to the beach. I sat behind a large SBS guy and after a couple of minutes I tapped him on the shoulder and asked him if he had been in a canoe before. When he replied that he had, on many occasions, I replied, 'Well, the idea is to move the water with the paddle not throw it all over me!' He was not amused. To be honest I think I was just nervous and had tried to break the tension.

We approached the shore and I felt the bottom of the canoe run aground on the sandy beach, within a split second my companion was out of the canoe and I quickly followed. The SBS men had a quick look round to make sure it was safe and us naval chaps stayed on the beach, close to the folboats.

Most of the SBS had been there before on a reconnaissance mission, so they were very familiar with the spot and the terrain.

Once we were all assembled on the beach, we were ordered to check all our equipment to make sure that nothing was left behind to be discovered by a German patrol or a lone beachcomber. The folboats also had to be concealed well away from any track and with this attended to, we began our ascent up the cliff path.

We were commanded by an SBS captain, it could have been Captain Patterson to whom I referred earlier, but I am not sure. His second in command was an SBS lieutenant, and there were a couple of sergeants, one of which I was ordered to stick to like glue as it was he who was to get me and the other naval chaps aboard the German craft.

It was imperative that we reached the summit of the hills overlooking the harbour and town before dawn. We set off in two single files up a rough path, through rocks and scrub, led by some of the SBS who had trodden this path before during their reconnaissance. I found it hard going carrying my gear as I had not been trained for this sort of caper, but I suffered no real distress.

At the summit, which we reached in good time, we were directed to some long abandoned rough stone structures, they could have been at one time shepherds' huts or similar. It was here that we settled down to rest up. Our assault upon the German landing craft was not due to take place until well after dark that night, when it was supposed that most of the population and German garrison would be asleep. However, later in the day, in groups of three and four, we moved up to a forward observation post overlooking the town and harbour. There we were instructed as to our own particular part in the operation and collective responsibility to the team.

In my own particular case, I was called forward on a second occasion and asked to describe in detail my own particular role in the undertaking. Looking down upon the small town and harbour, I could see that the German HQ was situated on our side of town just below our position, whilst the landing craft was secured to a mole on the far side of the town. If we had taken up a position in the hills overlooking the landing craft, it was possible that we could have been seen by someone in our present position.

We spent the day resting, checking equipment and talking over with one another our particular roles. During the afternoon, which was a Sunday, most of the lads, except a lookout, dozed off in the warm sunshine, but an incident occurred which woke everyone in an instant.

Voices and laughter were heard approaching our position and it soon became apparent that they were Germans, but quite some distance off, the sound being easily carried on the cool breeze blowing towards us in the hills. We were bound to be discovered as there was simply no time to disperse to any suitable cover nearby. A quick decision had to be made and it was decided to ambush them as we could see there were only two or three of them in the party.

The captain ordered us to take up our positions and made it clear that no shots were to be fired. With everyone at the ready, we waited, seemingly for ages, for them to arrive at our shelter. As the voices came closer I noticed the look of utter concentration on the faces of the SBS men and for a moment I felt sorry for the unsuspecting Germans about to walk into our trap.

Two hapless German soldiers, whose only weapons were canes, finally reached our shelter and we leapt forth from our concealed positions. I don't know who was the most taken aback, them or us, but it must have been them because one of the poor devils relieved himself with fright, he stunk like a polecat. They gave up without a fight and when we had them suitably under armed guard, we allowed the German to clean himself up the best way he could. These two were the first Germans I had seen in the flesh. They didn't look like superior troops to me and I think my confidence in the mission rose accordingly.

The two Germans, who appeared to be in their late thirties, were garrison troops out for a Sunday afternoon stroll and I doubt whether they would have put up a fight under any circumstances. They were very subdued, not sullen or arrogant as supposedly were most German combat troops.

There was no one in our outfit who could speak fluent German, but by a mixture of a few words of German and sign language, we learnt practically everything about the garrison, but not the purpose of the landing craft with its antenna and aerials.

The strength of the German garrison, which had been more or less assessed accurately by our CO, was now minus two. It was decided that two SBS would remain behind to guard the prisoners as the last thing we needed was for them to escape and raise the alarm.

When everyone in the town seemed to have settled down for the night we made our descent down a rough unmade path towards the German quarters. The plan was to skirt around this building or buildings, then creep along the front towards the mole, one or two of us at a time, but alas, this was not to be. I just followed the guy in front of me and have to admit that the butterflies in my stomach were going at a hundred miles an hour.

As I recall we split into two groups. One group went around the front of the first German building and the other group went around the back. Myself, together with my naval companions and the second in command, went with the group to the rear of the building. We had practically got around this building, which was surrounded by a 7ft wall of stone, when a dog inside the wall started to bark rather furiously and although we could not see it, we could tell that it was dashing about along the inside of the wall.

We stopped and the SBS sergeant next to me put his finger to his lips. Through holes and chinks in the wall, we saw a door open and silhouetted against the light was the figure of a German soldier holding an automatic rifle or machine gun. He began shouting at the dog who took no heed. We remained rooted to the spot, trying not to make the slightest noise in the darkness. However, the German either spotted or heard something from our direction because he let fly with a burst from his machine gun, spraying the wall from side to side. I could hear the bullets striking the wall in front of me.

All hell broke loose and some of our party made a dash to get clear. Germans rushed out of the building, firing into the darkness as they came. The SBS sergeant suggested that I push him up over the wall so he could get a shot at them. Because of the darkness I could hardly see the wall, but I located it with my outstretched hand and shoved the sergeant upwards with my right shoulder. At the same time I thrust out my left hand to steady myself on what turned out to be a gap in the wall. I fell through the small opening and cursed loudly and a German, on hearing the noise, sprayed a couple of bullets in my direction.

This was definitely dirty underwear time! I looked up to see the sergeant on top of the wall with his legs dangling on each side and called out to him to make sure he was alright. At which point a stream of bullets struck the wall close to him, 'Bloody hell,' he shouted, and immediately rolled back off the wall. By this time I had dragged myself back through the hole in the wall and to be honest for the first time I wondered what the hell I was doing there.

We now came under quite heavy fire and chunks of stone were flying off the top of the wall onto us crouching below. A larger weapon opened up, possibly 20 mm, and tracer bullets streaked through the darkness and ricocheted off the wall. The noise was quite unbelievable and in the distance could be heard the sound of sporadic gunfire as other members of our team engaged the Germans. You didn't need to be a genius to realise that our position was rapidly becoming untenable.

During a temporary lull in the firing, during which time I had not fired a single shot, our sergeant said he would try to find the lieutenant or captain in order to evaluate the situation and he ordered me to remain where I was. Bullets continued to bounce off the wall and after what seemed a lifetime he returned to say that as we had lost the element of surprise, it was unlikely that we would be able to continue with our plan. An understatement I thought, but he went on to tell us that the raid would be aborted at a suitable moment when repeated blasts would be given on a whistle. The whistle would be the signal for us to abandon our positions and make good our escape back into the hills towards our starting point. I asked him what was the drill and he answered, 'Run like bloody hell and keep your head down.'

When the whistle sounded I immediately stood up, removed my haversack with its deadly load of explosives, broke the ten minute time pencil, then like a cowboy with a lasso, twirled it around a couple of times and unleashed it through the wall opening towards the building. Five pounds lighter, I was off like a jack rabbit, but soon realised that whilst I was playing the hero, my companions had disappeared into the darkness.

With the sound of voices and machine gunfire behind me I headed in the direction which I hoped was the correct one. There were some darkened houses ahead of me and I started to veer to the left of these at about the same time as the explosive charge I had thrown went off. Unfortunately, I must have stumbled into someone's garden or vegetable patch and I crashed through some poles, netting and vines. The noise I made immediately attracted the attention of a burst of gunfire which had the effect of doubling my strength and I emerged from the garden trailing the poles and netting with me.

As more gunfire sounded behind me and a couple of tracer bullets went over my head, I wrenched myself clear of the debris and set off at a gallop. I have never run so fast over such a long period in my life. Eventually, I heard some of our party ahead of me so I redoubled my efforts to catch up and did not pause until I reached them and then I collapsed, totally out of breath.

I doubt whether I could have continued on for more than a few more yards, my heart was thumping like a hammer. I do not recall any fear — just a feeling of sheer exhaustion from my super human effort. However, relief was at hand because the half a dozen or so SBS that I had caught up with assured me that we would be alright and could take our time climbing up into the hills. Seemingly, the Germans would not attempt to pursue us into what could be an ambush, even so, small arms and larger calibre fire was still being aimed towards us.

After a short rest, we continued on our way upwards, and in the darkness tried to find the path which we had descended. Eventually we found it and reached our shelter at the summit and the two SBS lads we had left guarding the prisoners. They told us that they thought, after seeing the battle going on down below, that perhaps they would be the only survivors.

Our little group were the first to return and the others arrived shortly after us in small groups, it came as quite a relief to find us altogether without loss. There were, however, a few wounded, none too serious, mostly shoulders and arms, with just a couple who had been hit in their thighs, but they could all walk. Dawn was fast approaching so lookouts were posted and the rest of us settled down to await nightfall.

I found a corner to curl up into and I remember now the feeling as my blood coursed through my veins. I was in a turmoil and thoughts and questions continually entered my head. Thoughts of my wife and family at home. What was I doing here? Would the Germans come after us in daylight? Would they be waiting for us when we rendezvoused with our motor launch? Have our folboats been discovered? I can remember now thinking please let me get home safely. Eventually my exhausted body overcame my disturbed mind and I fell asleep and it was relief at last! I must have been out for three or four hours and woke up to find a beautiful morning with everyone fully alert. Nobody appeared to be at all apprehensive and when I remembered that most of my SBS companions had been in this situation or similar on many other occasions, it began to rub off on to me. I felt a lot more confident about the situation and looked forward to the night when we would make our descent to our original landing place.

During the daylight hours we did not detect any sign of an approach being made towards our shelter in the hills and shortly after nightfall we began making our way down to where we had concealed our boats. Our prisoners were quite docile and seemed fully resigned to their position.

We arrived at the beach and uncovered our folboats and waited. The rescuers arrived right on time and 'heaved to' at a distance of some four hundred yards or so from the shore. The sea was quite moderate and we set off towards the motor launch with our prisoners squeezed into two of the canoes. We had been unsuccessful in our mission, but I suppose that lessons had been learnt and we had returned with a couple of captives. Surely no operation of this nature can be deemed as unfruitful and strangely enough, I do not remember saying to myself never again. It is only now fifty years later that I wonder what the hell I was doing there.

On my return to our base schooner, *LS 9*, I settled down to my usual routine with no specific job to do. There was no debriefing session and I was not even asked by any of the officers about my part of the operation.

When I think back to the members of our team who were later caught and executed by the Germans a shudder still runs through my body. Our raid was very similar in many ways and just like them we were dressed in a nondescript fashion and if caught would probably have suffered the same fate.

Our two prisoners remained with us for a few days before being passed down the line for transit to a prison camp. They had seemingly enjoyed being with us and appeared loathe to leave, not knowing what their future treatment would be.

CHAPTER 32

After a few days I was informed that I was required back at the base in Beirut. Briefly, I was told that we had acquired an almost new MFV (Motor fishing vessel) and she was to be fitted out as our Headquarters Ship to replace the schooner *LS 9* and I was to be its engineer.

Such was our organization that no specific arrangements were made for me to get to Beirut, I just had to hitch a ride from any vessel making the trip.

I took passage on one of our smaller caiques which left Dereman and went to the small and lovely little harbour of Kiervasili, at the end of the Gulf of Doris and from there I hitched a ride on an ex-Italian motor launch. I believe that this launch was the one pinched by Captain Anders Lassen VC, from the Germans at Calchi after disposing of them with a few hand grenades. The launch took me to Casteloriso overnight where I reported to the Senior Naval Officer and requested passage to Beirut after showing him my written order and identity.

I was found a passage on board an ML leaving for Beirut via Cyprus, later in the day, which suited me perfectly as I would get a good rest and a swift, easy passage.

I had a gut feeling that everything was going along too easy and so it proved to be because we hadn't been under way for more than an hour or so when we altered course and headed for Alexandria. I was informed that I would be put ashore there together with four SBS chaps who were returning to their base at Zahle just north of Beirut.

The passage to Alex was smooth and uneventful and we secured alongside HMS *Mosquito,* which was the light naval forces base, about midday. The distance from Casteloriso to Alexandria was slightly less than the direct distance to Beirut, but our detour meant that I now had to endure another infernal train journey, accompanied seemingly by half the population of Egypt together with their livestock. With my mind racing ahead of my body, I thought of Haifa and Sonia and just how much I desperately needed that sort of therapy after my recent adventures.

I reported to the Regulating Office at HMS *Mosquito* and the first question I was asked was, 'What sort of outfit do you belong to?' This was because the only distinquishing part of what I was wearing happened to be a very well worn and forlorn petty officers cap, the rest of me was covered in khaki shirt, shorts, stockings and SBS desert boots. I did have my movement orders on a scrap of paper and that was it.

The chief in charge said, 'You must be one of Seligman's gang!' I was then informed that I could entrain for Beirut via Haifa the following day and I could get a change of shirt, shorts and stockings from the clothing store. So armed with these, I found the petty officers' mess where I bathed, had something to eat, saw a cinema show and then bedded down to dream of another bed in Haifa.

The following day, after a good nights sleep and hearty breakfast, I and the SBS lads, boarded a 30 cwt. truck and were driven to the railway station where we reported to the RT officer. Within minutes we were aboard the train and settled down on the hard wooden seats for the laborious journey that we all knew was ahead of us.

As usual the train was crowded and how the pedlars managed to get from one end to the other with their wares was beyond me. We trundled on, to Ismailaya, then El Qantara and El Arish, there were many more stops in between these well known places, God knows where, until we at last reached Haifa.

All through the journey I had been planning my stopover at Haifa. My travel pass simply stated that I was permitted to travel between Egypt, Palestine and Syria and had no dates of departure or arrival. I calculated that all I had to do on arrival at Haifa, was shove off to Sonia for a couple of days after which I could report to the station and continue my journey to Beirut.

Everything went according to plan and Karl and Sonia were seated under the umbrella in the garden when I walked through the gate. Her eyes simply lit up and Karl was overwhelming with his greeting. It was as if I were his long lost brother and he asked all sorts of questions — Where had I come from? Was I tired? How long could I stay? We sat at the small table with our cool drinks and Sonia continually pressed her knee against mine beneath the table, roll on nightfall I thought. As the evening wore on we engaged mostly in small talk in between listening to various radio broadcasts.

I told them I had been in Cyprus working on various boats and did not mention anything about my time in the Aegean. Not once did either of them ask any searching questions. I think they were just a lonely couple as they continually told me stories of their work, home and friends back in Austria. They were homesick, but alas they, unlike myself, could seemingly never return to their birthplace, bearing in mind that the Germans were at that time still masters of Europe. However, a light was beginning to appear at the end of the tunnel on the war front and radio broadcasts to that effect were becoming more optimistic. So having solved the situation for that day, Karl took himself off to his bed on the rear verandah and wished us both a good night.

A good night it most certainly was, the bed was just a necessary prop for the pantomime of perpetual motion. I had no thought of the morrow when the curtain would rise again on reality and I would have to go back to the war. I think I had just about had enough and I wanted to forget everything for a few hours at least. In the end I stayed for two nights and left promising to return and I honestly felt that would happen.

When I reported to the RT officer at Haifa, I asked for transport to Beirut. 'How did you get here?' I was asked, 'There hasn't been a train since yesterday afternoon.' I replied that I had been staying in the transit camp on the edge of town for a couple of days and that was it.

Within an hour or so, I was on the train for Beirut where I duly arrived. I checked into base and everyone, except Sgt Jones and 'Tanky' Rowlands, seemed to be new.

I was more or less told to get lost for a day or two and this I did. I reported early the next day, expecting to see the lovely MFV for which I had been sent down, only to be informed that the acquisition had not yet been finalised. The boat was at Port Said and I was told to go down and bring it back. A crew had not even been selected, but they wanted me to familiarise myself with the engines, fuel, spares and what have you. I was informed that it might be a week or even two before a crew arrived down in Port Said to bring her to Beirut.

This time I took my full kit with me before boarding that bloody train again and on the journey south my mind was occupied with trying to decided whether I could risk two or even three days with Sonia. I finally decided to leave my options open and to hell with it, you only live once!

Arriving at the station in Haifa, I asked if I could leave my kit in the stores there. With it safely stowed away in the baggage office, I took off for the 'Garden of Eden' and Sonia.

Three days later, sore and exhausted, I collected my kit and boarded the train again to rattle, roll and jolt my way to my destination, Port Said.

Port Said is definitely not one of my favourite watering holes. My previous visit was as a survivor from HMS *Medway*. On arriving at the station, I asked the RT officer for transport to the naval base and what a surprise awaited me there. One of the first people I set eyes upon was a chief petty officer who had been my landlord in Palmyra road, Gosport. He had been recalled to the Navy at the outbreak of hostilities and was now in charge of stores at Port Said.

So after reporting to the Regulating Office where I was checked in and told to report back the following morning, I went to the CPOs' and POs' mess, found a bed, took a bath, had a meal then proceeded to the canteen for a few pints with my friend to talk over old times.

The following day, rested and refreshed, I reported to the office where a messenger took me down to my MFV which was secured alongside. There were no officers or crew on board, just three or four maintenance people — one of whom was an engine room artificer who showed me all the ropes.

This boat was luxury indeed by the standards I had got used to, the space, cleanliness and newness of it all was overwhelming. There was a cabin aft for the crew with five bunks and kit lockers, so I immediately commandeered the best for myself.

I spent the whole of one day with the ERA getting the hang of things and finding out about obtaining fuel, spare parts and such like. When I said that I felt fully confident about everything, he suggested that we both see the base engineer officer in order that everything could be signed over to me. This we did and I took charge of the boat to await the arrival of a commanding officer, whoever he might be.

I moved all my kit on board and thought I would try sleeping in the crew's cabin aft of the engine room. It was down below with a small entrance hatch and short ladder. I decided to eat in the mess at the base because the small galley on board was not yet operational. However, before the arrival of our coxswain, who would be responsible for all food supplies, I thought I might try to obtain some tinned food from the victualling officer, this with an eye to the main chance.

With this in mind, I had a yarn with my friend, the chief, who in turn took me to see the victualling officer to whom I pleaded, saying that we had one hell of a job trying to get any decent food when we were up in the islands and was it possible that he could let me have some now to store away against any future contingency? I told him that until the CO and the others arrived I was in sole charge. He eventually said that I could have rations for the crew for one month providing I signed for it, kept it secure and turned it over to the coxswain when he arrived on board.

This suited me as I thought I could lose some of it amongst my engine room stores. I didn't intend to sell the stuff, because tinned food was always valuable when it came to bartering. I found that out when previously in Malta.

During the next week or so, I got to know the MFV from stem to stern and at times got to thinking of how much longer I could have stayed with Sonia. I soon got bored with just having a few pints in the canteen every night and was eager to get back up the line again to see what was happening.

The crew who were to take the MFV to Beirut duly arrived and within a couple of days we were off. I cannot for the life of me remember by name even one of the crew, perhaps because they were just a passage crew and not the permanent one. Our passage to Beirut was quite uneventful. We did not call in at Haifa, which was just as well, but I did look longingly towards the harbour as we sailed by quite close inshore.

As soon as we arrived at Beirut the alterations which had to be made to the vessel began immediately. The skipper's cabin was split into two, in order to accommodate the CO of any SBS men we occasionally had on board. The hold forward, normally a 'fish hold', was divided to provide a small operation's room and a wireless cabin with bunks. Also, as we were equipped with long range RAF cameras, a dark room was squeezed in somehow and any additional space was converted for storage or to take bunks. An Oerlikon 20 mm cannon was fitted forward, two .5 Colt Brownings were fitted to port and starboard in the waist and other gun mountings were placed at strategic points aft. Two extra wash basins were fitted on deck, fed from a forty gallon tank on top of the wheel house, there were just the two toilets, one on deck and one in the engine room.

The information we received daily from our caiques in the front line made us all anxious to get back up amongst it with our pals there, more especially as we now had our own HQ ship. It appeared that operations in the forward area were becoming more intense. The Germans were retaliating with increasing force, employing heavily armed schooners. They also had three or four destroyers operating in the Aegean and they were using better quality troops than the previous holding forces we had encountered.

One of our motor torpedo boat skippers was killed in a clash with one of the German destroyers and Alex McLeod on one of our Greek caiques fought a fierce gun battle with an armed German schooner which carried that very versatile gun of theirs, the formidable 88mm.

In May, work on our boat was completed and we began our shake down by carrying out exercises in Cyprus with the SBS. This continued until we could handle the various roles assigned to us blindfolded and were declared ready for the front line.

Suddenly, to us lower orders that is, we were given a shock as we heard we were to lose our charismatic CO, Adrian Seligman; not that many of us had seen a great deal of him of late, he was indeed a 'Will-of-the-Wisp' of the pimpernel type, but his presence always seemed to be felt.

The Admiralty, to their gain and to our loss, decided that they required Adrian to take command of a destroyer. His place as CO of the Levant Schooner Flotilla was to be taken over by Dougie Russell, a Lt Cdr, RNVR, who was the CO of Coastal Forces Base, Beirut. Although his time was officially up in the Middle East, he was anxious to remain in Beirut, simply because he had just married a very charming Hungarian girl. He had met her in Beirut and had fallen in love with her. If he had returned to England, she would not have been allowed to accompany him.

Nobody is indispensable, and with no disrespect to Dougie Russell, I, in company with many others, felt that things would never be quite the same. This for reasons other than the change of our commanding officer.

Our command, unit, outfit, call it what you will, was to me becoming more and more disenchanting. Here I was on this luxurious craft, divorced from the comradeship and togetherness of being with just four or five others on a tiny sailing craft, sneaking in and out of small inlets in various islands, eating, sleeping and living al fresco. The base at Beirut was not the easy going place of yore, not that respect and discipline was lacking then, but now everything had to be done by the rule book. The place seemed to be run by base 'wallahs' who never left there and had little knowledge of the privations endured by the lads when on operations. The whole place was seemingly becoming overcrowded with most of the faces largely unknown to me.

However, the first week in June we sailed away heading for our forward base, via Cyprus which was reached with nothing out of the ordinary happening and yet I did not feel at ease as I should have done on getting away from base and into the open sea once more.

It was after we left Cyprus and Paphos was well out of sight astern, that my uneasiness came to the boil. I was seated on the gunwale above the engine room hatch enjoying the feel of the open sea and the gentle roll of the MFV when the rhythm of my previously contented engine faltered and stopped. I was down into the engine room like a flash only to see that the casing of the fuel pump had cracked open, was red hot and had practically disintegrated.

It was impossible to see precisely what had happened, some internal part must have sheared off or come loose, shattering the whole assembly. There was absolutely nothing I could do except shut down and open the drain cocks on the exhaust manifold. I did this because the exhaust outlet was close to the water line on the port side and as we were rolling quite a lot, I was fearful of sea water entering the system. There was nothing the skipper, Dougie Russell, could do, other than to signal our position and ask for a tow. Knowing that it would be hours before anything turned up to help us, an awning was rigged as a sail on our tiny foremast and gun mounting and with a stiff breeze we were able to make a knot or so which helped prevent our rolling too much.

Our tow duly arrived to take us back to Beirut with our tails between our legs after having left there so triumphantly a short while before.

It was during our period in the hands of the engineers that I was informed that my time also was up in the Middle East having left the UK in December 1941 and it now being July 1944. It was indicated that I could apply to stay on out there, but the choice was not too difficult for me to make. I was homesick, missed my family and was disenchanted with our organization, which in my opinion was losing its piratical charm. I decided to go home.

CHAPTER 33

Saying goodbye to the base was not too difficult as the only people there that I really knew were just four lads who started in the unit from scratch with myself. There was Henry 'Chippy' Nineham, Sgt 'Tanky' Rowlands and ERA 'Jock' Andrews and last but not least, our general factotum, that Jack of all trades and procurer of anything and everything that was ever needed, Sgt Jones.

With the farewells over I obtained my rail pass and took off to, where else for heavens sake, Haifa, and I was determined to wangle as long as I possibly could there.

The RT staff at Haifa station were getting to know me by now so I dumped my kit with them and took off to *Chez Sonia* and to hell with the consequences. Live for today, tomorrow may never come was my motto then.

I was greeted with open arms and we were at it seemingly within minutes. Karl was resting out on the verandah on a sun lounger, although I doubt whether or not he would have minded or even cared had he been present. I had brought a few tins of goodies with me although food was not in short supply there, the corned beef, bacon and herrings were a welcome change to the menu. I told Sonia that I could stay for only three days, knowing from past experience that this would be the maximum I could take. The fact that it would surely be our last days together was an added spur for me to put my heart and soul into our every encounter.

Here , I must say that we had on a number of occasions and in some detail, discussed the aftermath of the war, especially since the tide had turned in our favour. She told me that when Karl died she would still be well off and would remain in Palestine. I had seen him deteriorate health wise during the short time I had known him. She asked whether or not I could stay with her and told me we would not want for anything. I was twenty-nine years old and she was twenty-seven.

We were very fond of one another and appeared to be compatible. She was really lovely, but seemingly insatiable, at the time I thought surely this would ease if we were together permanently. Every time we had these conversations, I always assured her that come hell or high water, I would always return to her and I really believed this to be so, that is until my last visit. I knew then that my place was at home, back in England.

Strange and difficult that it might be to understand, I have always been in love with my ladies, all of them, knowing immediately on seeing them for the first time that we could be in tune together.

Sonia had been compelled to live a very empty life, especially caring for Karl and yet she was just like my dear mother, forever singing quietly in Yiddisher when going about her chores and more so when making love. She seemed to be one of the most contented ladies I had ever met. Was it resigning oneself to fate? I don't know and now I was about to leave her, forever. This, as in Dorothy's case, was one of the most difficult decisions I have ever had to make and with all my heart I hope that she found someone to love and cherish her, for this is how I would have rewarded her.

Once again I found myself on a train with an aching heart, only the location was different. I felt exactly as I did on leaving Newcastle seemingly so many long years before. Just as then I felt like jumping off the train and running back to the arms of my beloved. Now as I look back to my thoughts at that time, I question why I did not do just that and the only answer that I can come up with is it was because of the discipline that had been instilled into me over the previous ten years or more.

This time my journey was not to Port Said, but to Alexandria where on arrival I was taken to a transit camp to await passage home to the UK and at that time not knowing that the UK as I had left it in December 1941 would be a far different place to the one I would be returning to in August 1944.

After a few days in the camp with nothing to do except eat, sleep and drink, I was just dying to get away from Egypt. I decided that it would be a damned long time before I set foot on those shores again. Finally, I got the welcome order to pack my kit and proceed to the docks at Alex to board ship. The ship turned out to be a two funnelled liner of the White Star Line, *The Highland Princess*, which pre-war used to ply between the UK and South America.

Having settled on board I immediately made friends with three other chaps and for practically the whole of the voyage, except for lifeboat drill, most of my waking hours were spent in playing cards.

Before the ship left Alex I had been a little apprehensive as thoughts of my last sailing from this port in a large ship, HMS *Medway*, entered my mind. Here I was on a similar size vessel which would also afford a lovely target for a U-boat, but as it turned out our passage to Liverpool was quite uneventful and we had just one alert after leaving Gibraltar and headed out well into the Atlantic in order to give the Bay of Biscay a wide berth.

What really surprised me during our passage was the amount of goodies which were available in the canteen on board, cigarettes of all brands and confectionery, sweets, chocolates etc. were unlimited. I spent all my available cash on these items, more especially on sweeties for my two little girls back home where sweets were rationed.

Apart from playing cards during my passage home, I had plenty of time to think about my future. My twelve years in the Navy expired in October and I had to decide whether to leave or sign on for another ten years, which would have entitled me to a pension. If I decided to stay, should I return to the submarine service, where brand new boats were being sent out to the Far East to combat the Japanese? The thought of another period of time overseas made me pause for thought, I was not sure I wanted to leave home again so I decided to leave my options open and play it from day to day.

Arriving at Liverpool, I disembarked and went through Customs. The customs officers turned a blind eye to the knowledge that the majority of us probably had about 1,000 fags each instead of the permitted 200. They sent us merrily on our way to our various destinations probably feeling that we deserved a break after two to three years in the Middle East.

During my journey to Plymouth, I had managed to send off a load of fags and sweets to Martha in Gosport during a stop and change of trains at Crewe, where I scrounged some packing material from the parcel office there.

After a frustrating journey to Devonport, with many stops due to the constant movement of large numbers of troops heading for France, I duly arrived in the barracks at HMS *Drake*. After formalities were completed, I was off to Martha and the children in Gosport for twenty-eight days leave.

Martha was waiting with my two little daughters at the door as I arrived and I really did feel at that time that it was good to be home. I tried to explain about my adventures since I had left, well, some of them anyway, but it was hard to sum up in a few words and I eventually gave up.

The England which now confronted me was indeed a far different England from the one I had previously known, it all seemed very strange.

The invasion of Europe was well under way and all activity was geared to this great enterprise. In the days that followed I witnessed large numbers of German prisoners being brought to Portsmouth and Gosport daily, a sure sign that our invasion was making progress.

I found it very difficult to settle down in the house, especially as I found that we had two Boom Defence sailors billeted with us. Unthinkable really, with just one cold water tap and stone sink in the kitchen and one outside 'thunderbox.' Our tiny house was home to Martha, myself, our two young children, her mother and the two other sailors.

It took a while for my two little girls to accept me, however, a supply of goodies soon brought them around and we began to get to know each other.

Unfortunately, the novelty of being home began to wear off, I was like a caged animal wanting to get back to wide open spaces.

I visited the submarine drafting office at Blockhouse during my leave in order to enquire about my returning there. I did not see one person I knew, however, I was told to apply at Devonport when my leave expired.

After twenty eight days leave I reported to Devonport and had still not decided upon my future, I just put off decisions from day to day in the knowledge that it would soon be October when I would have to decide about signing on again. After reporting I was given the job of driving one of the small steam driven naval pinnaces around the harbour. Twenty-four hours on duty, followed by twenty-four hours off. This meant that I could be stationed on shore and stay with my sister. Quite a good steady job until I ruined it.

CHAPTER 34

Foolishly, I applied for a progressive, which is a very small rise of pay which one is entitled to after being a petty officer for three years. I was informed that before I could have this small rise, I must obtain a boiler room watch-keeping certificate. I had applied once before, but I volunteered for the Levant Schooner Flotilla, so did not get it. I should have kept my mouth shut because as a consequence, I had to pack my bag and hammock and board the train for Rosyth in Scotland to join HMS *Venomous,* a sea going destroyer.

I was a little apprehensive about the task confronting me, but after telling the chief stoker that I hadn't a clue what to do, he assured me that my former experience as a stoker in a destroyer's boiler room would stand me in good stead. He explained that I would soon get to grips with things, plus the fact he would make a point of being with me for my first couple of watches.

So off we went into the North Sea escorting larger ships, such as cruisers, shepherding convoys and looking for U-boats. I soon settled down, growing in confidence about the job, until that is, what for me was another frightening experience.

It was during the forenoon watch and I was in the after boiler room, together with my stoker. He asked me whether or not I would be able to manage on my own whilst he went up to the fo'c's'le to replenish our supply of drinking water. I said I could and watched him disappear up through the air lock and out on to the upper deck. A couple of minutes passed and there was a thud against the port side of the ship, seemingly just where I was standing near to the fuel and water pumps.

My first reaction was that we were in a collision, but as it was broad daylight I thought perhaps we had rammed a surfacing U-boat. I did not notice any change to our speed, but I could feel that we were turning quickly to port and within seconds our Pom-Pom guns opened up, followed by one hell of an explosion, then another and suddenly all was quiet. Looking up, I saw my stoker enter the air lock to come down, I shouted, 'Where the hell have you been?' I must have been in a right state because the poor devil had only been gone five minutes or so.

It appeared that we had collided with a mine, one of a pair which probably were tethered together. Fortunately, they had drifted along our port side, dropping astern where at a safe distance, our guns opened up and exploded them. This was the final straw for me, I had been depth charged, bombed, torpedoed, shipwrecked, been in a fire fight with German soldiers and now nearly mined. All I wanted at that time was a bit of piece and quiet and I decided that the Navy would have to do without me.

Before returning to base we visited a number of places in Norway, including Stavanger and Kristiansund in Norway. I mention these two places in particular because I was asked, as an ex-submariner, to have a look at some U-boats which had apparently been abandoned by their crews.

These U-boats were guarded by what was a reconstituted Norwegian force and had not been entered since their abandonment. What was required of me was that I should go through them to see if anything looked out of the ordinary, for example booby traps etc. I momentarily forgot what I had said to myself when we had hit the mine about the Navy doing without me and agreed.

I was quite surprised to find everything so familiar, except naturally for the German names for different valves and switches etc., but the mere sight of them more or less told me their function. I think my only surprise was their passage way through the living quarters for the officers. Also, the conning tower was different, but on my walk through of about four U-boats with a British engineer officer, I could find nothing which did not appear to be in order and that was that. For my services, I did receive a commendation from King Olav of Norway which I still have in mint condition.

I loved Norway and its charming people. In spite of the way they had been treated, in company with other subjected peoples, they were bright and open hearted, possibly because they could feel freedom at last after the deprivation of their occupation. On a mercenary note, it was possible to obtain all sorts of favours for a bar of chocolate, cake of soap or a tin of food.

The war in Europe and the Pacific came to an end and I ended up at the shore base HMS *Cockrane,* at Rosyth. Decision time came and I signed the papers to go. In all honesty I had decided back in 1943 that provided I survived I would not remain in the Navy to qualify for a pension at forty. There were a number of reasons for this decision, the main one being I was confident I would find a job; also the Navy pension, introduced after the 'Invergordon Mutiny' would be a small one and my chances of getting a job at forty would be diminished.

So for the last time, I packed my bag and hammock and boarded the train to Devonport, there to await demobilisation. I imagined I would be one of the first to be demobbed as I was thirty-one years old and had served throughout the whole war.

When I arrived back at Devonport, I immediately walked into one of the cushiest jobs I have ever had in my whole life. Together with a stoker I took over the engine room of a large hospital launch which was mainly used for meeting ships arriving in Plymouth Sound with stretcher cases or VIPs, to ferry them ashore. On one occasion we went out into the Sound, near the Plymouth breakwater, to meet the USS *Augusta,* an American cruiser, carrying President Truman to the Potsdam conference.

The launch was a twin diesel affair with a large passenger space aft. The crew comprised of the stoker and me, plus, wait for it, three young Wrens. Their official duties were that of coxswain, bowman and stern sheet man, their unofficial duties were far different, in fact ones that could be performed lying down. But for once I had other far greater thoughts on my mind. As the date ofmy leaving the Navy approached so my mind became more and more confused with what I should do.

The closer the date came the more the turmoil within me developed. The same question burned away at me night and day, should I leave Martha and the girls and go to Dorothy or Sonia? I had to make a tremendous decision calling for the wisdom of Solomon. It was a decision that would decide my life and the lives of those I loved. Nobody could make it for me and I could not hope to explain the anguish I went through as the date of my leaving the Navy got closer and closer.

At times I lay awake for hours and felt as though the world was closing in on me. My mind continually returned to the night I had been in the fire-fight with German garrison on that remote island in the Aegean Sea. The thoughts that rushed through my mind that night when I just wanted to get home safely kept surfacing time and time again.

But I reasoned if I changed my mind and stayed in the Navy I could undoubtedly wangle periods of leave with Dorothy in Wallsend. She had responded very favourably to my letters when I arrived home and I did love her. But then there was Sonia in Haifa, which could have been heaven, but at what cost — time does not stand still and I was no Peter Pan.

However, difficult as it may seem to believe, my decision was to try and put my domestic life in order and make Martha and our two daughters my first consideration. It was my duty to love and protect the family that Martha and I had created. In my own selfish way I loved her and my children dearly. She was really the best wife anyone could have wished for, one that on reflection deserved a far better husband than I.

My last day in the Royal Navy arrived, October 22nd 1945, and in the blink of an eye I was dressed in my demob suit, standing at the dockyard gates.

I took one last look at the White Ensign fluttering in the breeze and a chill went up my spine as I am sure I heard the voices and laughter of all my old mates who had not made it home. I took a deep breath and stepped out through the gates for the last time and headed home to my family, hoping upon hope that I had made the right decision for everyone concerned. Only time would tell — but that is another story.

EPILOGUE

In the twilight of my life I often recall some traumatic and frightening periods and events from my past. However, I try to offset these by recalling the marvellous times I had with some wonderful people, in the main of course I refer to my ladies whom in all honesty I genuinely loved, albeit one at a time and impossible to list in order.

I now spend many hours in quiet contemplation dreaming of how things could have turned out differently, but always the romantic I very often sing quietly to myself the words of my favourite song, *This is all I ask,* which definitely seem to apply to me.

> Beautiful girls, walk a little slower when you walk by me
> Lingering sunsets, stay a little longer with the lonely sea
> Children every where, when you shoot at bad men, shoot at me
> Take me to that strange, enchanted land grown-ups seldom understand
> Wandering rainbows leave a bit of colour for my heart to own
> Stars in the sky, make my wish come true before the night has flown
> And let the music play as long as there's a song to sing
> And I will stay younger than spring.

Fred Matthews

SAILOR STOKER ODDBALL

Further copies of this publication may be ordered through your local bookshop or direct from Viper, The Studio, Rabbits Farm, Rabbits Road, South Darenth, Kent. DA4 9JZ. Telephone/Fax 01474 709843